HOW TO BUILD A PROGRAM

by

Jack Emmerichs

dilithium Press
Beaverton, Oregon

©Copyright, 1983, dilithium Press

10   9   8   7   6   5   4   3   2   1

Library of Congress Cataloging in Publication Data

Emmerichs, Jack.
  How to build a program.

  Bibliography: p.
  Includes index.
  1. Electronic digital computers — Programming.
I. Title.
QA76.6.E485 1983   001.64'2   82-14729
  ISBN 0-88056-068-1 (pbk.)

Printed in the United States of America

dilithium Press
P.O. Box 606
Beaverton, Oregon 97075

Contents

Introduction

"Before we proceed any further, hear me speak."
Shakespeare

This is a book on how to develop a computer programs for people who have had no previous experience with computers. It does not tell you how to write programs in BASIC, Pascal, or some other computer language, but rather how to develop the structure and the detailed logic of a program. Once this is done, the actual writing of the program will be much easier and you will make far fewer errors than if you simply start writing program statements.

If you have recently started writing your own programs but have had trouble understanding all the technical terms or how a program really works, then this book is for you. If you understand how computer programs work but not how they are developed from an original idea then this book is also for you. And if you are planning to buy a computer and want to know exactly what it takes to write your own computer programs, then once again this book is for you.

Since the development of the personal computer more and more people have become interested in writing their own computer programs. Even though there are many existing programs available right off the dealers' shelves, there are at least four reasons why sooner or later you will want to write your own programs:

1. There are always tasks that will interest you for which nobody else has written a program.
2. Even if someone else has written the program you need, it may not be exactly what you had in mind.
3. You will understand and enjoy your computer more if you know how to control it with your own programs.
4. Creating a well-written program can be an enjoyable and rewarding project.

This book will help you understand how to develop a computer program from an original idea through design, implementation, and actual use.

Contrary to popular myth, no magic words or secret formulas are required to produce a well-designed computer program that works. There are, however, a few skills and techniques which can make your programming more enjoyable and successful. The process of building a program is presented step-by-step. Each step is covered in a separate chapter that builds on ideas and techniques developed in previous chapters.

The program development procedure presented in this book is called *top-down structured programming*. It is used in projects ranging from a simple checkbook balancer for a personal computer to complex commercial applications written by professional programmers. The method is called *top-down* because you start with the overall requirements of the project and work down towards finer levels of detail until every last detail has been completed. It is called *structured* because the process of developing each level of detail is a well-defined procedure.

Appendix A contains a typical project plan for the development of a complete programming project. As each program design procedure is developed within this book, it is related to this project plan. This will explain how the steps relate to each other and to the project as a whole. By the end of the book, a complete BLACKJACK card game will have been developed as an example project. This may also serve as one of the first entries in your personal program library.

It has been my aim to keep this book as general as possible. Therefore, there are no discussions of specific computers or equipment. In general, your equipment will have some effect on how the final program is written, but not on how it is developed.

It is hard to make a programming book independent of specific programming languages. While the technique of structured programming is independent of any particular language, examples must be shown in some language or set of languages to be of any practical use. Therefore, most detailed examples (including the BLACKJACK program) are shown in the BASIC and Pascal programming languages.

BASIC is used for two reasons. First, it is the most widely used language in the personal computer field and, therefore, the one you will most likely encounter on a small system. Second, it is a very simple language. If a program can be written in BASIC, it can probably be written in any computer language. Unfortunately, specific versions of a computer language often differ from one computer to another. Therefore, explanations in this book will use the simplest versions of BASIC.

Pascal is used because it was designed specifically to use the type of structured design we will be using. Many examples will be clearer in Pascal than in BASIC. Pascal is rapidly becoming a very popular language and is already available on many small computers.

If you have a special interest in another language such as APL or LISP, you can still use this book to learn how to develop and write your own programs. In any case, you will want to use the instruction guide for your specific language and equipment along with this book to code your programs and get them running on your system. Remember, this book teaches you the principles of good program design and development. These principles will help you to program more easily and more reliably in any language.

1

What is a Program?

"A few strong instincts and a few plain rules."

William Wordsworth

The first step in learning how to develop a computer program is to know just what a program is. In this first chapter we define what a program is and give some examples. (Some of these will be found in unexpected places.) We will also develop the various components or building blocks of a program, examine their structure, and see how they can be combined into a single program. Finally we will look at some natural imitation on what can successfully be programmed.

I. DEFINING A PROGRAM

The computer itself has no built-in intelligence or ability to reason. It is extremely good at following instructions, however, and will do exactly what it is told to do. Forever! (Or until the power is cut off or the machine breaks.)

As long as the instructions can be carried out, the computer never questions them, no matter how outrageous they may be.

A list of instructions the computer follows to do a specific task is called a *program*. A program is stored within the computer's memory so that the machine can read it, and carry it out or *execute* it, one instruction at a time. Some computers can execute simple commands or a simple version of BASIC as soon as they are turned on. Such a machine contains a program for these commands or for BASIC stored permanently in its memory. This program starts to control the computer as soon as the machine is turned on. A computer without a program is like a seed without water —it has great potential but it just sits there.

The true power of the computer comes from two characteristics it has in following a sequence of instructions. First, no matter how boring or repetitious the instructions may seem to you and me, the computer executes them at high speed in a perfectly controlled manner for as long as necessary. Instrutions are followed in strict order; changing the order without being told to do so is beyond the computer's ability.

Second, a general-purpose computer uses a type of memory that allows you to change the instructions from time to time. This is quite different from most hand-held calculators and electronic games, whose instructions cannot be changed. These devices are restricted to the task for which they were originally built.

The purpose of this book is to help you develop computer programs. However, things will be easier to understand if we start with sets of instructions, or programs, that are a bit more familiar. From this point on, the term *program* will be used to mean any ordered set of instructions. The term *statement* will be used to mean a specific instruction within a program. The term *clause* will be used to mean part of a statement.

II. LOOKING FOR SOME EXAMPLE PROGRAMS

There are many examples of programs found in daily life, even though they may have nothing to do with computers. One of the more common examples is the recipe for oatmeal muffins shown in Figure 1.1.

This recipe contains a list of materials to be used and tells how to use them. If you follow each step correctly, the result will be oatmeal muffins. They will be just what

1   ¾ of a cup of old-fashioned rolled oats
2   ¾ of a cup plus 2 tablespoons of all-purpose flour
3   2 tablespoons of light brown sugar
4   1½ teaspoons of baking powder
5   ½ teaspoon of soda
6   ½ teaspoon of salt
7   1 teaspoon of cinnamon
8   ¼ cup of margarine
9   1 egg
10 ¾ of a cup of buttermilk

Combine the first seven ingredients and mix well.
Cut in the butter.
Beat the egg and the buttermilk together and pour it over the
    first mixture.
Mix only until it is well moistened.
Use a 12 pan greased muffin tin, filling each slot ⅔ full. Sprin-
    kle the tops with cinnamon sugar and bake at 425 degrees for
    15 minutes.

Figure   1.1. A Recipe for Oatmeal Muffins

the person who wrote the recipe had in mind. (They are,
by the way, quite good.)

The recipe uses a *language* that you must understand.
Notice that this language is slightly different from
standard English. Statements such as "½ teaspoon of
soda" and "Cut in the butter" are meaningful only if you
know what type of soda to use and what "cutting in butter" means. When you begin to work with computer programs you will need to learn the special languages in
which the instructions will be written.

Now let's look at a more complex program: the assembly instructions for an articulated frammis, a children's
toy which comes in a box marked "Some Assembly
Required." The assembly instructions are reproduced in
Figure 1.2. Read them through to get a feel for how they
control your actions as you assemble the frammis. It is
not important to understand each instruction the first
time through since you will soon be coming back to look
at specific instructions more carefully.

The illustrations for this set of instructions have not
been included here because we are not interested in how

to create graphic instructions, but rather how to create a step-by-step narrative.

While this set of instructions is more complex than the recipe for oatmeal muffins, it is probably not as complex as those discovered by unsuspecting parents trying to assemble a bicycle the night before a birthday party. These instructions do, however, contain examples of each type of statement that you need to construct computer programs.

III. GATHERING DIFFERENT TYPES OF INSTRUCTIONS

Let's take a closer look at each type of instruction — or statement — used in the assembly of the articulated frammis. These statements are the basic building blocks you will use later to construct a computer program.

A. Directive Statements

The simplest form of instruction in our example is the individual *directive* statement, for example:

OPEN THE PACKING CARTON AND REMOVE ALL OF THE PARTS

A directive simply states what is to be done. Such instructions are executed one after another in sequential order. In Figure 1.2, statement fifteen, the description of how to attach wheels to shafts, is a block of directive statements. Many programs (the recipe in Figure 1.1, for example) can be written using nothing more than directive statements.

B. IF-THEN Statements

A program becomes much more powerful if it can evaluate what is going on at the moment and *branch,* that is, do different things under different conditions. In a program, a condition is a question that can be answered true or false. For example, in Figure 1.2, statement two, "Are we assembling a model W frammis?" will be true or false depending on what has been packed in the box. The same instructions are packed with all models, so the user must determine which model is being assembled. Other condi-

FRAMMIS GENERAL CORPORATION
1 INDUSTRIAL PARK, EMERALD CITY, OZ 00100

ARTICULATED FRAMMIS MODELS A, B, AND W

< < <ASSEMBLY INSTRUCTIONS> > >

1. Open the packing carton and remove all of the parts.
   (NOTE: START INSTRUCTIONS HERE WITH #1)

2. If you have a model W frammis then make sure that you remove all of the parts that are packed under the foam supports at the bottom of the carton.

3. If any of the pieces listed on the enclosed parts list are missing from your carton then:

   • Repackage all parts.

   • Return the carton and its contents to the dealer for the missing parts or for a new frammis.

4. If you have a model B frammis and it contains the left handed hoop carrier, then bolt the left side frame support bracket holder arm to the frame holder arm position lock slot. Otherwise, bolt the right side frame support bracket holder arm to the frame holder arm position lock slot.

5. For each of the five wheels provided, do the following:

   • Snap a black rubber tire onto the wheel rim.

   • Fasten the wheel to one of the five lateral support frame carriage shaft ends as described in Instruction 15 (AT-TACHING WHEELS TO SHAFTS) below.

6. If you have a model A or model B frammis, skip ahead to Instruction 9 (THUS SKIPPING INSTRUCTIONS 7 AND 8).

7. Fasten a pulley to the upper pump pulley shaft and another to the lower pump pulley shaft as described in Instruction 15 (ATTACHING WHEELS TO SHAFTS) below.

8. Fit the V-belt provided around the two pulleys just installed.

9. Loosen the left trailing lever hold screw until the upper lift arm is free to move.

10. Turn the lift adjustment can until the lift adjustment indicators marked on the lateral support frame carriage shaft hous- .

ing as shown in Figure VII-I-A. Then tighten the left trailing lever hold screw back into place.

11. If the lift arm does not move freely between the lift arm assembly guides and the lateral support frame carriage shaft housing, go back to instruction 9 and try the adjustment procedure again.

12. The lift arm should also move freely between the trailing lever assembly guides located at the back end of the arm. If it does not, push the red self-alignment button on the right side of the upper head assembly for as long as the lift arm does not move freely in both sets of guides.

13. Install the fuse into the fuse holder clamps according to the following table:

> MODEL A: 10 AMP FUSE
> MODEL B: 15 AMP FUSE
> MODEL W: 13.4 AMP FUSE

14. The assembly of your frammis is now complete. See the operator's manual for instructions on the proper operation of your articulated frammis.

(NOTE: THE FOLLOWING PROCEDURE MAY BE USED ON ALL WHEELS.)

15. Attaching wheels to shafts:

- Insert a steel washer number 1277996-ABH/47 over the end of the appropriate shaft.

- Slide the wheel over the end of the shaft.

- Put a second steel washer number 1277996-ABH/47 and a castle nut number 2 on the end of the shaft.

- Tighten the castle nut and then back off one half turn.

- Put a cotter pin number CP-1 through the castle nut as shown in illustration VII-I-A.

- Continue with the assembly instructions from where you left off.

Figure   1.2. Articulated Frammis Assembly Instructions

tions are tested in statements two, four, six, eleven and twelve.

Statements of this type are called IF-THEN or *conditional* statements. The simplest IF-THEN statement has two parts: the condition to be tested, and the action to be taken when the condition is true. If the condition tested is true the THEN clause is executed; otherwise we skip the THEN clause and go on to the next statement. In statement two in Figure 1.2, the condition tested is whether this is a model W frammis. If it is true, then you must look for the extra parts in the bottom of the box. Note in statements six, eleven and twelve that in an informal language such as English, the word THEN may be implied. In a formal computer language, the THEN will usually be included in some form.

IF-THEN statements can be made more powerful by testing several conditions in one statement. This is called a *conditional expression.* Instruction four in Figure 1.2 contains a conditional expression that combines two simple tests: do you have a model B frammis, and do you have the left-handed option. The AND connecting the two conditions means that both conditions must be true before the THEN action is taken. If the two conditions were connected by the word OR it would mean, "when either condition is true, take the THEN action." If one of the conditions were preceded by the word NOT it would mean "the condition must NOT be met for the THEN action to be taken." Thus, "not-condition" is true just where "condition" is false. Here are several complex IF-THEN statements containing conditional expressions using AND, OR and NOT:

IF you have a model B frammis AND it contains the left handed hoop carrier THEN bolt the right arm to the slot.

IF you have a model A frammis OR you have a model B frammis THEN skip to instruction 9.

IF you have some frammis parts left over AND you are NOT fed up with this project yet THEN reread the instructions to see where these parts should have been used.

How to build conditional expressions so they mean exactly what you want them to mean will be covered later.

It is important to realize that conditional expressions are only a convenient way to create more powerful IF-THEN statements. For example, the following simple conditional statements have the same meanings as the three examples just given:

IF you have a model B frammis THEN IF it contains the left handed hoop carrier THEN bolt the right arm to the slot.

IF you have a model A frammis THEN skip to instruction 9.

IF you have a model B frammis THEN skip to instrution 9.

IF you have some frammis parts left over THEN IF you are NOT fed up with this project yet THEN reread the instructions to see where these parts should have been used.

As you can see, AND can be replaced by using one IF-THEN statement as the THEN action of another IF-THEN. A group of several IF-THEN statements can be used to replace OR.

A more powerful type of IF-THEN statement is called IF-THEN-ELSE. An IF-THEN-ELSE tells what action to take when the condition tested is false as well as when it is true. In Figure 1.2, for example, statement four states that the right side frame support bracket holder arm is to be used if the conditional expression is false. This simple addition of a clause changes the IF-THEN statement into an IF-THEN-ELSE statement. Here are some more examples of IF-THEN-ELSE statements:

IF you have a left handed model B frammis THEN bolt the left arm to the slot, ELSE bolt the right arm to the slot.

IF you have a model A or B frammis THEN skip to instruction 9, ELSE fasten the pulleys and the V-belt.

IF you have some frammis parts left over THEN reread the instructions to see where these parts should have been used, ELSE consider yourself very lucky and relax for a while.

Again it is important to realize that the ELSE clause only helps make the IF-THEN statement easier to use. The following pairs of instructions produce exactly the same results as the three examples just given:

IF you have a left-handed model B frammis THEN bolt the left arm to the slot.

IF you do NOT have a left handed model B frammis THEN bolt the right arm to the slot.

IF you have a model A or B frammis THEN skip to instruction 9.

IF you do NOT have a model A or B frammis THEN fasten the pulleys and the V-belt.

IF you have some frammis parts left over THEN reread the instructions to see where these parts should have been used.

IF you do NOT have some frammis parts left over THEN consider yourself very lucky and relax for a while.

Yet another way to expand the power of an IF-THEN statement is to include several instructions in the THEN (or ELSE) clause. However, since this requires some statement types that we have not looked at yet, we'll return to it a bit later. For now, just note that a simple IF-THEN statement is powerful enough to create all of the fancy IF-THEN-ELSE examples presented so far.

C. GOTO Statements

All of the statements examined so far have been set up to follow each other in normal sequential order. Sometimes, however, it is necessary to leave your current place in a program and use statements located someplace else. An example of this is shown in Figure 1.2, statement six, where several upcoming instructions may be skipped depending on the model frammis being assembled. This is an example of a GO-TO statement appearing as the THEN clause of an IF-THEN statement. The form GO-TO is usually shortened to GOTO. A GOTO statement is the simplest way to move from one place in a program to another. It simply tells you which instruction to execute next.

The GOTO statement is exactly what we need to allow an IF-THEN statement to control several instructions in the THEN clause. As we saw earlier, statement three in the frammis assembly instructions contains such a list of THEN actions. To accomplish the same thing, the IF-THEN-GOTO is used to skip a block of instructions when those instructions are not to be used. The test must be for conditions that are just the opposite (NOT) of those desired if the block of instructions were to be used. This is because we are now testing when to jump around the instructions rather than when to execute them. The following two sets of instructions produce the same results:

Complex IF-THEN

1. IF you have a model W frammis THEN
   - Fasten the pulleys to the shafts
   - Fit the V-belt to the pulleys.
2. Next instruction.

Simple IF—THEN with GOTO

1. IF you do NOT have a model W frammis THEN GOTO instruction 4.
2. Fasten the pulleys to the shafts.
3. Fit the V-belt to the pulleys.
4. Next instruction.

Another GOTO statement is found in Figure 1.2, statement six. That statement tells you to bypass items seven and eight if you have a model A or model B frammis. The GOTO statement can go to another IF-THEN statement to create AND condition expressions. A simple IF-THEN-GOTO is all that is absolutely necessary to create any type of complex IF-THEN-ELSE statement.

GOTO statements can be dangerous, however, if they are used too often in a program. It is easy for a programmer to get lost in a maze of GOTO statements and not be able to tell when particular parts of the program will be used. The problem is not the going to; it is that you lose track of where you are coming from. Therefore, in this book GOTO statements are only used to construct other types of structured statements or to handle error conditions that require special action. In a language such as Pascal that was designed around structured programming techniques, entire programs can be written without the use of a single GOTO statement. In fact, in some languages GOTO is not allowed at all! In BASIC, however, GOTO is necessary to build some structured statement types.

D. Simple Loop Statements

We mentioned earlier that one characteristic of a computer is that it does not mind boring and repetitive tasks. The easiest way to program a repetitive task is to create a *loop* in which the same instructions are executed over and over. In the frammis assembly instructions (Figure 1.2), statement five creates a loop. The items within the loop will be executed five times, once for each wheel.

A simple loop can be created by a GOTO statement that refers back to an earlier instruction. For example:

1. Snap a rubber tire onto one of the steel wheels.
2. Fasten the wheel to one of the lateral support frame carriage shaft ends as described in statement 15.
3. GOTO instruction 1.

This loop has a major problem, however — there is no way to get out of it! Clearly, you would stop when you ran out of wheels or shafts. But a computer is not that smart! Usually the only way to stop the machine is to interrupt the program or to shut the whole thing off and start over.

Therefore, every loop must have some kind of control mechanism that tells when to stop executing the loop. The simplest type of loop control uses a counter. The counter is a mechanism that counts the number of times the loop has been executed. An IF-THEN statement exits the loop when some upper limit has been reached. This can be accomplished in the previous example by changing instruction three:

1. Snap a rubber tire onto one of the steel wheels.
2. Fasten the wheel to one of the lateral support frame carriage shaft ends as described in statement 15.
3. IF five wheels have been attached, GOTO the next statement ELSE GOTO instruction 1.

You can create a loop with a counter using a simple IF-THEN and GOTO combination. The counter itself must be increased for each pass through the loop and may be used by instructions within the loop. A complete set of instructions for the assembly of the five wheels in the previous example, therefore, may look like this:

1. The first shaft to work on is number 1.
2. IF the current shaft count is greater than 5 then GOTO instruction 7.
3. Snap a rubber tire onto a steel wheel.
4. Fasten the wheel onto the current shaft as described in statement 15.
5. Add one to the number of the current shaft count.
6. GOTO instruction 2.
7. The next instruction.

A loop with a counter is so useful in computer programming that most programming languages provide a special set of instructions for it. BASIC and Pascal use the FOR/NEXT statement. PL/1 and FORTRAN use the DO loop. Loop structures vary widely from one language to another, but all of them share the following control features:

• The first instruction and the last instruction to be controlled by the loop must be identified.
• The counter to be used must be defined.
• The beginning and ending values of the counter must be defined.
• The increment — that is, how much to change the counter each time through the loop — must be defined.

The most common counting increment within a loop is one, and the value one is usually assumed if no increment is given. It is helpful, however, to be able to count by some other value such as five or ten. Particularly useful is the ability to count backwards by using a negative increment. For example, the loop might count from ten down to zero by a minus one.

The general form of a simple loop, showing all the control features, is:

> For the loop counter changing from a-starting-number to an-ending-number by some-increment do the following:
> The statements to be performed in the loop.
> Increment the loop counter and do the next iteration.

E. DO-WHILE and DO-UNTIL Statements

There are two kinds of simple loops that are not controlled by counters. These are the DO-WHILE and DO-UNTIL statements. In each case a condition is tested once during each pass through the loop. This condition controls whether or not the loop will be performed again. It is important to realize that you may not always know ahead of time how many executions such a loop will require. The adjustment procedures in the frammis instructions are such loops. Some languages allow you to exit simple counter loops for conditions unrelated to the current value of the counter by using a special EXIT statement. The process is easier to understand, however, if you use a loop that is controlled by a condition in the first place.

The DO-WHILE statement performs the loop as long as the stated condition is true. Frammis assembly instruction twelve is really a DO-WHILE loop:

WHILE the arm is out of adjustment, DO the adjustment.

The test for the condition, which is similar to the IF clause of the IF-THEN statement, is at the front of the loop. If the arm is already free to move, the adjustment process will never be performed. As long as the upper lift arm is not moving freely in both sets of guides, however, the adjustment process continues.

The DO-UNTIL statement performs the loop as long as the stated condition is false. Frammis assembly instructions nine through eleven form a DO-UNTIL loop:

DO the adjustment UNTIL the arm is in adjustment.

The test for the condition is at the *end* of the loop. Therefore, if the condition is never false, the loop is executed once (before the condition is checked the first time). In Figure 1.2, for example, the arm adjustment controlled by statements nine through eleven is made at least once. Depending on the success of the adjustment, statement eleven determines whether another execution of the loop is required.

The problem with DO-WHILE and DO-UNTIL loops is that there may be no guarantee that the conditions tested will ever be met. In the above examples, what happens if the arm cannot be adjusted? No doubt after many attempts, the customer will storm back to the dealer and try to dispose of the entire frammis. The adjustment process finally stopped only because the person following the instructions has a natural counter: a frustration level which cuts off the action of the loop. Since a computer has no frustration level, it would be stuck in the loop with no way out.

If you have any doubt whether a loop will terminate properly, you can add a counter to the condition expression to set an upper limit on the number of passes made. If the limit is exceeded, the program should leave the loop with some sort of error message.

F. Subroutine Calls

Sometimes a block of instructions needs to be repeated in several different places in a program. In this case no single loop controls all executions of the repeated statements. It is inefficient to repeat this block of instructions every time it is needed. What we need is a single location for this block of instructions, some way of getting to it whenever it is to be used, and a way to return to the main program after the instructions have been executed

While assembling a frammis, for example, there are two places where you must attach wheels to shafts. The detailed instructions for attaching wheels are contained in instruction fifteen. Actually, this is a block of six separate instructions that are all referred to by the single statement fifteen. It is, in fact, a little program all by itself. This block is referred to, or *called,* in statements five and seven. To get back to the main program, the last instruction in statement fifteen tells you to return to the place in the program where the call was made. For example, when the call is made from statement seven, you perform the group of instructions in statement fifteen, then return to the end of statement seven and continue on into statement eight.

Small program segments like this one that may be invoked from anywhere in the program are call subroutines. In this book, the statement that transfers control to the subroutine is a CALL statement, and the statement used to return to the location of the call is called a "RETURN".* Like the GOTO, the CALL statement is a way of moving from one part of the program to another. Unlike the GOTO, however, the CALL always remembers where it came from and returns there when the subroutine has executed.

It is possible to have one subroutine call another subroutine. Each subroutine remembers where to return when it is finished. As each subroutine is called, control of the program moves down the chain of connected routines. And as each routine ends, control is returned back up the chain until it finally reaches the call to the first subroutine. This allows you to write blocks of instructions in several levels of detail, with each level calling a lower level whenever greater detail is required. As we shall see later, this is the foundation of the top-down structure that *top-down structured programs* use.

G. SELECT-A-CASE Statement

Occasionally it is necessary to select one specific action from a table of several possible actions. In Figure 1.2, for example, statement thirteen selects the proper fuse instal-

---

*The terms subroutine, CALL (and GOSUB), and RETURN are used in BASIC. Pascal uses different terms for the same ideas. See your programming language manual for details.

lation for the model you have. This is an expanded type of IF-THEN structure in which there are several possible values for the condition tested, rather than just "true" or "false". An action is then specified for each value of the condition.

This general structure is called SELECT-A-CASE, or simply CASE. The CASE statement requires a specific item which may have a variety of values, and a table that lists the action to take for each value of the tested item. There may be a catch-all listing in case the item tested does not have any of the listed values. Here is another CASE statement in a more formal format:

    IN CASE the frammis-model is
        A: CALL A-routine
        B: CALL B-routine
        C: CALL C-routine
        W: CALL W-routine
        END of statement

Note that the actual instructions are subroutine calls. Each subroutine may contain as many statements as necessary to process the appropriate case. The item "frammis-model" may assume the value of any frammis model. This value is compared with the list of values in the table and the appropriate call statement is executed. The program then continues with the next instruction after the end of the CASE statement.

Each option in the table can be replaced by a separate IF-THEN statement. For this reason, many languages do not have specific CASE statements. When the CASE statement is available, as it is in Pascal, it is much more efficient than multiple IF-THEN statements. However, when it is not available, as in BASIC, you can use multiple IF-THEN statements to achieve the same result.

H. STOP or END Statement

The final thing that a program needs is a logical indication that its job is finished. This requires a STOP or END statement. The actual statement differs from one language to another, and some languages have both. In BASIC, for example, STOP means stop processing but be ready to continue, while END means the program has ended. In other languages, END may simply mark the end of some block of code, not the end of the program. And in some languages, such as Pascal, the end is indicated by the structure of the program rather than by a specific statement. In this book we will use the name STOP because it works in many languages.

In the frammis instructions in Figure 1.2, statement fourteen states that the instructions have been completed. Note that it is *not* the last statement in the program, since the subroutine for attaching wheels appears after the last regular statement. If statement fourteen were not present, the subroutine in statement fifteen would be incorrectly executed an extra time after statement thirteen. Furthermore, the RETURN at the end of statement fifteen would not know which CALL statement to return to.

In addition to ending the current program, statement fourteen tells the reader that there is another set of instructions to be used now that this one is done. Having the end of one program start the execution of another program is called chaining. Not all languages allow chaining, but it can be quite useful if available. You should be aware of how the language you are using indicates that the end of the program has been reached and that processing should STOP.

I. Comments and Data Definitions

There are two additional types of information that appear in the muffin recipe and the frammis assembly instructions. *Data definition* statements, such as the ingredients list in the recipe, define the data items used in the program. *Comments* such as the notes in parentheses in Figure 1.2, are not executed by the program. They contain information to help explain the program to someone reading it.

The form of data definitions varies from language to language. For example, BASIC will be able to understand some types of data in your program with no separate definition needed. (Special types of information discussed later do require special definitions.) The Pascal language, on the other hand, requires *all* data items in a program to be defined before they can be used. The best way to explain data definition statements is by examples. Therefore, we will introduce these statements as they are needed throughout this book.

Comments are available in almost all languages. A comment is ignored by the computer and has absolutely no effect on the running of the program. It is simply used to make the program more meaningful to someone reading it. As we will see, comments are very important in helping you remember what each part of a program is doing and how it relates to the other parts. Wise and liberal use of comments is a good habit to develop.

IV. THE STRUCTURE OF THE STATEMENTS

The nine types of statements that we have just looked at are all that you need to write well-structured programs. Each statement can be considered a single block of instructions to be combined with other blocks in the building of a program. Each statement has a single entry point at the beginning and a single exit point at the end. This allows different types of statements to be combined in sequence, with the end of one statement connected to the beginning of the next. Such a structure is easy to understand since you always know where you're going and where you're coming from.

There is one exception: the GOTO statement. A GOTO has a single entry point at the beginning, but the exit point can be any place in the program.

Unlike CALL, GOTO leaves no trace of where it came from. There are two uses for GOTOs in structured programming: to handle error conditions, and to build other structured statements not available in a particular programming language. Therefore, for the rest of this book, GOTO will be considered only as a part of other instructions, and not as a statement in its own right.

This leaves us with eight statements to use in building our programs. Figure 1.3, parts A-H, show the structure of each statement we have discussed.

Note that in each diagram, the part shown in a heavy outline has a single entry point (IN) and a single exit point (OUT). These entry and exit points are the only places where structured statements interact with each other. By connecting blocks of statements only at these

IN and OUT points, you do not interfere with the internal controls of the more complex statements. Many detailed and often hard-to-remember rules that were once taught as programming guidelines are all taken care of simply by plugging together the appropriate statements like Tinker Toys.

Each block in heavy outline can be treated as a *black box;* that is, a process that has a single entry, performs some function without our having to know how, and has a single exit. This black box may itself contain any statement or group of statements. This means that the THEN actions of an IF-THEN-ELSE statement, for example, may be a DO-WHILE, subroutine call, or any other type of statement.

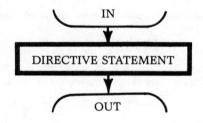

Figure   1.3-A. Directive Statement

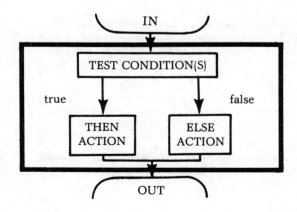

Figure   1.3-B. If-Then-Else

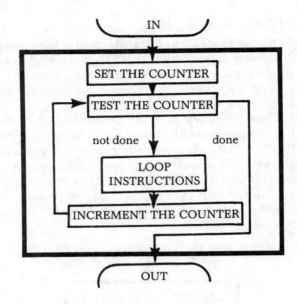

Figure 1.3-C. Loop with a Counter

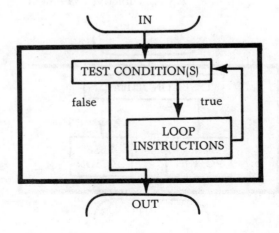

Figure 1.3-D. Do-While

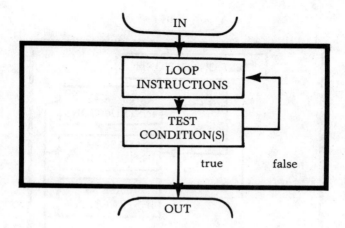

Figure 1.3-E. Do-Until

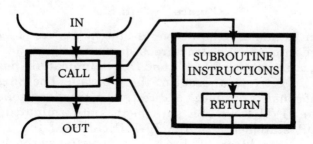

Figure 1.3-F. Subroutine Call

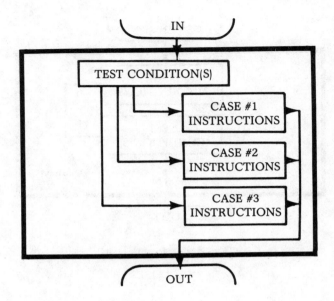

Figure 1.3-G. Select-A-Case

Figure 1.3-H. Stop

An example of how several statements can be combined into a single structure is shown in Figure 1.4. This diagram contains START and DONE indicators showing how to get into and out of the program. The program itself consists of a block of directive instructions, followed by an IF-THEN-ELSE statement, and terminated by a STOP statement. In the IF-THEN-ELSE, the THEN clause is a block of directive instructions; the ELSE clause is a subroutine call. The subroutine itself is a DO-WHILE statement.

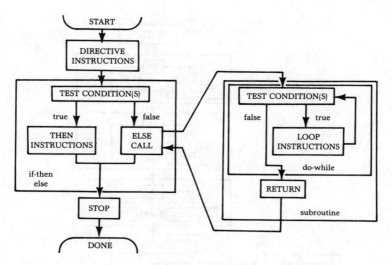

Figure 1.4. Complex Statements

Blocks of instructions can be built up in this way to the level of detail needed. A final example of combined instructions is shown in Figure 1.5. This is a diagram of the frammis assembly instructions in Figure 1.2 showing the structure of each of the instructions.

This process of breaking large blocks down into smaller blocks all having the form of a structured statement has given structured programming its name. In like manner, the building of a program from discrete structural blocks has given this book its name.

V. SOME NATURAL LIMITATIONS

In general, any set of instructions can be written using structured statements. There are, of course, limitations to what can be accomplished with a properly developed program. For example, some sets of instructions are so large that it may not be worth the effort to develop them. Federal income tax instructions can fill whole books and are written by a large staff of people.*

It is easier to fill out a single tax form by hand than to write a computer program that contains all the tax

---

*No doubt the instructions would be easier to understand if they were written as structured statements.

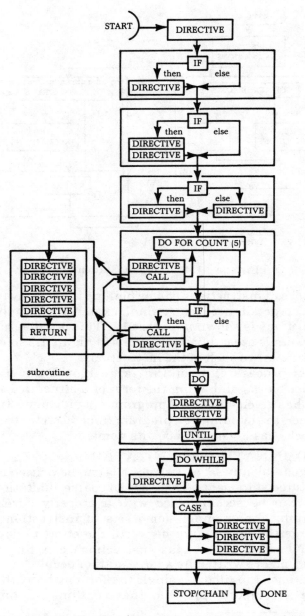

Figure 1.5. The Structure of the Assembly Instructions

instructions. It is more likely, however, that size limitations will become a problem when you try to fit a large program into the available memory of a small computer. There will always be complex and fascinating projects that are just too big to fit into your computer.

A more basic problem arises when a process is so hard to define that a set of instructions cannot be written for it at all. For instance, how does one judge the quality of a painting, symphony, or play. Even more difficult is understanding the creative process that produces such art in the first place. It is true that computers have generated art, music, and poetry, but these efforts have not yet shown the creative genius of a true artist. There are also problems in which information is always incomplete, such as stock market strategy. In such cases a person must use intuition or make educated guesses. A complete list of instructions is simply not possible. So far, problems that are ill-defined and those with insufficient information have been very difficult to solve by any program.

These difficulties, however, are limitations on programming in general, not only structured programming. If you can define a process using a group of specific instructions, it will be most easily programmed using structured statements.

VI. REVIEW OF MAJOR IDEAS

This chapter has dealt with defining what a program is and how it is used. The important points to remember are the following:

- A program is an ordered set of instructions or statements.
- All programs can be made up of the following types of statements:

DIRECTIVES
IF-THEN (ELSE)
SIMPLE LOOPS
DO-WHILE LOOPS
DO-UNTIL LOOPS
SUBROUTINE CALLS
SELECT A CASE
STOP

- The GOTO statement is not to be used except to construct one of the above statements, or to exit the program under very severe error conditions.
- In addition to these instructional statements there may also be data definition statements and comments within a program.
- Each type of structured statement has one entry point and one exit point.
- Each block of statement composed of structured statements also has only one entry point and only one exit point.
- Any statement or block of statements may be plugged into such a block of controlled instructions. The available types of statements may be plugged into each other or strung together sequentially to make a very complex program. The flow of instructions within such a program, however, will still be easy to understand.
- This technique, called *structured programming,* has been used to build large commercial systems and has proved useful on programming projects of all sizes. It works!

2

Consideration For *Computer* Programs

"And now I see with eye serene
The very pulse of the machine."
William Wordsworth

Now that you have seen how to write programs for people, you're naturally eager to learn how to write programs for computers. Before jumping right into this, however, we need to take a quick look at how a computer works and the type of language required to write instructions for it. Remember from Chapter One that any set of ordered instructions is called a program. By the end of this chapter you will be able to understand why computer programs are written as they are and how they work. If you are already familiar with various data types, constants, variables, arrays, assemblers, compilers, interpreters, and how all of these things relate to each other, this chapter will be a review. You may simply want to skim it to be sure you understand all the ideas presented here.

In this chapter we will examine the different types of information used by a computer and how it uses them. We will learn what is meant by *computer language,* how such a language differs from natural spoken languages, and how you can use a computer language to write programs. Finally we will look at a simple program written in two common computer languages to see what it looks like when it is all put together.

I. THE TYPES OF FUNCTIONS
PERFORMED BY COMPUTERS

The instructions that we have seen so far, like the muffin recipe with its mixing of ingredients and greasing of pans, are just fine for a human with hands working in a kitchen or workshop. Unfortunately, they are of no use at all to a computer. We must make a short side trip into the inner workings of the machine itself to understand why. You will find that it is easier to understand the programs you write if you understand what they do while running. Fear not, however, for this will only be a short introductory trip and there will be no quiz at the end.* Rather than picking a specific computer to examine, we will look at functions found on most small computers on the market today.

The computer is made up of two basic components, the *memory* and the *processor,* along with various minor parts which help the memory and the processor work together. The memory is a large collection of electronic switches that can store information in patterns of ON and OFF settings. The processor contains circuits much like those in a powerful calculator. It uses information stored in memory to solve a problem, then communicates the results to the outside world — that is, you! This organization is shown in Figure 2.1.

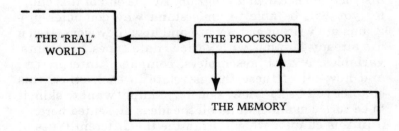

Figure   2.1. The Computer's Organization

---

*If you want to learn more about computers in general, the references at the end of this book offer more detailed information.

While a general-purpose digital computer may be an amazing piece of equipment, its functions are really quite limited. In fact, most of the time it is simply moving things around in memory as directed by the program. To understand how information is used by the processor, we must take a closer look at how it is stored in memory.

A. What Computers Work With

The information in memory is kept in individual chunks called *bytes*. Each byte contains eight little electronic switches called *bits*. Each bit is either on or off like a light bulb. Thus, a single byte can be represented like this:

The use of actual lights in early computers to display information in this way led to the popular image of flashing lights on a computer console. In today's machines, these lights have mostly been replaced by more efficient means of communication, but many people are still disappointed by a computer that has no flashing lights.

By convention, bits that are ON are represented by the digit one (1) and those that are OFF are represented by the digit zero (0). For example, the following five bytes can be used to represent the numbers zero through four:

00000000	00000001	00000010	00000011	00000100
0	1	2	3	4

There are 256 possible combinations of the eight 1's and 0's in a single byte. Each byte can be thought of as a single item of information available to the computer. Bytes may be used in a variety of ways to record all the information that the computer will use. Some common uses for a single byte include:

- A single instruction to the processor. Many computers are therefore limited to a total of 256 instructions.*
- A whole number from 0 to +255. Notice that zero makes up the 256th symbol.
- A single printable character, including upper and lower case letters of the alphabet, the digits "0" through "9", and various punctuation marks.
- One of a string of bytes making up a larger unit. For example two eight-bit bytes taken together contain sixteen bits. This gives a total of 65536 combinations of 1's and 0's. Sixteen-bit numbers are often used in BASIC and Pascal for integer whole numbers from -32768 to +32767. You will see the numbers 256, 32768, and 65536 frequently when dealing with computers.
- The location of another symbol in memory. Usually such locations are made up of two bytes together.

Any location in memory may be used to store any byte. Each memory location has an address ranging from zero up to the last location in memory (perhaps 65535). Each byte in memory is referred to by its address, just as houses along a street are referred to by their house numbers.

Recall that a byte may be used in more than one way. For example, most small computers use the same byte to represent the number 33, the exclamation point (!) character, and a machine instruction of some sort. The computer must be told how to interpret each byte. For example, it must keep the numbers and characters straight and not try to add a symbol that represents a letter of the alphabet to one that represents a number. Fortunately, the programming language will take care of most of this.

When bytes are used as information by a program, they are called *data*. The prime function of the computer is therefore *data processing*.

B. How Computers Process Information

Just as a calculator can only perform those functions for which it has a button, a computer can only use the

---

*Some of the newer small machines, use more than one symbol for each instruction.

information in its memory in ways that have been built into the processor's circuitry. Each operation that the computer can perform is called a *machine instruction*. All of these instructions together make up the computer's *instruction set*. The instruction set usually includes the following types of operations:

- Move a byte from one memory location to another.
- Add or subtract two bytes.
- Compare two bytes to decide if the first is less than, equal to, or greater than the second.
- Start executing instructions at some location, possibly based on the results of a previous comparison.
- Start executing a subroutine of instructions at some location, or return from a subroutine.
- Input a byte from or output a byte to a device such as a keyboard or display.

Additional instructions are usually available for special operations that are beyond the scope of this discussion. The more instructions the computer has, the more powerful it is. However, the limited set of instructions on a small computer is still sufficient for a great many programming tasks.

The real power of a computer comes from allowing its instructions to be modified as a program proceeds. This is much more flexible than other types of calculating devices such as electronic games, in which the programs are permanently wired into the machine's circuits. Just as the person assembling the articulated frammis read and followed the instructions in the preceding chapter, so the processor reads one instruction after another and branches, loops or calls a subroutine depending on conditions at the moment. Each machine instruction includes the address of any data it will be working with, just as the frammis instructions included the names of the parts.

II. GETTING DATA AND INSTRUCTIONS TOGETHER

The job of a program is to manipulate the data stored in memory by using the available instructions. However, you will normally not specify data in a programming language as patterns of 0's and 1's. Therefore, our next task is to examine how data is included or identified in a programming language.

In order to illustrate examples of data types that may be manipulated by your program, we will return once again to the mythical articulated frammis built in the first chapter. One of the many wondrous functions that the frammis performs is to shuffle and deal a deck of cards. In fact, included with the frammis is a special deck of cards designed to be used in the simple game of Fish.

As in a regular deck, the upper left corner of the face of each card shows the value of the card starting with the Ace and ending with the Jack, Queen, and King. Under this value is the symbol of the card's suit: Spades, Hearts, Diamonds, or Clubs. This information looks the same if the card is turned upside down. The color of each card is the same as in a regular deck of cards. However, in the center of each card there is a picture of a different fish instead of the normal pips or face-card pictures. On the back of each card is a fancy picture of a sea monster from an old seafaring map and the name of the manufacturer. The manufactuer's information and the front and back of the Seven of Spades is shown in Figure 2.2.

Deck no. 15389

Figure 2.2. A Typical Card Used in the Game of Fish

The deck includes the normal fifty-two playing cards. There are no jokers, but there is an extra "card" that contains the rules for the game of Fish.

In the following discussion we will use the information on these playing cards to illustrate the types of data that may be used in a computer program and how that data may be organized.

A. Numbers

The most common type of data is simply a number. Numbers, or *numeric data,* are used extensively in programs dealing with things that may be counted, such as dollars and cents. And almost all programs use numbers to count loops and control the structured statements that we developed in the first chapter. Numeric values may be manipulated by the rules of arithmetic like addition and division. Numbers can also be compared to see which of two numbers is the larger.

Numbers may be either exact values like the number of cards in a deck or approximate values such as one third (approximately 0.33333). Using arithmetic on approximate numbers may result in some peculiar answers. For example, because 0.33333 is slightly less than one third, you may find that dividing one by three and then multiplying the answers by three, which should result in an answer of one (1.00000) actually results in the unexpected answer of 0.99999.

The deck of cards used in our game of Fish is identified on the back with the number 15389. The value of each card may be represented by the number one through thirteen, with the Jack, Queen, and King being eleven, twelve, and thirteen, respectively. In like manner the suits can be represented by the numbers one through four. The number of cards may then be calculated by multiplying the number of values in a suit by the number of suits:

$$\text{CARDS} = \text{NUMBER OF VALUES} \times \text{NUMBER OF SUITS}$$

or

$$52 = 13 \times 4$$

B. Characters and Strings

The next most common type of data is *character data* consisting of the upper and lower case letters of the alphabet, the numerals from "0" to "9", and various punctuation marks. Because this type of data includes both letters and numerals, it is often called *alphanumeric data*. A data element made up of several characters grouped together is called a *character string* or just a *string*. Strings are used to represent the names of things, to display instructions on a terminal screen, or to print headings and titles on reports. All of the text in this book started out as strings of character data in a small computer. The spaces between the words are not just empty places but the *space* character.

Note that the "1" in this case is not the value of the number one, but rather the character "1" which may be printed in a string of text such as "1234 Dusty Road". To a computer the difference between the value one and the character "1" is an important distinction and will lead to problems if it is not well understood. Therefore this book will always refer to the *number* one when referring to the value one and the *character* "1", in quotes, when referring to the printable character.

Unlike numeric data, character strings are never approximate values and are not processed arithmetically. Strings can be moved from place to place, grouped together into longer strings, broken down into shorter strings, or printed as output. Strings can also be compared to one another and sorted into some specific order (e.g. alphabetically).

The manufacturer's name and address on the back of our cards is represented as three strings of printed characters. The names of the suits may be represented by strings: "SPADES", "HEARTS", "DIAMONDS", and "CLUBS".

There are many other types of data that a program may use. For example, the color of each Fish card is a special item which has one of two values: red or black. The picture of the fish on each card is an item of *graphic information* and the representation of a picture in a computer is called *computer graphics*. The subject of computer graphics is a complex and fast-growing area of programming applications. If your computer provides some graphic characters, you may be able to show symbols for the four suits on the terminal screen.

In most cases, however, additional types of data will be represented by numbers or strings of characters. For example, the colors red and black could be represented by the numbers one and two, or by the characters "R" and "B". The names of the fish in the pictures could be represented by fifty-two strings of descriptive text.

One special type of data that we will use from time to time is called a *switch* or *flag*. A flag has only two possible values: *true* and *false*. It may be represented by the numbers zero and one (like a bit), or by character values of "T" and "F". In BASIC it is usually represented as a numeric variable using zero for false and minus one for true. In Pascal a flag is a special type of data called a BOOLEAN* variable.

For the rest of this book we will deal mostly with numeric data and character strings, with an occasional flag thrown in to control the processing.

III. HOW THE DATA TYPES ARE USED

The data in a program can also be classified as *constant* or *variable*. The value of a constant never changes, like the name and address of the manufacturer on the back of our cards. In contrast, a variable may take on several, perhaps hundreds, of values during a single program execution.

A. Constants

Constants can be either numeric or string. Numeric constants are usually written using numerals:

5
–1.50
45.20

This is because 5 is always 5, never –1.5 or any other value. In the frammis assembly instructions there is a loop which controls attaching wheels to shafts that has

_____

*Named after Boolean Algebra, the branch of mathematics which deals with true and false values.

to be executed *exactly* five times. Notice that the 5 is considered the *number* 5, not a character.

Character string constants are usually written between quotation marks or apostrophes, for example:

"Leviathan Playing Card Company"
"1234 Dusty Road"
"Do you want another card?"

Note that the characters "1234" in quotation marks are considered as a string of characters just like "Road", not numeric data.

B. Variables

Variables are data elements whose values must be able to change while the program is running. The way variables are written varies from language to language. In this book, variable names are usually written as a single word. Just remember that when you write the actual computer code for the program, you may have to use different names (especially in BASIC). Each variable in the program must have a unique name to avoid confusion. It helps if the name indicates how the variable will be used. For example, the value of a card may have the variable name VALUE. Notice that the name does not indicate what the value of the card will actually be. In this case, it could be any value from one to thirteen. In fact, it may be each of these values before the program finishes.

Both numeric and string variables are given variable names. In some languages the name indicates the type of the variable. In most versions of BASIC, for example, string variable names end with a dollar sign. A1 is a numeric variable, A1$ is a string variable. (Notice that these would be different from the *string constants* "A1" and "A1$".) Variable names usually have to start with a letter to distinguish them from numeric constants.

For our deck of Fish cards, the following variable names might be used:

VALUE   The face value of the card (numeric).
SUIT   The suit of the card (string).
COLOR   The color of the card (string).
FISH   The fish pictured on the card (string).

There are strict limits on what values may be assigned to a given variable. You cannot assign numeric values to a string variable, and vice-versa. Numeric variables usually have lower and upper limits on the values that can be assigned to them. For example, Pascal and many versions of BASIC contain *integers* that may only be a whole number from -32768 to +32767. Numbers like 0.333333 are usually called *real* numbers. These may be either single precision numbers, which hold seven or eight significant digits, or double precision numbers which hold up to seventeen significant digits. String variables usually have a limit on the number of characters that may be assigned to them. Within these limits, however, variables may be set equal to any legal value you desire. A variable may have a constant value or the current value of any other variable of the same type. For example, to set the proper COLOR for a card once the SUIT is known, the following IF-THEN-ELSE statement could be used:

If SUIT IS EQUAL TO "SPADES" OR SUIT IS
    EQUAL TO "CLUBS" THEN COLOR IS EQUAL
    TO "BLACK"
ELSE
    COLOR IS EQUAL TO "RED"

C. The Primary Types of Data

So far we have discussed the primary types of information available, numbers and character strings, and their use as constants and variables. All of this may be summarized in Figure 2.3.

It is important for you to understand Figure 2.3 before you start writing computer programs. If you have any questions about types of data, constants and variables, please review this material before continuing.

IV. ORGANIZING DATA

A. Data Structures

There is a final technique for organizing data we need to discuss. This is the idea of gathering together several related items of information and treating the group as a

DATA USES / DATA TYPES	CONSTANTS	VARIABLES
NUMERIC	5 – 1.50 0.3333	VALUE A1
CHARACTER	"VALUE" " – 1.50" "Hello"	NAME A1$

Figure 2.3. The Primary Data Types and Uses

new data type. Such a new data type is called a *data structure*. Notice that a data structure is always made up of a group of existing data types. The data structure will have its own name assigned, just as other data types do. As you may have guessed, our deck of cards is made up of data structures.

Each data element in a data structure is called a *record*. In general, a record may contain any number of data items. Once the format of the record has been established, all other records of the same type will have the same format. The items required for a single record for one of our cards are the VALUE, the SUIT, and the FISH. (The COLOR can always be figured out from the SUIT so we don't need to keep track of it for each card.) Therefore, all 52 CARD records will have the following format:

```
VALUE   (numeric    - one to thirteen)
SUIT    (character   - "SPADE" will be black
                      "HEART" will be red
                      "DIAMOND" will be red
                      "CLUB" will be black)
FISH    (numeric    - one to fifty-two)
```

When all of the records are gathered together they make up a more complex data structure called a *file*. In our case we will call the file a *deck*. Usually all the records in a file are of the same type, but this is not necessary. There may be special records that give information about the deck itself such as the "card" in the front of the deck that contains the playing instructions for the game of Fish.

B. Arrays

A data structure that is made up of repetitions of a single type of data is called an *array*. Items in an array are usually indicated by the name of the array followed by the item's position in the array written in parentheses. The number in parentheses is called the *index*. This is a very convenient data structure. For example, we can assemble the fifty-two fish from our deck into an array of fish. Then, instead of needing fifty-two variable names, FISH1 through FISH52, we have just the single array name FISH containing FISH(1) through FISH(52). The seventh fish would be FISH(7). This is called a *one-dimensional array* because only one index is required to identify each item in the array:

FISH(index)
  ⌐ The index indicates which fish
   you are using and will have a
   value from 0 to 52

Some computer languages (BASIC, for example) do not lend themselves to working with records. If this is the case we may wish to represent our deck of cards as three arrays: one for values, one for suits and one for fish. Each array would contain fifty-two entries, one for each card. The seventh card in the deck would then be made up of VALUE(7), SUIT(7), and FISH(7). All of these arrays are one-dimensional arrays because they require only one index.

VALUE(index)
SUIT (index)
FISH (index)
  ⌐ The same index indicates which
   card you are using.

All of this information could be combined into one data structure by using an array with two indexes: one index for the card number, and one index to indicate which of these three data items for each card is being used. This is called a *two-dimensional array*. Since an array cannot contain both numeric and string information we will have to use the same type of data for all of our information. SUIT must therefore become a numeric variable, with values of one to four. In this two-dimensional array, the first index will indicate the card in the deck as before; it will have a value from one to fifty two. The second index will indicate which item about the card is being used as follows: one for the VALUE, two for the SUIT, and three for the FISH.

Therefore, the three arrays VALUE, SUIT, and FISH will be replaced by the new two-dimensional array DECK. The value of the first card in the deck will be DECK(1,1). The suit for this card will be DECK(1,2). The fish will be DECK(1,3). The value, suit, and fish for the seventh card in the deck will be DECK(7,1), DECK(7,2) and DECK(7,3). The format of the array DECK is as follows:

DECK (cardindex, itemindex)

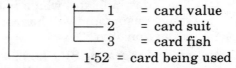

```
                    ┌──── 1      = card value
                    ├──── 2      = card suit
                    └──── 3      = card fish
            └────────────── 1-52 = card being used
```

The development of more complex data structures can go far beyond the scope of this book. It is possible to have arrays with many dimensions, records that contain arrays, arrays of records and so forth. Generally, the only limit to how fancy the organization of data becomes is the imagination of the person organizing it.

One last use of an array will be mentioned here because it is often used to save space and simplify large programs. You will notice that in the two-dimensional array just developed, we lost the ability to print a card's suit as a character string. The suit is now kept as a number from one to four. If we still want to have the names of the suits available we can put them in a small array of strings called SUIT. SUIT will be a one-dimensional string array with four entries: "SPADES", "HEARTS", "DIAMONDS", and "CLUBS". An array holding common values like this is often called a *table*. The suit name can be looked up in the table just as you would look up a train departure in a time table or a mathematical value in a table of numbers.

SUIT can be used with DECK to determine the suit of a card as follows: First look up the number of a card's suit in DECK, and then look up the name of the suit in SUIT. For example, let's call the name of the suit SUITNAME. To print the name of the seventh card's suit, find the number of the suit using:

$$NUMBER = DECK\ (7,2)$$

This will be a number from one to four. The name of that suit number will be:

$$SUITNAME = SUIT\ (NUMBER)$$

This will be the appropriate entry in the table and can be printed on the terminal. This two-step process can be shortened by using the following expression:

$$SUITNAME = SUIT\ (DECK\ (7,2))$$

This can be expanded to a more general form by re-placing the constant 7 with the variable CARD. Now the name of the suit for the card represented by the variable CARD will be

$$SUITNAME = SUIT\ (DECK\ (CARD,2))$$

One advantage of all this is that instead of repeating the four character strings for the suits thirteen times as we did when we had three arrays with fifty-two values in each array, we only need to define them once in the small table. When dealing with very long character strings this can save a lot of space. The second advantage of this organization is that instead of having lots of variable names for the different cards and suits in the deck, there are only two: DECK and SUIT. Any specific cards can be identified by assigning the proper values to the indexes for these arrays.

Another table could be created to hold the names of the card values including "ACE", "JACK", "QUEEN", and "KING". In practice, programs are often full of tables containing special values that can be looked up when needed.

We shall now change our focus from how the data is organized to when it will be used in a program. Do not worry if you still do not completely understand all of the ideas about data structures just presented. We will go over this material again during the examples developed throughout the book. For now it is sufficient that you understand the importance of organizing a program's data in the proper way.

V. HOW DATA IS USED BY A COMPUTER PROGRAM

There are four ways that a computer program may use the data at its disposal: (1) allocate room for the data in memory, (2) get any necessary input from the outside world (the user), (3) perform the necessary calculations on the data, and finally (4) make the results available to the outside world (output). The allocation of space for data may or may not be done automatically by the computer, depending on the system being used. The other three operations, however, are the basic functions of most computer programs. The flow of data through a program can be shown in a picture called a *data flow diagram.* Here is a simple diagram showing the primary flow of data through a program:

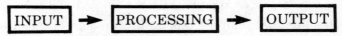

A. Data Allocation

The first thing a program has to do is make sure that it knows what data it will be working with and where to find it. The first part of the muffin recipe is a list of all the ingredients that will be needed. This allows the baker to arrange everything to be used before starting. In like manner, a computer program must define each item of information and where it will be stored in memory. The amount of memory required will depend on the type of data used. For example, it will take more room to store a string that is 25 characters long than to store a single number. The program must therefore keep track of data, its location in memory, and perhaps its length.

Constants are defined as part of the program by the user and stored in memory when the program is loaded into memory. However, the contents of variables will not become meaningful until the program is run and the variables are set to some specific value.

B. Getting the Input

It is possible to create programs which do not require any information from the outside world. The muffin recipe is such a program. Every time it is executed the same result is produced. The only way to alter the output is to alter the program. Most programs, however, are written to produce appropriate results based on changing information so you don't have to rewrite the program every time your problem changes. This means that some information must be entered into the program by the user when the program is executed. Clearly, the program must be written to ask for this input.

Most programs receive information from a computer terminal, magnetic tape drive, or some other piece of equipment. The most common form of input device for today's small computer is a terminal keyboard, cassette tape, or floppy disk drive. Each piece of data must be properly identified by the program and stored in its appropriate place in memory.

Some programs, such as loan payment calculations, may require only a small amount of data at the beginning. Other programs such as computer games, may require constant information about what the player wants to do next. It is usually quite important that the program check all input for errors. Any conditions for which an invalid value could be entered should be checked and handled by appropriate error messages and the user asked to enter the correct value. Since the computer does exactly what the program tells it to do with the data it receives, a common expression among experienced programmers is "garbage in, garbage out!" Therefore, checking input is very important.

C. Processing the Data

Usually the bulk of a computer program is concerned with performing the necessary operations on the data it has been given. Numbers are calculated, variables are changed, values are compared, and a final result is obtained. This may be a simple one-time operation as in the muffin recipe, or it may be repeated over and over for changing conditions as in a computer game.

D. Reporting the Results

A program would be worthless if it kept the results of all this work to itself. It is therefore necessary to record or display the results of the program in some way. This is usually done on a computer terminal, printer, or some other form of display device. In some cases the results of a computer's operation will directly control other machines like assembly line robots. The most common form of output device for today's small computer is a terminal screen. Most systems will also provide permanent copies or storage on a printer, cassette tape, or floppy disk. As with input, the output operation may happen only once or it may happen continuously.

Now that we know what a computer can do, what types of data it can use, and how the data will be used, it is time to look at how to talk to the computer itself.

VI. HOW INSTRUCTIONS MAY BE WRITTEN TO BE UNDERSTOOD BY MAN AND MACHINE

So far in this book, all the programs have been written in English. This seems reasonable because people reading the book will be able to understand them. As we have seen, however, computers are not controlled by English but by a special and limited set of instructions. If we agree that the computer can "understand" only these few instructions, then we can express a significant programming problem as follows: the programmer and the computer do not understand the same language and therefore do not understand each other.

In fact, the problem is quite similar to that facing two people who do not speak the same language. The alternatives are: one person learns the other's language, both persons learn a third language, or constantly translate between languages through an interpreter. As we shall see, many computer languages have been developed to help implement these solutions.

A. What is Meant by a "Computer Language"

Spoken or "natural" languages such as English have evolved from the needs of people who wish to convey feelings, thoughts, fears, humor, and endless wonderful and subtle things to each other. These languages are therefore rich in descriptions, full of contradictions, and unbelievably large and difficult to learn. (Fortunately we learn our own tongue when we are too young to know how difficult it is!) By contrast, the sole purpose of a computer language is to express a set of instructions as precisely as possible. Such a language requires clarity and formal structure, but has no need for such interesting attributes as description, emotion, or humor. In this language it must be impossible to make a correct but contradictory statement. A computer programming language therefore exchanges the capabilities of a natural language like English for clarity and precision.

While there are hundreds of computer languages in use today, they can generally be grouped into the following three categories: machine languages, assembler languages, and high level languages. A machine language is designed along with each new type of computer that is built. It consists of all the instructions that are directly understood by that computer. Assembler languages are closely related to machine languages, but translate most of the numeric representation of a machine language into alphanumeric code that the programmer can more easily understand. High-level languages are not closely related to any specific computer. They translate the programmer's ideas into whatever machine-language program is needed.

B. Machine Language

The numeric instructions that make up a computer's instruction set also make up its machine language. These are the only instructions that the computer can really use, so all programs must sooner or later be translated into a series of machine language instructions.

The following examples show actual machine language programs that simply add the numbers one and two and store the result in the first location in memory (location zero). In English, the process could be expressed as "calculate one plus two." These programs only figure out the addition; printing the answer would require additional steps. The first program is for the Intel 8080 microcomputer and the second is for the Motorola 6800 microcomputer:

```
8080:   62    1    198   2    50    0    0
6800:   131   1    139   2    151   0
```

Listing 2.1. Two Machine Language Programs to Add One Plus Two

The first program would be stored in memory as the following set of on and off bits in 7 bytes of computer memory:

```
00111110
00000001
11000110
00000010
00110010
00000000
00000000
```

This is just fine for the electronic switches in the computer, but it is almost impossible for a human being to use. Another disadvantage of machine language programs is that the instructions for different computers will usually be quite different. As this example shows, even a simple program may vary greatly in content and length. Programs written for one computer cannot be easily moved to another.

C. Assembly Language

So much for learning the computer's language. It is also impossible for the simple-minded computer to learn a language as complex as ours, or for the two of us to learn a third language. The next best thing is to translate from one language to another.

This translation can be carried out by the computer itself, using a special program that reads instructions in some form convenient to the programmer and then converts them to programs in machine language for the computer. The first translation programs allowed the use of code words and expressions instead of numbers for writing instructions. The actual instructions were much the same, but in a form a human could understand. These programs were called *assemblers* because they assembled instructions of a more English-like form into machine language programs. Such programs are still used today.

The assembler takes care of much of the bookkeeping and details required to write a program. Each machine instruction is represented by a short abbreviation that is easier to remember than its numeric value. The instructions are written down one line at a time with English comments, which are ignored during translation, to make the program more readable. Any location in memory where data or part of a program will be located may be given a name meaningful to the programmer. The assembler then translates the program written in this "language" into the actual machine language instructions and addresses.

To write our example addition program in assembler language we will have to add a step to define the variable FRED. The program in Listing 2.2 is written for the Intel 8080 computer; it will create the machine-language program shown in Listing 2.1. A value of one will first be moved to the part of the processor, called A, that performs arithmetic. A value of two will be added to this. The result, still in A, will then be stored in FRED. While this may still look strange to you, there are several improvements here over the machine-language program. Each instruction has its own line. The comments, which all start with a semicolon, provide a running commentary in English about what is going on. An instruction such as STA FRED is easier to understand than the machine instruction 50 0 0. And the data and program location names are easy to identify and use.

Still, this is a long way from "add one plus two." Each instruction line of the assembly-language program creates one complete machine instruction, so you still have to know exactly how the processor works. The programs still will not be easy to move from one computer to

another. Clearly, a more powerful translation program
will be needed to make the computer easy to use.

```
; THIS IS THE 8080 ASSEMBLY LANGUAGE PROGRAM TO ADD 1+2.
; Author: Jack Emmerichs       Last Changed: 1/01/82

          ORG 0     ; SET THE ORIGIN FOR VARIABLES TO ZERO
FRED:     DS  1     ; FRED, DEFINE STORAGE OF ONE BYTE

          ORG 1     ; SET THE ORIGIN FOR THE PROGRAM TO ONE
START:              ; START OF THE PROGRAM
          MVI A,1   ; MOVE INTO A, ONE
          ADI 2     ; ADD TO IT, TWO
          STA FRED  ; STORE THE ANSWER IN FRED
          END       ; END OF THE PROGRAM
```
Listing 2.2. Assembly Language Program to Add One
Plus Two

D. High-Level Languages

High-level languages are translation programs that
allow you to write instructions in a form much more like a
natural language. As you might expect, such programs
are far more complex than assemblers. Usually many
machine instructions are needed to carry out one simple
function. The programmer no longer needs to know the
inner workings of the machine, since the translation program allocates space for data and creates the appropriate
machine instructions.

It is important to realize that there is no particular
magic in the form of the language itself. The syntax used
is merely a formal way of describing meaningful input to
the translation program. It is the translator itself that
changes the programmer's instructions into a working
machine language program.

Listing 2.3 shows our simple one plus two addition program written in four high-level languages. Notice how
much easier they are to understand than the previous
examples. Here we do not need to know where numbers
are stored in memory, although we may still have to
define the variables that will hold them. In languages
that do not require you to define variables before they are
used, the translator will allocate space for each variable

as it is first encountered. The programmer has little or no control over how this is done.

BASIC and Pascal were chosen as examples because they are the most popular languages used with today's small computers. On larger computers FORTRAN is the most common scientific programming language and COBOL is the most common business language. These examples, by the way, are not complete programs but just enough to show what each language looks like.

Now this shows real progress. These instructions are much easier for people to understand. Furthermore, programs written in these languages are usually quite easy to move from one machine to another. The programmer's original instructions, with perhaps a few changes, are simply translated again for the new machine.

```
BASIC:
            REMARK    BASIC uses short variable names
            REMARK    and does not require that they
            REMARK    be defined ahead of time.

            REMARK    Do calculations

            F = 1 + 2
```

```
Pascal:
                  (*  Pascal requires data definitions
                      and allows long variable names    *)

            VAR   FRED: INTEGER;

                  (*  Do calculations  *)

            FRED := 1 + 2;
```

```
FORTRAN:
      C           FORTRAN looks like BASIC but allows
      C               longer variable names.

      C               Do calculations

            FRED = 1 + 2
```

```
COBOL:
   *     COBOL uses longer data definitions and
   *           English like sentences.

   01 FRED     PICTURE 999.

   *        Do calculations

   ADD 1, 2 GIVING FRED.
```

Listing 2.3. High-Level Programs to Add One Plus Two

The advantages of high-level languages are so great that virtually all applications are now written using one of them. The rest of this book will deal exclusively with high-level languages.

As with most good things, of course, there is a catch to all of this. The biggest problem is that once your instructions are not limited to a particular piece of equipment, the language may change from time to time. This allows for improvements in the language, but also allows for conflicting versions of it since not all manufacturers may develop their "improvements" in the same way. Over the years most high-level languages have developed several *dialects*. This is why programs that are published for general use, like BASIC games and the examples in this book, may not work on your computer.

A second problem is that the translation program is not as efficient as a program written in machine language. Therefore, programs that must run very fast or use very little memory are usually still written using an assembler. This is particularly important in small computers where speed and memory size are limited. The translation programs themselves, for example, are usually written in assembly-languages.

E. Compilers and Interpreters

There are several ways in which a high-level language may work. Most large computers use translation programs that read the programmer's instructions once and convert them into a new machine-level program. This type of translator is called a *compiler*. The translation, which is quite complex, is done only once. Most Pascal systems use a compiler.

Another approach, often used on small computers, is to translate each line of the high-level program as it is being run. This is somewhat like a tourist using a guide book to speak a foreign language. Each time you have to say something, you look it up in the book again. Such programs are called *interpreters*. Since the translation is done continuously, interpreted programs often run quite a bit slower than compiled programs. Interpreters are easier to write, however, and may require less memory than a compiled program. Most small BASIC systems use interpreters.

A compromise between these approaches is the *semi-compiler*. This is a program that compiles most of the input program into machine code (or something very similar). Another smaller program, called a *run-time* package is stored in memory along with the semi-compiled program. Most of the complex parts of the program are then handled as subroutine calls to standard routines in the run-time package. This offers much of the simplicity of an interpreter and the speed of a compiler.

VII.EXAMPLE COMPUTER PROGRAMS FOR A REAL APPLICATION

Now that we understand what a high-level computer language is, let's look at some actual examples.

As a simple example that will use much of what we have just discussed let's develop a program to look up the value and suit of a card in our Fish deck and print this information on the terminal screen. The input from the terminal will be a number from one to fifty-two indicating the position of a card in a new unshuffled deck. The number one represents the Ace of Spades at one end of the deck, and the fifty-two represents the King of Clubs at the other end. The output will be the value and the name of the suit for the card number entered. The program will require the table of suit names developed earlier and another table for value names. Instructions in English to do this are given in Figure 2.4.

1. Get the number of a card in the deck. Be sure it is a valid number from zero to 52.

2. If the number entered was zero, end the program.

3. Figure out the card's suit by knowing that the cards are kept in sequential order and that the first thirteen cards are spades, the next thirteen are hearts, then come diamonds, and finally clubs.

4. Figure out the card's value by knowing that after each group of thirteen cards the value sequence starts over again. Remember that a one is an ACE and that eleven, twelve, and thirteen are JACK, QUEEN, and KING.

5. Report the suit and the value found for the card.

6. Continue looking up card values until a card number of zero is entered.

Figure   2.4. An Example Problem Statement

Even though this looks quite specific there are still some procedures left undefined. How should the input information be requested? How should an invalid card number be handled. How should the knowledge of the deck's organization be used to find the suit and value? This much freedom in a set of instructions for people probably works quite well, but it will not work for the computer. No one has yet developed the programming instruction: "You know what I mean."

The instructions shown in Listing 2.4 are much more specific. Each instruction has been written in one of the statements developed in the first chapter. Notice that it sounds like instructions that "any dummy" could follow. This is the very thing we are looking for since the computer is a world-class dummy. Figure 2.5 shows a diagram of these instructions.

Listing 2.4 is not an actual program in any computer language. An actual program in a specific programming language is called a *program listing* or *program code*. It is so close to being a program, however, that it is called *pseudo code* or *sketch code*. Structured programs are developed in this format because it is fairly free-style, easy to work with and not tied to a specific language.

```
PROGRAM MAINLINE:

    DEFINE THE VARIABLES
    LOAD THE TABLE OF SUITS
    LOAD THE TABLE OF VALUES

    DO LOOP
        DO LOOP
            PRINT THE QUESTION ASKING FOR INPUT
            GET A CARD #
            IF THE CARD # IS NOT VALID THEN
                PRINT AN ERROR MESSAGE
        UNTIL THE CARD # IS VALID

        IF THE CARD # IS NOT ZERO THEN
            CALL THE REPORT ROUTINE

    UNTIL CARD # IS ZERO

END MAINLINE
STOP PROGRAM




REPORT ROUTINE

    CASE CARD # OF
         1 TO 13:   SUIT IS 1
        14 TO 26:   SUIT IS 2
        27 TO 39:   SUIT IS 3
        40 TO 52:   SUIT IS 4
    END CASE

    VALUE = CARD #
    DO WHILE VALUE IS GREATER THAN 13
        SUBTRACT 13 FROM VALUE
    END DO WHILE

    PRINT VALUE_TABLE(VALUE), SUIT_TABLE(SUIT)

RETURN
```

Listing 2.4. Example Problem Statement

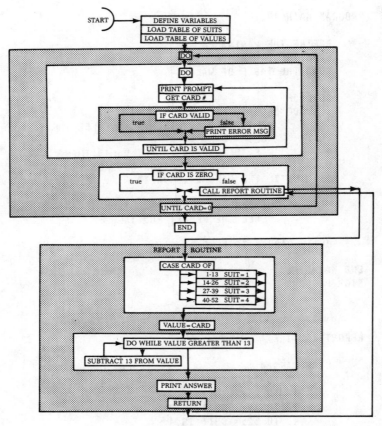

Figure 2.5 The Structure of the Example Problem

Once the program is developed in sketch code, it is easy to translate it into final program code in the language being used. The structure shown in Figure 2.5 shows how these instructions relate to those developed in Chapter 1. From now on we will use sketch code rather than structure diagrams because sketch code is easier to work with and looks more like the final program listings.

The programs shown in listings 2.5 and 2.6 are the card lookup example as finally written in the BASIC and Pascal computer languages. Comments in the listings refer to items of interest to the specific languages.

The sample programs listed in this book will need little comment. However, here are a few things to keep in mind as we go along.

Programs in this book are written with major parts in a specific order. At the beginning is a comment that identifies the program, who wrote it, and when it was last changed. This will be followed by definitions of all variable names that are not self-explanatory. BASIC programs will have the kernel of the program, called the *mainline* at the beginning followed by the subroutines that it uses. Pascal requires that all routines be defined before they are used, so the subroutines will be listed first with the program mainline at the very end.

In all programs, arrays are defined showing the type of data used in the array, how many dimensions there are, and how large the indexes may be. In Pascal this is done in the VAR section in which all variables are described. In BASIC the DIM statement is used to define arrays.

Every line of a BASIC program is numbered. You can go to (GOTO) or call (GOSUB) any instruction by using its line number. Any line starting with the key word REM is a remark. The two arrays are given dimensions in line 140. They are loaded with values using the READ statements in the loops from line 180 through 230 and the DATA statement in lines 150 through 170. Each execution of a READ statement uses the next constant in the DATA statements. The structured DO-WHILE, DO-UNTIL, and CASE statements have been constructed from simple IF-THEN-GOTO statements. The PRINT statement displays output on the terminal. INPUT reads variables from the terminal. This is a reasonably standard version of BASIC and should run on any system that allows arrays of character strings — such as the Radio Shack TRS-80.* BASIC programs in this book are written in this version.

Pascal is a free-form language that does not require a set format for each line of the program. Statements are separated from each other by a semicolon (;). There may be several statements on one line, or a single statement

---

*TRS-80 is a trademark of the Radio Shack division of Tandy Corporation.

```
10    REM  This is the card printing example written in BASIC
20    REM     Author: Jack Emmerichs
30    REM     Last changed: 1/01/82
40    REM
50    REM     Variables used will be:
60    REM        S$    SUIT TABLE      V$    VALUE TABLE
70    REM        S     SUIT NUMBER     V     VALUE NUMBER
80    REM        C     CARD NUMBER
90    REM        X     GENERAL COUNTER
100   REM
110   REM        NOTE: Some BASIC'S need a CLEAR statement here
120   REM     DEFINE THE TWO ARRAYS AND LOAD THEM WITH VALUES:
130   REM
140 DIM S$(4), V$(13)
150 DATA "SPADES","HEARTS","DIAMONDS","CLUBS"
160 DATA "ACE","2","3","4","5","6","7","8","9","10"
170 DATA "JACK","QUEEN","KING"
180 FOR X=1 TO 4
190   READ S$(X)
200 NEXT X
210 FOR X=1 TO 13
220   READ V$(X)
230 NEXT X
240   REM
250   REM     GET THE CARD TO USE AND EDIT IT
260   REM
270 PRINT "Enter a card number or zero if done: ";
280 INPUT C
290 IF C>=0 AND C<=52 AND C=INT(C) THEN GOTO 350
300 PRINT "*****  Please enter a proper card number."
310 GOTO 270
320   REM
330   REM     NOW PROCESS THE CARD
340   REM
350 IF C<>0 THEN GOSUB 410
360 IF C<>0 THEN GOTO 270
370 END
380   REM
390   REM     SUBROUTINE TO REPORT THE CARD'S VALUES
400   REM
410 S=1
420 IF C>13 THEN S=2
430 IF C>26 THEN S=3
440 IF C>39 THEN S=4
450 V=C
460 IF V<=13 THEN GOTO 490
470 V=V-13
480 GOTO 460
490 PRINT "   The card is the ";V$(V);" of ";S$(S);"."
500 RETURN
```

Listing 2.5. Example Program in BASIC

```
(*  This is the card printing example written in Pascal.
            Author: Jack Emmerichs,   Last Changed: 1/01/82      *)

PROGRAM DEMO (INPUT, OUTPUT);           (* Declare files & data    *)
    VAR
        SUIT:           ARRAY [1..4] OF STRING [8];
        VALUE:          ARRAY [1..13] OF STRING [5];
        CARD:           INTEGER;
        SUIT_NUMBER:    INTEGER;
        VALUE_NUMBER:   INTEGER;


    PROCEDURE REPORT;                   (* Report subroutine       *)
      BEGIN
        CASE (CARD-1) DIV 13 OF
            0:  SUIT_NUMBER := 1;
            1:  SUIT_NUMBER := 2;
            2:  SUIT_NUMBER := 3;
            3:  SUIT_NUMBER := 4;
        END;                            (* End of CASE statement   *)

        VALUE_NUMBER := CARD;
        WHILE VALUE_NUMBER>13 DO
            VALUE_NUMBER := VALUE_NUMBER - 13;

        WRITELN (OUTPUT, '  The card is the ',
            VALUE[VALUE_NUMBER],' of ',SUIT[SUIT_NUMBER],'.');
      END;                              (* End of REPORT routine   *)

BEGIN                                   (* Start:   load values    *)
  SUIT[1] := 'SPADES';          SUIT[2] := 'HEARTS';
  SUIT[3] := 'DIAMONDS';        SUIT[4] := 'CLUBS';
  VALUE[1] := 'ACE';    VALUE[2] := '2';    VALUE[3] := '3';
  VALUE[4] := '4';      VALUE[5] := '5';    VALUE[6] := '6';
  VALUE[7] := '7';      VALUE[8] := '8';    VALUE[9] := '9';
  VALUE[10] := '10';    VALUE[11] := 'JACK';
  VALUE[12] := 'QUEEN'; VALUE[13] := 'KING';

  REPEAT                                (* Mainline of program     *)
    REPEAT
      WRITE (OUTPUT,'Enter a card number or zero if done: ');
      READLN (INPUT,CARD);
      IF (CARD<0) OR (CARD>52) THEN
          WRITELN (OUTPUT,
                  '***** Please enter a proper card number');
    UNTIL (CARD>=0) AND (CARD<=52);

    IF CARD<>0 THEN                     (* Now process the card    *)
        REPORT;
  UNTIL CARD=0;
END.                                    (* End of program          *)
```

Listing 2.6. Example Program in Pascal

may be several lines long. All variables and subroutines must be defined before they are used. The statement

PROCEDURE REPORT;

defines the report subroutine. Notice that the CASE statement has been changed to calculate the precise suit of the card rather than using the range of values shown in the sketch code. Of course, this is not the only way to write the program. For example, you could replace the CASE statement by the single line:

SUIT NUMBER :=((CARD-1)DIV 13) +1;

The REPORT routine is called in the third line from the end by simply using the word REPORT. Anything between the character pairs "(*" and "*)" is a comment. Pascal has no feature like the READ and DATA statements in BASIC to load the arrays, so the program starts (at the comment BEGIN:) by loading the arrays with the appropriate values. The WRITE and WRITELN statements display output on the terminal and the READLN statement reads variables from the terminal. The LN at the end of a READ or WRITE statement indicates that it is reading or writing a complete line of information. The standard input and output files defined in the PRO-GRAM statement are used for these operations. This example is written in UCSD Pascal* which allows character strings as a variable type. Other versions may not allow strings. All Pascal programs in this book will be written in UCSD Pascal.

By this time you should be able to understand what each statement of each example program does. Use your system's programming manual for specific explanations of various statements.

VIII. REVIEW OF MAJOR IDEAS

This chapter has dealt with considerations unique to writing instructions for computers. The following major ideas should be well understood before you continue with the rest of the book:

---

*UCSD Pascal is a trademark of the Regents of the University of California.

- The only thing a computer does is to manipulate information in its memory and communicate the results to the outside world. A relatively small number of instructions control its operation.
- The primary types of data that a programmer deals with are numbers and strings of characters. In some languages other types of data may be available.
- Data in a program consists of constants, which never change, and variables, which are referred to by name and may have any value that is appropriate for the variable's data type.
- Data structures may be developed to organize related data elements into arrays, records, files, or other data types.
- Machines and programmers rarely use the same language. There is usually a translation program used to convert statements in a programming language into a machine-language program. Most applications, including the examples in this book, use high-level languages.
- High-level languages come in various dialects so that programs that run on one computer may not run on another. Your program may have to be modified to run on a computer using a different version of the same language.
- The instructions for a program must be very specific so that the computer which only does just what it is told to do, can perform them.
- Once you know what your program must do, the instructions can be developed using a sketch code regardless of the language being used. The final program will then be written in the actual programming language from this outline.

3

When Should a Program be Written (The Feasibility Study)

"Begin at the beginning."
Lewis Carroll

I. THE START OF A PROGRAMMING PROJECT

In the first two chapters we developed many of the tools needed to write computer programs. Now that we have the tools with which to work, we can start learning how to use them. We will do this by plunging right into a program development project. This is where the fun of programming really begins.

Enthusiasm for the project is usually quite high at this point, and there is a natural inclination to sit right down at the terminal and start programming. Unfortunately, this is much like running into the kitchen and throwing together various ingredients to see if oatmeal muffins will emerge. While there may be bakers who can do this on occasion, it is certainly not recommended if you want a consistently high quality product without a lot of frustration and false starts.

In this project we will use the *top-down* design method described in the first chapter. This method involves much more planning and design before we start to write any programs. Then, when we do start programming, it will go much more quickly and with fewer difficulties.

Large commercial projects that are developed over several months or years are often broken into several smaller pieces. While there is no need to be quite as formal when working with a few small programs or with a project of personal interest, it is not a bad idea to deal with these projects in smaller pieces as well. However, the same technique can help you to be successful in your personal programming, and therefore to enjoy it more.

The entire life of a program or system of related programs, from the time someone thinks up the project until it is no longer used, is called the *project life cycle*. The life cycle of a moderately sized project is shown in Figure 3.1.

The first step of the project, called the *feasibility study*, defines what is to be done and determines if it is possible. This planning step is often skipped in small projects, and the results often suffer. The *general design* is where the program really starts to take shape. The major items of data and the primary program functions are defined and related to each other. In the *detail design*, the general design is fleshed out and specific details are filled in. A dictionary of all data items is developed, and the sketch code for the program itself is written. It is not until the *implementation*, however, that programs are actually written in a programming language, tested, and run on the computer. The amount of time and effort usually spent on each step of the project is represented by the corresponding area on the chart.

The boundary between one step and another is shown as a slanted line because there may be no clear-cut point where you stop doing one thing and start doing another. The first step develops a definition of the overall functions to be performed. The project should then have a reasonably smooth progression of ever more detailed refinement until the final program has been finished. Details worked out at one level of development may force change in previous design ideas, so there is some movement back and forth along the development path. The idea, however, is to perform each step well enough that backtracking is held to a minimum. When all the design steps are finally completed, the programs are written in the implementation step. The boundaries between steps are used primarily as check points to review the status of the whole project.

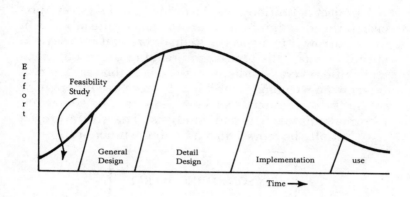

Figure 3.1. A Simple Project Life Cycle

Once the program is in use you will usually think of enhancements or corrections that would make the program even better. This often leads to changes in the original design and may even lead to a whole new project. If you work with a program long enough you are likely to find yourself at the beginning of a new project life cycle.

To show how these steps in project development work, each succeeding chapter of the book will cover one step of the project. This chapter begins at the beginning by determining what it is we want to do and if it feasible to do it.

II. IDENTIFYING THE PROBLEM

The most important thing to remember at the beginning of a project is that the statement of the problem must be specific. "Let's fix something to eat" may get you out of your chair and into the kitchen, but it is too vague to do much more than that. Once in the kitchen, you face the real decision: what to fix.

A project definition must be refined until it is very precise. If the idea that first occurs to you is quite broad, you must narrow it to a specific item, or break it into several specific items. This process of breaking broad functions down into several smaller functions is at the very heart of top-down development, and will be developed more fully in the next chapter. For now, let's take a somewhat informal approach to our analysis. The entire project may initially be represented as a single function:

> FIX SOMETHING TO EAT

Staring at the cupboards, we realize that we still do not know just what to do. Therefore we refine the problem definition to include three specific actions: fix something cold to drink, make some oatmeal muffins, and assemble a platter of sliced cheese and apples. The single function of FIX SOMETHING TO EAT has not been changed, simply refined.

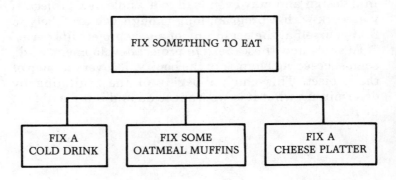

As you can see I have not defined any new functions, but simply refined the original function. All of the functions at the lower level of this structure are connected to the higher level function. Most of this looks better, but FIX A COLD DRINK is still too vague. We need to know what type of drink to fix. A more precise refinement is as follows:

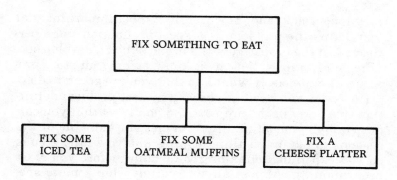

This time we have improved the problem definition by being more specific. We can now further refine the problem definition by breaking each function down into several sub-functions. This top-down process is to be continued until the entire project is stated in terms of specific functions that are clearly understood.

In many cases the project as originally stated will turn out to be more than you really want to do. The overall function may then be redefined to reflect this change. In the case of fixing something to eat, we may decide that some oatmeal muffins would be enough for now. The project is then redefined as follows:

FIX SOME OATMEAL MUFFINS

In a large commercial programming project this process of defining the problem may take months to complete. Often the future user of the program does not really know what the problem is or what is needed to get the job done. On a small project this process may be done rather informally. For example, walking into the kitchen, looking for a snack, and deciding to fix some muffins may only take a few seconds. Defining a programming project may take a few days while you talk to other people interested in what you are doing, sketch out ideas of your own and try alternate problem statements. Regardless of how long you spend, however, it is most important that you define the problem as a specific function to be performed. If the project covers a broad subject, develop specific sub-funtions. You must know before you start programming precisely what it is that you are going to do.

However, you need not have a perfect problem definition this early in the project. And don't feel that you can not change your mind after you get started. One of the reasons to put off writing the programs to a later step is so you can finish changing your mind before you start programming. Almost anyone will develop a more specific idea of what must be done as the design progresses. What we want at the beginning is a specific idea of what we will work towards. If that goal must be modified along the way, fine.

A. What Are We Going To Do?

Most successful programming projects start with a problem. Your interest in the problem leads you to investigate what is required to solve it and, eventually, to develop a solution. You are more likely to be successful on those projects that you are interested in than on those you start simply because you feel like writing a program. Therefore, for the remainder of this book, we shall try to define an interesting goal, develop a program for that purpose, and use the example as a side benefit as we go along.

Our project should be large enough to serve as a comprehensive example, but not too complex for an introduction to program design. It should deal with a subject that most readers will find familiar and easy to understand. Finally, it should produce a program that is fun and easy to use.

Hey! I've got a brilliant idea — let's develop a program that will be able to play cards with us! I wonder if we could get the Frammis to deal the cards for it?

Most projects start at about this level of detail. Now let's refine this into something usable.

B. The Problem Statement For Our Example

So far our "brilliant idea" is only a vague notion: have the computer play cards with us. This idea must be developed to include specific functions required to play any game of cards, or it must be narrowed down to a more specific sub-function of card playing. Figure 3.2 shows a few of the sub-functions that could be developed.

There are many ways to sub-divide the function of "playing cards". Some games may fit under more than one "object of the game" category and under more than one "number of players" group. If we considered all examples for all types of card games for any number of players, we would end up with hundreds of functions to define. Perhaps it would be easiest to pick a specific card game and concentrate on that.

We should avoid overly complex games like Panguingue which may not be widely known. We should also avoid games that depend too heavily on remembering the play of the cards. Computers are perfect at remembering what they have done, and it is no fun to play with an opponent who never makes a mistake.

After considering various card games we find that the version of poker called Blackjack (or Twenty-one) has all the characteristics we need. The game is known to most people and has fairly simple rules. The part of the dealer is particularly well defined. And the game requires only the dealer and one other player. Therefore, the first reasonable statement of our project will be the single function:

```
HAVE THE COMPUTER PLAY
A GAME OF BLACKJACK
```

This can be further refined by defining what part the computer will play and whose rules will be used for the game. Most people who play Blackjack at a casino play against a permanent dealer. It may be most natural, therefore, to have the computer play the part of dealer so that we can play against it. The game will be developed

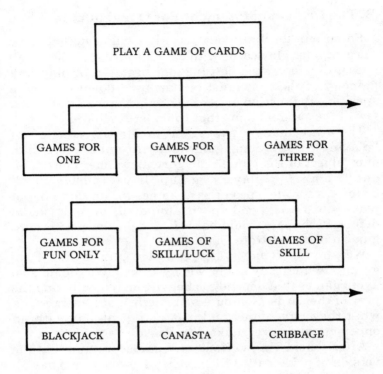

Figure 3.2. Major Functions of Playing Cards

according to the rules for the game of blackjack, with a permanent bank, stated in *Hoyle's Official Rules of Card Games* (Fawcett Crest Books, New York, 1968).

We have now narrowed our original idea down to a single specific function, rather than refining it into more detailed sub-functions. This single function may be stated as:

> HAVE THE COMPUTER PLAY
> THE PART OF THE DEALER
> IN A GAME OF BLACKJACK
> ACCORDING TO HOYLE

The object of our project will be to develop one or more programs, along with their associated data, that satisfy this problem statement. Such a group of programs and data may be called a system.

The term *computer system* is used in different ways by different people. In its fullest sense it encompasses all equipment, programs, data, and procedures required to perform a particular function. In this book we will not deal with the equipment (called hardware) or how it is used. Instead we will focus on the programs (called software) that work on the hardware. We will therefore use the term software system or simple system to refer to the programs and data developed to run as part of a complete computer system. Our objective, then, is to develop a software system to play the part of the dealer in a game of Blackjack according to Hoyle. We shall call this the "Blackjack system" for short.

III. CAN IT BE DONE?

This takes care of the first part of the feasibility study: deciding what it is that we are going to do. The next step is to see if what we want to do is possible to do. There are two general areas to consider when checking the feasibility of a project. First, determine whether the available equipment can perform the required functions. Second, determine whether you are capable of writing the program or programs for the job. Like the original problem definition, this process may require anything from a few moments thought to a detailed investigation.

A. Is It More Than My Equipment Can Handle?

Until you have written some programs that reach the limits of your computer, you will have trouble answering this question for sure. There are some things to consider when starting a new program: (1) Will there be enough memory to store the program and data (and, with BASIC, perhaps a separate interpreter or run-time package); (2) Will the computer operate fast enough to make the program usable.

Most small computers are sold with relatively small amounts of memory to reduce the initial cost of the machine. However, you can usually add memory capacity up to some maximum amount. With a bit of experimentation you will soon have a good idea of the size program that will fit in your memory. A well known law of programming states that no matter how much memory you have, there will always be a project that interests you that is slightly too big for your machine.

Speed of execution presents a different kind of problem. There is usually no way that the speed of a computer can be increased. The most common difficulty arises when the computer has to check a lot of information in a short time, as in an interactive game. This is most likely to happen in a system using an interpreter. Speed of execution and program size are the reasons that almost all of the programs developed by the manufacturer as part of a computer system are written at the assembler language level.

The considerations of storage space and execution speed also apply to information stored outside the computer itself on magnetic tape or disk units. These units are called external storage devices and can hold large amounts of data. The size of files stored on such devices can be estimated by calculating how much space will be required for each item in the file and multiplying that times the number of items to be stored. For example, if an average recipe requires 500 characters and you want to save 500 recipes in a file, the file will require space for 250,000 characters (500 times 500 equals 250,000). The speed of external devices is much slower than the speed of the computer, and tape storage is much slower than disk storage.

On occasion there may be other pieces of equipment to consider. If reports are to be generated you must have a printer capable of displaying the appropriate characters on paper large enough to hold your reports. A printer with no lower case letters, for example, would not be a good choice for producing business letters. Other projects may involve home-made equipment such as simple robots, model railroad controllers, or almost anything else. If you plan to use equipment like this be sure you know its limitations at the beginning of the project.

B. Is It More Than I Want To Tackle Right Now?

The second area to consider when evaluating the feasibility of a project is to determine if we are capable of writing the programs. This is a very subjective evaluation. The object is to separate long, demanding projects that will turn into frustrating failures from reasonable projects that challenge us with new knowledge and expanded capabilities.

The most important rule is to understand the statement of the problem. If you developed the problem definition yourself, as explained above, this should not create difficulties. If you see a problem in a magazine article or get an idea from another person, however, be sure you really understand what is to be done before you begin. Few things are as frustrating as working on a project that you do not understand.

The next thing is to decide if you have enough time to work on the project. If you start a major project that will require lots of planning, programming, and evaluation when you have barely enough time for what you are now doing, you may never have time to finish it. You are your own best judge about how much time you have, but remember that programming requires reasonably long stretches of time for uninterrupted thinking and working.

A final item to consider is how much new material you will have to learn in order to understand and complete the project. A project to move a robot around a room may require a knowledge of electronics, machine design, geometry, and several other disciplines. It is certainly not required that you understand everything about all of these items at the start, but you will certainly have to learn about them as you go along. Try to pick projects that involve areas that you already know something about or that you have wanted to know more about. If you have to learn too much new material that does not interest you, you may lose heart and not finish. This takes the enjoyment out of programming very quickly.

The time to consider these matters is now — before the problem occurs. Of course, you can't foresee the unforeseeable. The best time to consider stopping any project in favor of one more likely to succeed is as soon as you are aware of the problem. The goal of the top-down approach is to identify insurmountable problems as soon as possible to avoid wasting time on a project that cannot be completed.

C. Can The Blackjack Program Be Done?

The tests for a project's feasibility can now be applied to our Blackjack project. This game has actually been programmed by many people; it should work well on most of today's small computers. The main difficulty is in graphics. If a complete game with nice screen displays is developed, it may be too large for some computers with a minimum amount of memory. We may have to develop a scaled-down version of the program for smaller machines. Such a scaled-down version would reduce the use of arrays and character strings in the program, since these are often limited in small computers. There are no timing requirements in the game, so speed should be no problem. And, finally, there will be no files stored on external devices.

The development of the Blackjack programs should not be too difficult for a beginner. Anyone who does not know the rules of the game will have to study two pages in the *Official Rules of Card Games* (Appendix B of this book). The program will not take long to develop, but offers plenty of opportunity for artful design and elegant programming.

It should come as no surprise that there are no compelling reasons not to continue with the project.

IV. FINDING ADDITIONAL HELP

Now that we have decided what we are going to do, the next step should be to see if someone else has already done it. Traditionally, computer programmers have spent much of their time re-inventing programs that have already been developed and tested. Even if nobody else has done just what you wish to do, there may be portions of your project that have already been developed.

In many cases, there may be programs for your computer commercially available that will suit your needs. Today's computer stores usually carry a large selection of software products that can be used right off the shelf. If you can get the program listings, you may be able to modify the program to suit your specific needs. This is most often possible for small systems using a BASIC interpreter, since here the original programs run directly on the computer. Programs that are developed with a compiler or semi-compiler are usually not sold with the original program listing and are therefore very hard to modify. Be very careful about modifying somebody else's programs, however. This will surely nullify any warranty that the programs may have. Furthermore, if you sell or give away your changed programs you are probably infringing on the original author's copyrights. If you want to change another person's programs, make an extra copy so you can save the original and be sure that you only use the modified program yourself.

The next place to look for help would be in books and magazine articles about programming. There are many magazines that offer articles each month on solving programming problems. They may also answer common questions sent in by readers. Even if you don't find items on the project at hand, you may learn something that will be of use later. Magazines are also an excellent way to keep up to date on what programs are currently available from your local dealer or directly through the mail.

In the case of our Blackjack program we could no doubt buy any one of several available programs and have it work just fine. However, developing the program ourselves will be more instructive. Besides, there is always the feeling that "I'd rather do it myself." As long as you are only programming for fun, this attitude is quite acceptable. When you are interested in having a quality final product with a minimum of wasted effort, however, remember that there are several places that you can turn for help — including buying the whole program right at the start.

V. REVIEW OF MAJOR IDEAS

This chapter has served two purposes. First, it defined a programming project as a cycle that can be broken into several steps — from a feasibility study at the start, to the use of the final product at the end. It then took us through the first step of our Blackjack project. The following are the major points covered in this chapter:

- A programming project is easier to manage if it is broken into the several steps shown in the Project Life Cycle.
- The first step of the cycle is to develop a specific statement of the problem as a function to be performed, and to determine if the function is possible.
- A vague problem statement can be refined by breaking it into specific sub-functions, by reducing the scope of the original idea to such a sub-function, or by a combination of both techniques.
- Once a specific project has been chosen, the available equipment should be checked to see if it is capable of supporting everything that is to be done.
- Your own time and interest as a programmer should be considered.
- As a first step towards developing the project, look for any help from existing programs or articles about programming that may apply.
- The primary reasons for all these preparations are (1) to know before starting exactly what is to be done, and (2) to identify as soon as possible any projects that are not feasible or desirable.

4

What Should the Program Do? (The General Design)

"Build from the bottom up and not from the top down."

Franklin Delano Roosevelt

"The heresy of one age becomes the orthodoxy of the next."

Helen Keller

One of the major objectives of the previous chapter was to identify what sort of software system we are going to develop and to define its overall function. In this chapter we continue this process by breaking the high-level function down into smaller sub-functions until every task to be performed has been defined in terms of many simple functions. We will also define the types of data required, identify where they will come from, and determine how they will be used. When we are finished with this second step —— the General Design —— we will know everything that the system must do, how many programs will be required to do it, what information must be needed, where this information will come from and how it will eventually be used.

Just as there are many ways to classify card games, there are usually many ways to organize a complex programming function. The design developed in this book is not the only "correct" solution. After you have completed several of your own programming projects you will no doubt develop your own programming style — that is, your personal method of completing the steps of a system design. The procedures used in top-down structured design follow a well-ordered path of development, but they are independent of the programmer's style.

There are two ways to begin developing our Blackjack project. One is to start by defining what we want as the final output, then develop the input and functions required to produce this output. The other approach is to start with the functions that must be performed and then to develop the data that these functions will use as input and output. Before the General Design has been completed we will have to work on the functions and the data, so we might as well start with the easiest one. This usually depends on whether the project is primarily *data processing,* in which the data is most important and the processing is relatively simple, or *procedure processing,* in which the procedures (functions) performed are most important and the data is relatively simple.

In the case of the Blackjack project we will start by analyzing the functions to be performed because we are primarily interested in the procedures for playing the game. Besides, we have such a nice list of them in the *Official Rules of Card Games.* Keep in mind, however, that we also could have started with data requirements.

I. BREAKING FUNCTIONS INTO SMALLER UNITS

The object of analyzing the functions within our system is to break each complex function down into several simpler ones. The job of each complex function then becomes one of coordinating the operations of its sub-functions. If these sub-elements are still quite complex they can, in turn, be broken down into their own sub-elements. This process continues until everything that must be done in the system is defined in terms of a number of simple operations. Each of these operations, called a module of the system, performs a single, well-defined function. The job of the system as a whole will be to control the operations of these modules. During the implementation stage, each module will be translated into actual computer code.

There are two general principles to keep in mind when deciding how to break a complex function into smaller sub-functions:

1. Every operation within a single function should be directly related to all the other operations within that function.

2. The operations of one function should not be directly related to the operations of any other function.

The structured programming statements developed in the first chapter are excellent examples of these principles.

A. Strength and Coupling

The extent to which operations within a single module relate to one another is called the module's strength. Each module should perform only one function. A DO-WHILE statement, for example, does not contain any operations used by a DO-UNTIL statement or any other type of statement. If any extraneous operations are found within a module, they should be moved to another function or the whole module should be further refined into smaller sub-elements. This will be very important later on when you are trying to understand what a particular part of the system is doing.

The extent to which two modules are independent of each other's processing is called the coupling between them. Like the programming statements, each module in the system should have one entry point and one exit point. This will usually take the form of a subroutine CALL and RETURN. When called, each module should perform a single well-defined function and return, regardless of the status of other modules in the system. This will also be very important later if changes have to be made to a part of the system. If one function needs to be changed, there should be no side effects in or from functions which are coupled to this one.

In a well-designed system, all modules should be as high in strength and as loosely coupled to each other as the programming instructions themselves. In real life, it is not often possible to achieve these goals completely, but we shall keep them in mind as we develop our Blackjack system.

II. DEVELOPING THE SYSTEM'S STRUCTURE

When a system is defined in terms of functional elements and sub-elements showing what controls what, it takes on the form of a hierarchy. This structure is usually drawn as a tree, similar to Figure 4.1.

Each function in the system is represented on the chart by a single box containing a descriptive label. The function of the whole system is shown in one box at the first level of the chart. The sub-elements of each module form the next lower level of that module's branch. A module is made up of all its sub-elements and any procedures required to control the operations of those sub-elements. As the chart branches out into the lower levels, all of the complex functions of the system are defined in terms of simple "low-level" operations. Each complex function will usually have from two to eight sub-elements. The length of each branch of the chart depends on the complexity of the functions defined in that part of the system; there need not be any relationship between the number of levels reached in the different branches. The last module in each branch must be a single, simple function.

When discussing the relationships between modules in a hierarchy, the following terms will be used: (refer to the module names in Figure 4.1)

A is the parent of B and H.
B and H are siblings to each other.
B and H are offspring of A.
D has all three of these relationships with its neighbors.

Other relationships such as aunts, uncles, and cousins are usually avoided because they are not precise.

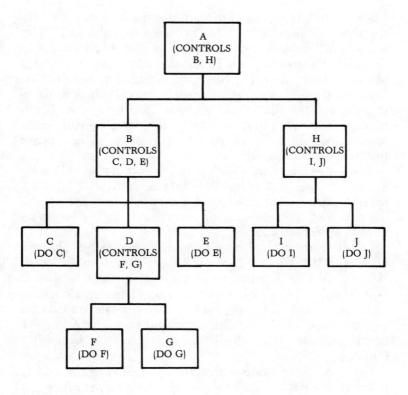

Figure 4.1. A Structural Hierarchy

Any module in a hierarchy may have several siblings and offspring, but it must have only one parent. It is possible to have a single offspring if the execution of a function is so complex that the control of that single module constitutes a high-level function.

Each module on the chart can use its offspring by calling them as subroutines. In the hierarchy shown in Figure 4.1, function A can call function B and function H to complete its tasks. These functions may be called in any order and as often as necessary to perform function A. Each of these functions may, in turn, call their sub-elements, but that is of no interest to function A. Each module is coupled to its offspring and its parent by calls and returns but has no direct connection to any other function in the system.

There are cases in which a function may be called by more than one higher level module, or "parent." This is a more complex structure called a network. In this case the branches of the tree can converge at the lower levels as shown in Figure 4.2.

In this structure, G may be called from either D or H. However, it always returns to the module that called it. When a module is called from many places in a system it is referred to as a utility subroutine. Complex networks are often drawn with the utility subroutines grouped in a separate section of the chart without showing all of the connections to them. This keeps the chart from becoming cluttered.

Developing a system design by breaking functions down into a network offers the following advantages:

- Everything that the system must do will be defined during this design phase.

- At the complex higher levels of the system you do not have to worry about the details of how things will be done. Each sub-element is simply invoked with a subroutine call.

- When working with low-level processes of the system you only have to deal with one reasonably simple operation at a time.

- Functions that are to be used in several places in the system can easily be identified.

- A clear relationship is established between all the operations in the system.

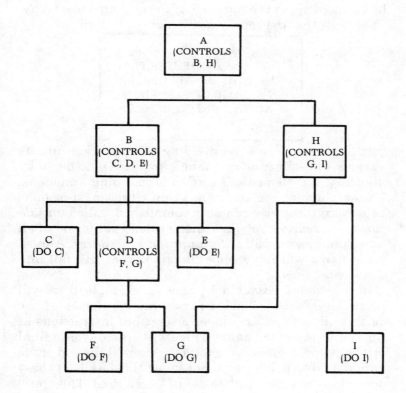

Figure 4.2. A Structural Network

A. The Initial Structure Of Our Blackjack System

It is now time to develop the first few levels of our Blackjack system. We will start by breaking the system's primary function down into its first level of sub-elements.

The beginning of the General Design will pick up where the previous chapter left off by using the project's problem statement as the top level of the system's hierarchy. Therefore, the first representation of our design is:

> HAVE THE COMPUTER PLAY
> THE PART OF THE DEALER
> IN A GAME OF BLACKJACK
> ACCORDING TO HOYLE

It is now time to start dividing this function into its various sub-elements. A common practice is to begin by allowing for elements called housekeeping functions. These functions include things that either must be done before anything else can be accomplished, called *initialization procedures,* or what must be done at the end of all other processing, called *termination procedures.* Almost all systems will have some functions that will fall into these categories.

In the case of a Blackjack game, for example, there will be requirements to load arrays with the names of the cards and to show the player a screen of instructions at the beginning of the game. There will probably be a final message and some scoring totals to show at the end of the game. At this point we do not know the details of these operations but they will no doubt be required. Therefore, the first two levels of our system structure looks like this:

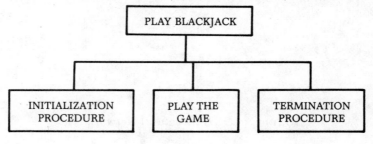

The overall system function has been restated as PLAY BLACKJACK to keep things simple. The initialization and termination procedures, whatever they may eventually contain, have been split off from the actual playing of the game. We can now concentrate on developing the game, knowing that whenever an initializing or terminating function is found it can be put under these new functions.

B. A More Detailed Structure For Our Blackjack System

Now comes the fun part — where do we go from here? There are no set rules or specific procedures for developing a system's structure. This is why each programmer will develop a slightly different design. Just how does one actually go about it?

The design process becomes somewhat easier with practice, so don't be surprised if what looks easy in this example becomes a bit harder when you are working on your own. Approach the general design as a puzzle in which you must find all of the pieces as well as put them together. So grab a pencil and plenty of blank paper and get started. The design process presented in this example will be the actual procedure that the author used to develop the Blackjack program.

The first thing to do is to identify as many functions as we can in some organized way. This may be done by working from the first function to be performed through to the last, or by using any other order that helps organize our thoughts. However, always look for the highest level of abstraction first. Then work from the top of the structure diagram down toward the bottom, leaving the details to be worked out later.

Since our goal is to play Blackjack according to Hoyle, let's start by reading the rules of the game in the Official Rules of Card Games. These rules are shown in APPENDIX B at the back of this book. As each new function is encountered, it will be written down on a sheet of paper without worrying (yet) about how one function relates to another. For the game of Blackjack, the first list of functions might look like this:

- SETTING UP A DOUBLE DECK OF CARDS
- SHUFFLING THE CARDS
- BETTING
- DEALING THE HANDS
- TAKING CARE OF NATURALS
- DRAWING FOR THE PLAYER'S HAND
- DRAWING FOR THE DEALER'S HAND
- SETTLING BETS
- RESHUFFLING THE CARDS
- SPLITTING PAIRS OF CARDS

This covers the points in the rules and is almost in sequential order for the actual play of the game.

Once the initial functions have been identified, they must be organized in some way. The first thing to do is to look for duplicated functions. In this case shuffling the cards and reshuffling the cards could no doubt be combined into a single shuffling function. We can indicate that this is sometimes required during the deal of the hand by changing the function DEALING THE HANDS to read DEALING AND RESHUFFLING.

When duplicates have been eliminated, the list of functions should be organized by grouping related items together. One that stands out from the rest is SET UP A DOUBLE DECK OF CARDS. This will only be done once before the first hand is played and is not really a part of the game. It is an initialization function and will be listed under the first major sub-function of our chart. Another function that stands out is shuffling. This is done at the start of the game and between some hands, but not between every hand. All the other functions are used during the playing of a single hand of blackjack and can be grouped together.

Everything except setting up the deck will be listed under the PLAYING THE GAME on the chart. Also, SPLITTING PAIRS OF CARDS is listed after the handling of naturals and before the players start to draw cards, since this is when splitting pairs is normally done. There are no termination procedures yet.

Remember that these observations and changes are one person's way of organizing the first list of functions. While it follows the general pattern of eliminating duplicates, organizing by groups and then putting the groups in order, the details of each of these decisions are quite personal. This reorganization results in the following modified list of major functions:

INITIALIZATION PROCEDURES
- SETTING UP A DOUBLE DECK OF CARDS

PLAYING THE GAME
- SHUFFLING THE CARDS
- PLAYING A HAND OF BLACKJACK
  - BETTING
  - DEALING AND RESUFFLING
  - TAKING CARE OF NATURALS
  - SPLITTING PAIRS OF CARDS
  - DRAWING FOR THE PLAYER'S HAND
  - DRAWING FOR THE DEALER'S HAND
  - SETTLING BETS

TERMINATION PROCEDURES

Notice that this is a tabulated list using indentation to indicate relationships, rather than a structural hierarchy. The format used to show structural information is not as important as the information itself. However, these functions can also be shown, using somewhat shorter module descriptions, as the structural chart in Figure 4.3.

There is more to playing a game of cards, however, than we have considered so far. This is because the rules we have been using as listed in Appendix B are for people who know something about playing card games. Common activities such as keeping track of the chips won and lost, or how the dealer and player talk to each other during the play of the game, are left to the reader's common sense. In a computer program however, we must define *all* aspects of the game in detail.

A good way to identify any parts of the game that may have been overlooked is to play an imaginary game. While you play, keep track of everything that the comput- 1eeds to do to play the game. In most projects analyz- an imaginary "dry run" will help identify all of the iired functions. The following scene represents my

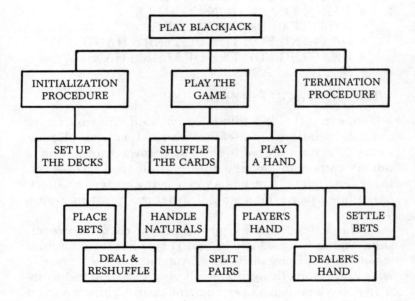

Figure 4.3. An Alternate Format for Displaying Functions

imaginary session at the Blackjack table with the computer playing the part of the dealer:

> Upon approaching a gambling table at a casino, I ask the dealer what the game is and how it is played. In response, the dealer tells me that it is a Blackjack game and informs me of the rules being used. This sounds interesting, so I purchase a supply of chips from the bank and sit down to play the first hand. The dealer shuffles two decks of cards together and lets me cut the cards. The first hand is completed and, of course, I win.
> Several more hands are played while I win some and lose some. Finally, I decide to take a small break. At this time, I would like to see how I am doing, so I ask the dealer how much I have won or lost and how long we have been playing. If I have won lots of money or if I am running short of chips, I may want to cash some in or buy some new ones at the bank. At this point I decide to have the deck reshuffled because the person watching over my shoulder is good at keeping track of the odds and it makes me nervous. Once I am alone at the table, however, I will let the deck go as long as possible without being shuffled so that I may try keeping track of the odds myself. After about forty-five minutes I get bored and decide to quit. The dealer thanks me for a fascinating game, tells me how I did, cashes in the last of my chips (if I have any left) and bids me good-bye.

As you can see, little of this has to do with the actual play of the hands. These interactions with the dealer and the bank make the game more enjoyable, however. If we make them part of our system, it will feel more like a friendly game of cards. If you were designing the game for yourself you would no doubt come up with your own personal touches.

To provide these interactions we must add the following functions to those we have taken from Hoyle's rules:

- SHOW INSTRUCTIONS ON HOW THE GAME IS PLAYED
- DEAL WITH THE BANK
- REPORT ON HOW THE GAME IS GOING

- SHUFFLE THE CARDS ON DEMAND
- QUIT THE GAME AND SHOW HOW THE
  PLAYER DID

All of these functions seem to have about the same importance in our session at the table as playing another hand of cards would have. At any point, for example, we may wish to buy chips, see how we are doing, reread the instructions, or play another hand of cards. After the completion of any of these activities we may again choose among any of these options. This suggests that perhaps the major function PLAY THE GAME should be changed to SELECT THE NEXT ACTIVITY. This function will include the activities listed above, as well as playing a hand of cards. The one exception is the final status display and good-bye message at the end of the game. This is a termination procedure and will be listed under that function on the system structure chart. You may have noticed that we have added another function in which shuffling is to be done. Since this is the third time this function has shown up, SHUFFLE THE CARDS will become the first utility subroutine. It can be called from anywhere in the system.

If we reorganize things in this way the major functions can be represented as follows:

INITIALIZATION PROCEDURES
- SET UP A DOUBLE DECK OF CARDS

SELECT THE NEXT ACTIVITY
- SHOW INSTRUCTIONS ON HOW THE GAME IS
  PLAYED
- DEAL WITH THE BANK
- REPORT ON HOW THE GAME IS GOING
- SHUFFLE THE CARDS ON DEMAND
- PLAY A HAND OF BLACKJACK (to include all of
  the details developed in Figure 4.3)

TERMINATION PROCEDURES
- QUIT THE GAME AND SHOW HOW THE
  PLAYER FARED

UTILITY SUBROUTINES
- SHUFFLE THE CARDS

All of this information can now be added to the system's structural network. In the final network, functions that have only one sub-element (such as the INITIALI-

ZATION PROCEDURE) are usually combined with the sub-element and renamed to indicate the one thing that they do rather than being "broken down" into a single detailed item. At this stage, however, we will show all the items that we have developed so far. This illustrates more clearly what we have done and allows additional functions to be easily added, if necessary. We can simplify the structure later after everything has been included. In the meantime, the system structure now looks like Figure 4.4.

This is a good approximation for the structure of our system and seems to contain everything needed to describe the whole game. Some of these functions will no doubt be broken into still further detail as the design progresses. Dealing with the bank, for example, will have to allow for buying new chips and cashing in existing ones. We have developed the major functions, however, and it is time to step back and consider what we have done so far.

C. A Look At What We Have Done

Whenever you take time out to consider the project as a whole, it is a good idea to see if you are still satisfied with the way everything is going. It is easier to correct things now than it will be later on. There are very few guidelines for this type of introspective analysis. However, if you ever start to feel vaguely dissatisfied with the project, stop then and there, find out what is bothering you, and see what you can do to fix it. In the case of our Blackjack game things seem to be progressing nicely and we have not run into any significant problems yet. So far, so good, so let's continue.

In a large system with many complex functions, there is often more to be done than one program can easily handle. When this happens, each module is usually divided into several different programs, each one simple enough to be easily understood and small enough to fit the computer's memory. Such programs usually share information by creating data files on external storage devices. Each program within the system takes care of its own task, just as each module within a program takes care of its own function. For very large applications, such as the computerized accounting systems for large corporations, entire systems of programs work with each other;

each system performing a specific but complex task. The structural hierarchy of a complete computer installation may look something like Figure 4.5.

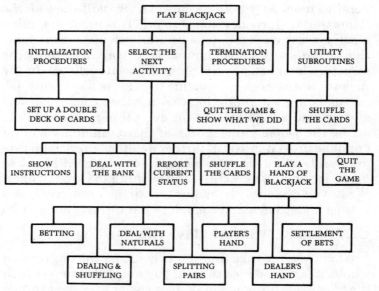

Figure 4.4. The Expanded Structure Diagram

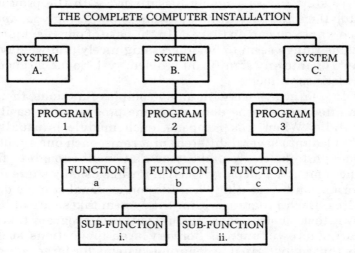

Figure 4.5. The Computer System Hierarchy

The number of systems, programs, functions and subfunctions in any part of the system, and the number of additional levels of sub-functions along any branch, will of course depend on the details of the installation. Even a system as small as an individual's personal computing applications can contain all of these elements.*

Once we have defined the major functions, we can decide how many programs our system will require. Our Blackjack "system" will consist of just one program.

D. A Look At The Process We Have Used

While we are taking time out to review what we have done, we can make some observations about how the top-down method we have been using has worked and what we have gained by using it.

The greatest advantage of this design approach is that you don't lose track of the overall objective while dealing with the details. This is in marked contrast to the way many small projects are developed. Often the designer becomes buried in specific parts of the system without knowing how (or if) these parts will eventually be used. For example, it would have been most interesting at the beginning of our project to write a little program to shuffle and deal the deck of cards. We may not have realized then, however, that we would eventually be using a double deck that could be shuffled or dealt independently. The original program would no doubt have required rewriting to make these changes. As it is, we can now work on any part of the system without worrying about whether or not it will fit with the whole.

A second advantage of top-down design is that the structure of the system is developed around the functions that must be performed. If any of these functions require modifications at some later time, it will be easy to see where the changes should be made. It will also be easy to change one function without changing anything else.

---

*Things will work best if everything is developed from the top down, of course, but this is usually quite hard to do because programs or systems are usually added piecemeal as a person becomes interested in them over a long period of time.

A third advantage is that we have already done a better job of documenting how the system will work than many programmers do for an entire project. When the time comes for changes to be made — and that time always comes — it will be crucial to have a written guide to show how the system works, especially if you eventually develop several different projects and can't keep all the details in your head at once. As we continue developing our Blackjack game, we will continue adding its documentation as well.

There are two minor disadvantages to this method of development. The first is entirely psychological: it is frankly more fun to jump right in and start programming than it is to take the time to figure out how things should be done in the first place. Please know that your patience will pay off handsomely. There will be far less re-development and frustration due to design changes. It's no fun to take apart something that has already been done, and programs that have been heavily modified usually do not work as well as ones that operate as they were originally designed. Persevere during the early design steps because the final writing of the programs will be more fun than ever.

The other problem deals with the fact that we are developing the project for the programmer's benefit rather than for the computer's benefit. In the early days of computer programming, machines were small and expensive. Programming time, however, was relatively easy to come by, so programmers spent much effort developing efficient programs that made the fewest demands on the equipment. Today things are just the other way around. Even small personal computers can have reasonably large memories and run relatively fast. The time available for program development, however, has become very expensive.

Top-down structured programming was developed to smooth program development for the programmer at the expense of the computer. This means that while our Blackjack program will be easy to understand and write, it may not be quite as efficient as one written to make the best possible use of the equipment. For most programs this is not a major problem. But you should be aware that we are not necessarily developing the most efficient program from the computer's point of view.

We should mention here that there can be exceptions to the top-down direction of design. In some projects, it may be necessary to experiment with some specific detailed functions to see if the project is even possible. The system will then be developed down toward these specific modules. Working from the top and bottom toward the middle, as it were, usually results in changing both the higher system structure and the detailed routines before everything works together. This is to be avoided if possible, but sometimes it is necessary.

Now that we know basically what the system is going to do, it is time to consider the information required by the system. This will include data gathered from the outside world as input, data maintained within the system for its own use, and data to be displayed to the outside world as output.

III. DEFINING THE FLOW OF DATA IN THE SYSTEM

Remember that in the beginning of this chapter, we decided to develop the system's functions first, then to look at the data requirements. You will usually work back and forth between the functions and the data used throughout the project's development. The following is an initial look at the data required by the Blackjack program.

The initial analysis of a system's flow of information starts by defining everything that we want the system to produce as output. From this we can define all the data required to give us that output and the functions needed to develop it. Finally, we define what information is needed as input and what information can be included in the programs as consultants. In the case of the Blackjack program, we have already defined much of this from the official rules of the game and from the dialogues based on an imaginary session with the game. It is now time to look at the output from the system in more detail.

We can begin working with the system's information requirements in much the same way as we began working with the system's functional requirements — start writing down everything that comes to mind. To maintain some order during this process, we can go through each function looking for any information that should be displayed. The following list is a first attempt to identify the system's output:

Start the game. (initialization)
- Show a screen welcoming the player to the game.

Select the next activity.
- Show choices and ask for the next thing to do.

Show instructions.
- Print standard screen (or screens) of rules.

Deal with the bank.
- Ask if you are buying or cashing in chips.
- Show the current amount you have won or lost.
- Indicate when the player's limit has been reached or when the bank has been broken.
- Ask for the number of chips to buy or cash in.

Report on the progress of the game.
- Show the amount that has been won or lost.
- Show the number of hands played so far.
- Show the number of hands won and the number of hands lost.
- Show the percentage of hands that have been won.
- Show the average amount won or lost on each hand.

Shuffle the cards.
- Print a simple message stating the cards have been shuffled.

Play a hand of blackjack.
- Ask for bets to be placed.
- Indicate when there is not enough money to cover a bet or when a bet is below the minimum or above the maximum.
- Cards must be shown when dealt, some face up and some face down.
- Indicate that the dealer has a natural.
- Ask if any pairs are to be split.
- Ask if players want another card.
- Show the playing of the dealer's hand.
- Show amounts won or lost for the hand.

Quitting the game (termination).
• Show the game status report.
• Show a good-bye message.

From this list we can identify the following specific data items that must be available to the program.

Start the game.
• "Welcome to the game" message.

Select the next activity.
• "The following choices are available" messages.
• "What next" question.

Show instructions.
• Standard rules message.

Deal with the bank.
• "Buy or cash in" question.
• Total amount of money won or lost.
• Player's credit limit.
• Bank's credit limit.
• "How much to buy or cash in" question.

Report on the progress of the game.
• Total amount of money won or lost.
• Total number of hands played.
• Total number of hands won or lost.
• Percentage of hands won or lost.
• Average amount won or lost per hand.

Shuffle the cards.
• "The cards have been shuffled" message.

Play a hand of blackjack.
• "How much to bet" question.
• Current value of player's chips.
• Minimum bet.
• Maximum bet.
• Cards — value and suit must be shown.
  • The remaining deck.
  • The dealer's hand.
  • The player's regular hand.
  • The player's second (split) hand.
• The back of the dealer's first card.
• "Dealer has a natural" message.
• "You won" message.
• "You lost" message.

- "Split your pair" question.
- "Take another card" question.
- Amount won or lost during this hand.

Quitting the game.
- "Good-bye" message.

Unfortunately this list is organized by the functions of the system rather than by any criteria derived from the data items themselves. We would know more about the information we will be using if this list were grouped together by similar types of information. In looking over this list, the data items seem to fall into four general groups.

The first group includes any message which asks the player a question, such as:

"WHAT DO YOU WISH TO DO NEXT?"

This is called a prompt message because it prompts the user to enter some sort of information. This message is usually followed by some sort of input processing to receive and check the user's answer to the question.

The second group includes general messages such as the rules of the game. These messages do not change, can be displayed at any time, and are not dependent upon any other type of processing.

The third group includes items like the minimum and maximum bets. These items, will not vary throughout any single game, but they may be changed from time to time between games for the sake of variety. These will probably be implemented as variables that are defined during the initialization procedure. By changing one value in this procedure, the item will be changed for the whole program. We can call these items *static variables* because they do not change during execution of the program.

The last group contains items like the total amount won or lost, that can change from one value to another throughout the game. These variables may be entered as input or calculated from other information. They may be stored throughout the game or they may be re-calculated just before they are displayed. We can call these items *dynamic variables* because of the way they change.

We can now reorganize the data items into these four categories. Any items that were duplicated have been eliminated.

The list also indicates items that can assume negative values. For example, the total amount won or lost can be saved as the total amount won, where positive values indicate winnings and negative values indicate losses. These items are followed by the indicator (+-).

Prompt Messages.
- "What next" question.
- "Buy or cash in" question.
- "How much to buy or cash in" question.
- "How much to bet" question.
- "Split your pair" question.
- "Take another card" question.

General Messages.
- "Welcome to the game" message.
- "The following choices are available" message.
- Standard rules message.
- "The cards have been shuffled" message.
- "Dealer has a natural" message.
- "You won" message.
- "You lost" message.
- "Good-bye" message.

Static Variables.
- Player's credit limit.
- Bank's credit limit.
- Minimum bet.
- Maximum bet.
- the value and suit of any card.
- The back of the dealer's first card.

Dynamic Variables.
- Total amount of money won (+-).
- Total number of hands played.
- Total number of hands won (+-).
- Percentage of hands won (+-).
- Average amount won per hand (+-).
- Current value of player's chips.

- The remaining deck.
- The dealer's hand.
- The player's regular hand.
- The player's second (split) hand.
- Amount won during this hand (+-).

This list shows clearly the types of output that we will be using. Notice that the deck of cards has been listed even though we were concentrating on output information. It is now time to add the rest of the internal data required to produce all this output, as well as the items that will be entered by the player. At the same time we will make additional refinements in the overall organization of the data.

Most of this data is easy to understand just the way it is listed. An exception to this is the data representing the hands held by the dealer and the player. Since, each hand contains more than one card, we will probably use arrays to hold this information. We may use three one-dimensional arrays or one two-dimensional array, but it is a little too early in the design to specify this. At any rate, it will certainly be necessary to keep track of the number of cards in each hand, so these values will be added as new data items. Because there will be several hands, the card counts may also be kept in an array.

The prompt messages indicate that two types of information will be entered by the player: selecting an item from a list such as YES or NO, or the available functions; and entering an amount to buy, cash in, or bet. We shall therefore add input variables to store the answer to a choice question and the answer to an amount question.

There is one more type of output that should be in every program — the error messages. In the next chapter we will discuss the types of errors that can occur and how they are handled, but at this point, we can state with certainty that there will be error messages.

Before adding this new information to our list of data items, let's re-examine how the data is organized. So far we have shown the data as indented lists. The major types of data can also be shown as a hierarchy:

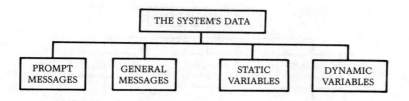

The prompt messages can be further divided into choice prompts and dollar amount prompts to go along with the two types of input that we have developed.

The dynamic variables can also be divided into two types. Some of these items, like the total number of hands played or the total amount won or lost, must be saved throughout the game. We will continue to call these items dynamic variables. Other items like the average amount won or lost per hand can be recalculated each time they are needed. We will call these items *transient variables* because they need not be kept when they are not being used.

In looking over the new structure, two changes seem indicated for data shown in our indented list. The back of the dealer's first card is not really a variable, so it will be moved to the group of general messages. The value and suit of any card can be calculated at the time the card is displayed, so we will move these items to our new category of transient variables. The structure of the major types of data is now shown in Figure 4.6.

Now we can fill in the lower levels of this chart with all of the data items that we have identified so far. Remember that this is still the *general* design phase of the project; we do not need to identify in detail every item of data that will eventually be used. Our current data structure looks like this:

Choice prompt messages.
• "What next" question.

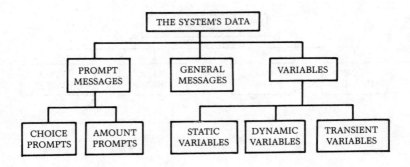

Figure 4.6. A Better Structure for the System's Data

- "Buy or cash in" question.
- "Split your pair" question.
- "Take another card" question.

Amount prompt messages.
- "How much to buy or cash in" question.
- "How much to bet" question.

General messages.
- "Welcome to the game" message.
- "The following choices are available" message.
- Standard rules message.
- "The cards have been shuffled" message.
- "Dealer has a natural" message.
- "You won" message.
- "You lost" message.
- "Good-bye" message.
- The back of the dealer's first card.
- Error messages.

Static variables.
- Player's credit limit.
- Bank's credit limit.
- Minimum bet.
- Maximum bet.

Dynamic variables.
- Total amount of money won (+-).
- Total number of hands played.

- Total number of hands won (+-).
- Current value of player's chips.
- The remaining deck. (an array)
- The dealer's hand. (an array)
- The player's regular hand. (an array)
- The player's second (split) hand. (an array)
- Amount won during this hand (+-).
- Answers to choice questions.
- Answers to amount questions.
- The number of cards in each hand. (an array)

Transient variables.

- Percentage of hands won (+-).
- Average amount won per hand (+-).
- The value of a card.
- The suit of a card.

Remember that this is only one way to organize the information. As the project continues there will be occasional requirements for new data items. However, this gives us a good idea of the types of data required and how each item will be used.

A. A Look At What We Have Done — Again

Let's reflect a moment on the data structure that we have developed. We have identified all of the data requirements that we could at this point in the system's development. Items that are related to each other have been assembled into separate data structures. In our case, the deck of cards and the hands dealt for a game have been gathered into arrays.

This part of the design would also gather data into any appropriate files and records if they were required. We have also identified in general terms how each data item will be used. This has been easy to do because our system does not require a great variety of information.

In a large, complex system there may be many layers to the data structure, just as there may be many layers to the functional structure. In fact, data structures usually have a richer variety of details than functional structures. They will also vary greatly from one application to another. The major levels of information are usually organized in a similar fashion to Figure 4.7.

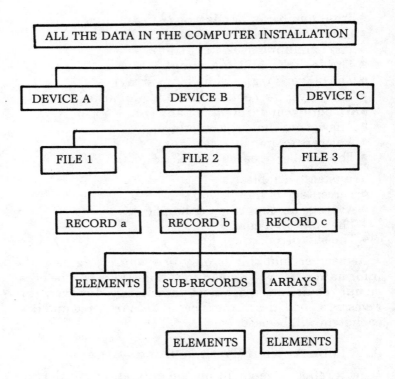

Figure 4.7. A Computer System Data Hierarchy

In this figure, a device is an external storage device like a disk drive or a magnetic tape unit; a file is a collection of records; and records and arrays are the data structures discussed in Chapter 2.

There are many many variations upon this theme: files that span more than one device; arrays and records that contain sub-records and sub-arrays; and unique data organizations for tables, data bases, or other special applications. At the bottom of the hierarchy, however, will always be the data element that represents one item of data such as a number or a character string. Our program, which contains only data elements and perhaps a few arrays, will use only a small number of the many possible data structures.

IV. ANOTHER LOOK AT THE PROGRAM'S STRUCTURE

As we worked out the data structure of our system, we certainly thought more about how the system should work. Therefore, let's return to the functional structure of the system and see if it can be improved. The most likely place for improvements is in the area of user input-how to get it and how to process it. This function depends on what is to be entered, and how the system's input has been more precisely defined.

One of the most important parts of any computer system is the part that receives information from the user. Since this information may contain errors, it must be checked for correctness and any errors must be handled in some way. The details of identifying and handling errors will be dealt with in the next chapters. For now, we can simply say that there will be some sort of error processing in the system.

According to the system's data structure in Figure 4.6, there are two types of input: a choice of one item from a list of available selections, and a numerical amount of money or number of chips. These functions may be required while dealing with the bank, betting, playing a hand, and perhaps by other parts of the system. It will make the program simpler if we can concentrate all of the input functions into a few general input-processing modules so the error handling can be concentrated in these modules.

We can satisfy all of these requirements by creating two new utility subroutines; one for entering choices and one for entering amounts. Each module will include all editing and error-handling functions required to ensure the validity of the incoming data. The rest of the system can then simply assume that all the data available is valid.

Generalized input-handling subroutines are quite common in well-designed computer systems, so it is not surprising that such modules would show up someplace once the input requirements were known.

There do not seem to be any other new functional requirements, so we can add these new modules to the structure to obtain the final system structure for the general design as shown in Figure 4.8. This structure along with the final data structure in Figure 4.6 are repeated in Appendix C which contains the results of this general design.

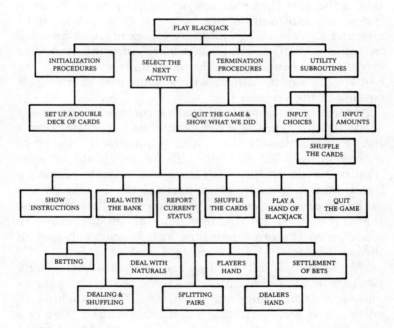

Figure   4.8. The General Design System Structure

V. DEFINING THE SYSTEM'S ENVIRONMENTAL STRUCTURE

We have reached the point in our design where the structure of the system identifies all the required functions in a reasonable organization, and all of the information required to support these functions. Before completing the general design we should see if the system requires anything beyond computer programs and the information they will process. These requirements may be thought of as the "environment" in which the system will operate. This includes items like special data handling or storage equipment, test equipment or any other items that must be designed, developed or tested for the system to operate.

In the case of the Blackjack system there are no special environmental requirements. If there were any such requirements, we would develop the functional description of each of these items just as we developed the descriptions of our system's program and data structures. All elements of the project should now be defined and there should be a definite structure to both the system as a whole and to its component parts.

VI. REVIEWING THE DESIGN AND THE CHAPTER'S MAJOR IDEAS

The objective of the general design is to identify and organize the basic structure of the system. This should be followed by a decision: proceed with the detailed design, return to a previous step because of problems that have been uncovered during the design or cancel the project if it does not seem reasonable to continue. This kind of review is similar to the project analysis at the end of the previous chapter. In fact, such a review should occur at the end of each phase of the project's development.

If the system function has proved too vague or ill-defined to be developed into a reasonable structure, you can end the project here or repeat the analysis in the previous chapter. You should also reconsider the project if the system has expanded during the general design to more than you want to deal with. Don't worry about having to rework part or all of a design. It is a rare system design that never needs backtracking at some point.

In the case of our Blackjack program, no such problems appear. The general design has expanded the detail of the overall functions without changing the original objective — to play a game of Blackjack according to Hoyle. The system's functional and information requirements are easy to understand and seem complete enough to proceed to the next step: the detailed design.

The following ideas represent the major points of this chapter:

- You may start the design by working either with the system's functional structure or with its data structure.
- Both of these structures can be defined as a hierarchy or a network which have the following characteristics:
  - The structure is made up of separate modules that are developed from the top down.
  - The top level of the structure is a single module.
  - The modules at each level control (or are made up of) their sub-elements at the next lower level.
  - In a hierarchy a module may have only one parent, while in a network it may have several.
  - The bottom level of each branch will always be a single simple function or data element.
- The functional structure (which is usually a network) may be developed as follows:
  - Each module should have a high internal strength and be loosely coupled to its relatives.
  - The first level of sub-elements will usually consist of an initializing routine, a program mainline, and a terminating routine.
  - Start by listing all the major functions. Try an imaginary dry run of the system.
  - Eliminate all duplicate functions.
  - Organize the functions into related groups with about 2 to 8 sub-elements in each group.
  - Put the groups in the approximate order in which they will be used.

- Gather any utility sub-routines into their own group.
- Repeat this cycle until there are no more functions to be broken down.

- The data structure (which is usually a hierarchy) may be developed as follows:
    - List all of the output required from the system.
    - Develop the data within the system required to produce this output.
    - Develop the input to the system required to maintain this data.
    - Organize related items into files, records, arrays, and other sub-structures.
    - Within these structures, organize the types of data being used.

- You may work back and forth between the data and functional structures.

- In practice the development will not always be strictly from the top down, but the final design should be presented in a top-down structure.

- There is no one "correct" way to develop a project — your own personal style should be used.

- From time to time you should stand back to see how you are doing. If there are problems, fix them before continuing.

- If there are environmental requirements beyond those we have shown in our project, they should be developed along with the program functions and data structures.

- There should be an overall project review before proceeding to the detailed design.

- Having found no serious problems at this stage we will proceed.

5

How Will the Program Work?
(The Detailed Design)

"Everything takes longer than you think. Whenever you set out to do something, something else must be done first."

Corollaries to Murphy's Law.

Now that we know what our system is going to do, it is time to start filling in the details of our program. However, those of you who just made a mad dash for your computer terminal should come back and sit down. There is one more step to complete before we actually write computer code in a programming language. This extra step is the detailed design. In this step, the Blackjack program and the data it uses will be further refined and written in terms of the structured instructions we developed in Chapter One. This will allow us to write the first draft of the program in an English-like sketch code like that used at the end of Chapter Two. It will be much easier to develop the program's detailed logic in this "very high-level language" than it would be to start programming immediately in a specific programming language — even a reasonably high-level one.

The first thing we must do is to refine the system's data structure and compile it into a data dictionary. This dictionary will contain a listing for each variable data element and data structure in the system. Each listing will include the variable's name, data type, and allowable values. Each data structure will be broken down into constituent sub-structures and elements. Each entry in the dictionary will also have a written description stating how the item is to be used. Constant values will not be included because there is nothing about them that will change.

The second step of the detailed design is to translate each module of the general design into sketch code, starting at the highest level and working down to the lowest subroutines. Each module will be treated as a separate little program, showing exactly what steps are required for the module to work. As the development progresses, there may be changes made to the general design. If we did a good job on the previous step, however, these changes will be minimal and will consist mainly of new details that must be added.

The development of the system's data and functional description in this step is simply a continuation and refinement of the general design process. When we have completed the detailed design, the whole program will be expressed in a well-structured, very high-level language which can then be easily translated into an actual computer language.

I. DEVELOPING THE DATA DICTIONARY

Following the top-down practice of beginning each task at the most general or highest level, we will start the data dictionary with the most complex data structures identified in the general design. In a complex system of programs, this will usually be data files and the records that comprise them. In our case, the most complex structures that we identified were the arrays used to keep track of the cards remaining in the deck and the cards in the player's hands. The deck of cards is the heart of any card game, so this seems like a good place to start.

We saw in Chapter Two that if we simply keep track of a number for each card, we can calculate its suit and value with a simple bit of programming. Furthermore, we want to store as little data as possible so our program will run in computers with a small memory. The simplest way to represent a deck of cards will be therefore an array of numbers from one to fifty-two. For the double deck in the

Blackjack game we will use an array of 104 numbers which may each have a value of one to fifty-two. We can call the array DECK and represent it in the data dictionary like this:

DECK   NUMERIC ARRAY (1 TO 104)
               OF NUMBERS 1 TO 52

Arrays are also required for the dealer's hand and the player's hand. The player can split a pair of cards into two hands so there must be two arrays for the player. Now for an interesting question: How many cards can there be in one hand? We know there will be at least the two cards that are dealt at the beginning of the hand. We must allow room for the maximum number of cards that might actually be dealt in a hand, without wasting space for cards that will never be required. The most cards one player may be dealt would be a collection of cards with the lowest possible values until the total value of the hand exceeded twenty-one. Since we are using two decks, the largest hand possible is:

CARDS DEALT	VALUE OF CARDS
8 ACES	8
7 TWOS	14
15 CARDS	22 POINTS

The arrays must therefore be large enough to accommodate fifteen cards per hand. The other array that was identified in the general design was one to keep track of the number of cards contained in each hand. This must have three entries that may each contain values of zero to fifteen.

The data dictionary can now be updated to include all the arrays in the system, listed alphabetically:

DEALER	NUMERIC ARRAY (1 TO 15)	OF NUMBERS 1 TO 52
DECK	NUMERIC ARRAY (1 TO 104)	OF NUMBERS 1 TO 52
HANDCOUNT	NUMERIC ARRAY (1 TO 3)	OF NUMBERS 1 TO 15
PLAYER1	NUMERIC ARRAY (1 TO 15)	OF NUMBERS 1 TO 52
PLAYER2	NUMERIC ARRAY (1 TO 15)	OF NUMBERS 1 TO 52

We can now go through the rest of the data elements from the general design and define their attributes. The first three categories of data are constants and can be ignored. We therefore continue with the static variables.

The credit limits and bet limits will all be numeric data elements. The credit limits will be called BANKLIMIT and PLAYLIMIT. To make the game interesting there should be lots of money available, so we should allow for BANKLIMIT of several thousand dollars. The player should have a lower limit than the bank because few players have the resources of a casino. The lower and upper bet limits will be called MINBET and MAXBET, respectively. These values should be set to limit each round of betting to an interesting but reasonable amount. The static variables will therefore be defined as follows:

BANKLIMIT	A NUMBER FROM 0 TO 10,000
PLAYLIMIT	A NUMBER FROM 0 TO 2,000
MINBET	A NUMBER FROM 0 TO 10
MAXBET	A NUMBER FROM 0 TO 500

Using the same type of reasoning, we can also define the characteristics of the dynamic variables. Note that some of these items can be either positive to indicate the amount won or negative to indicate the amount lost.

The arrays have already been defined. The rest of the dynamic variables are:

AMOUNTWON	A NUMBER FROM -2,000 TO +10,000
HANDSPLAYD	A NUMBER FROM 0 TO 1,000
HANDSWON	A NUMBER FROM -1,000 TO +1,000
CHIPS	A NUMBER FROM 0 TO 12,000
WONTHISHAND	A NUMBER FROM -500 TO +500
CHOICE	A NUMBER FROM 1 TO 10
AMOUNT	A NUMBER FROM -10,000 TO +10,000

The high and low values are guesses at this point, but are close enough to indicate which numbers will be large or small and which must be negative. The remaining variables in the system are defined as follows:

PERCNTWON	A NUMBER FROM -100 TO +100
AVERAGEWON	A NUMBER FROM -500 TO +500
CARDVALUE	A NUMBER FROM 1 TO 52
CARDSUIT	A NUMBER FROM 1 TO 4

When all of these items are combined and alphabetical, we have the first draft of the data dictionary. We will not worry about the program's error message at this time since error messages are usually constant character strings and do not appear in a data dictionary. A comment which contains the verbal description from the general design can be added to each entry giving us the preliminary data dictionary shown in Figure 5.1.

This version of the data dictionary contains only those items identified in the general design. As the detailed design progresses toward levels of increasing detail, we may require additional entries. As each new item is developed, it will be added to the dictionary so that the listing is always kept up-to-date. This will help prevent duplication of data items that have already been defined but have been temporarily forgotten.

Now that the data dictionary has been started we can begin developing the sketch code instructions for our program.

II. DEVELOPING THE PROGRAM INSTRUCTIONS

Here we are at last, well into the fifth chapter of this book on programming, and we are finally ready to do some actual programming. It has been a long wait, but now the top-down method of program design really begins to pay off. For example, we don't need to wonder about where to begin. As the names *general design* and *detailed design* indicate, this step will develop the details of the system. We can narrow our attention to a small part of the program without worrying about how it relates to the system as a whole.

In Appendix C, we see that the top module of the system controls the initialization procedures, the selection of the activities within the program, and the termination procedures. It will also contain the utility subroutines. To start at the top, we should first develop the instructions that control these procedures.

AMOUNT	NUMBER FROM	-10,000	TO +10,000
answer to amount questions			
AMOUNTWON	NUMBER FROM	-2,000	TO +10,000
amount won during this hand			
AVERAGEWON	NUMBER FROM	-500	TO +500
average amount won per hand			
BANKLIMIT	NUMBER FROM	0	TO 10,000
bank's credit limit			
CARDSUIT	NUMBER FROM	1	TO 4
the suit of a card			
CARDVALUE	NUMBER FROM	1	TO 52
the value of a card			
CHIPS	NUMBER FROM	0	TO 12,000
current value of player's chips			
CHOICE	NUMBER FROM	1	TO 10
answers to choice questions			
DEALER	NUMERIC ARRAY	(1 TO 15)	FROM 1 TO 52
the dealer's hand			
DECK	NUMERIC ARRAY	(1 TO 104)	FROM 1 TO 52
the remaining deck			
HANDCOUNT	NUMERIC ARRAY	(1 TO 3)	FROM 1 TO 15
number of cards in each hand			
HANDSPLAYD	NUMBER FROM	0	TO 1,000
total number of hands played			
HANDSWON	NUMBER FROM	-1000	TO +1000
total number of hands won			
MAXBET	NUMBER FROM	0	TO 500
maximum bet			
MINBET	NUMBER FROM	0	TO 10
minimum bet			
PERCNTWON	NUMBER FROM	-100	TO +100
percentage of hands won			
PLAYER1	NUMERIC ARRAY	(1 TO 15)	FROM 1 TO 52
the player's regular hand			
PLAYER2	NUMERIC ARRAY	(1 TO 15)	FROM 1 TO 52
the player's second (split) hand			
PLAYLIMIT	NUMBER FROM	0	TO 2,000
player's credit limit			
WONTHISHAND	NUMBER FROM	-500	TO +500
amount won during this hand			

Figure 5.1. The First Draft Data Dictionary

A. DEVELOPING THE PROGRAM'S MAINLINE ROUTINE

Within a program, a group of instructions that perform a single function is called a routine. As we have already seen, a routine that is controlled by a higher level of the

system may be called a subroutine. The highest level routine in a system is called the mainline since it controls the main divisions of the program. The actual instructions in a program are often called the program's logic or code. We will, therefore, start developing the logic for the Blackjack program's mainline routine.

The utility subroutines are controlled by modules throughout the system, rather than by the mainline routine. They have been included at the highest level of the system's organization chart primarily for convenience. We will develop the utility subroutines after we know more about when they will be called and how they will be used. This leaves a mainline routine that must control the initialization procedures, the selection of the next activity, and the termination procedures.

In the mainline routine, we only tell when these functions are to be executed, not how they will work. The functions themselves are not performed within the program's mainline, but by subroutines called by the mainline. Because the mainline controls the highest levels of the program from start to finish, the start-of-program and end-of-program conditions should be shown with the routine's instruction. Combining all of these ideas with the instructions developed in Chapter One, the mainline routine for the Blackjack program can be represented by the following sketch code:

```
PROGRAM: BLACKJACK

    START (MAINLINE)
        CALL INITIALIZE
        CALL SELECTACTIV
        CALL TERMINATE
    END MAINLINE

    END PROGRAM
```

This looks so simple that it hardly seems to be worth all the effort that we went through to develop it. The whole routine only has three instructions in it! Well, there's nothing wrong with that. The primary objective of our method of development is to produce accurate programs that are easy to understand and use. It would be difficult to get much easier to understand than three simple sub-

routine calls. Granted, most programs will have a somewhat more complex mainline routine. There is, however,
nothing wrong with our simple mainline. Be thankful
that we are off to an easy start; things will get more complicated soon enough.

Just as we developed the program's data into a data
dictionary, the development of the program's logic produces a functional dictionary made up of the sketch code
listing for every routine in the program. Each reference to
a particular routine must use its proper subroutine name,
just as each reference to a data item must use its proper
variable name. Note that we chose a name for each routine that is descriptive of its function. Using the names
we have just developed, the high level structure of the
system can be shown in Figure 5.2.

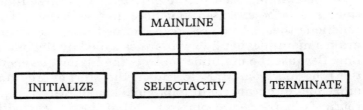

Figure 5.2. The High-Level Structure of the System

B. Developing the Second-Level Routines

Now that the first-level module has been completed, we
can develop the second-level modules: the three subroutines that are called from the program's mainline.

The initialization routine must load initial values into
data tables and other variables. We won't know the
details of these operations, however, until we know what
these tables and variables will be or how they will be
used. These operations must be developed and added to
the initialization routine as the design progresses. In the
meantime, though, we can include the initial greeting to
the player and indicate that the routine must set up a
double deck of cards. The details of this operation can be

specified later on when we know more about how the deck will be used. The initialization routine will therefore start out looking like this:

INITIALIZE

    SET UP THE DOUBLE DECK OF CARDS
    SET UP INITIAL VALUES FOR STATIC
        VARIABLES
    PRINT THE GREETING TO THE PLAYER
    WAIT FOR A<RETURN> TO CONTINUE

RETURN

There is no need to specify the exact greeting message at this point. It will probably require a series of output statements to print the message on the terminal screen. The player has to have enough time to read the message, so the program should stop until told to continue. The most common way to do this is to end the message with an instruction for the player to press the RETURN key to continue. We always show the name of specific terminal keys between angle brackets (<>); in the above listing, for example, <RETURN> means the RETURN key.

Since this is all we know about this routine at the moment, let's continue to the next one. Notice that we are somewhat flexible about the top-down order of program development. The high-level initialization routine will not be completed until quite a bit of work has been done on the lower levels of the program. The top-down approach should be used as a general guide, not as an iron-clad rule that cannot be broken.

Moving along this level of the system structure chart, we find the next module to be SELECT THE NEXT ACTIVITY. The routines that we have developed so far have been very simple. This one will be a bit more complex, however, for now there are decisions to be made and loops to be controlled. One of the easiest approaches to a more complicated function is to try writing instructions that could be understood by a person. Then, we must be sure that the instructions match the formats developed in Chapter One.

In this case, we want the routine to do the following:

- Display the choices for the next activity on the terminal screen.
- Get the player's choice using the INPUT CHOICES utility routine (which has yet to be developed).
- If the choice is to quit the game, then we should return to the mainline and then to the end of the program.
- If the choice is not to quit the game, we should call the subroutine that performs the function of the player's choice.
- This process should be continued until the player chooses to quit the game.

Notice that this routine only selects the proper activity. At this point we do not care how the activities are carried out. And we do not need to worry about the player making a meaningless selection, because that will be taken care of by the INPUTCHOICES routine. We are only concerned with having the player make a choice and then activating the proper part of the program based on that choice. This is a good example of how the modules can be strongly bound and loosely coupled. Everything needed to select a function of the program is in this module, but its processing is not concerned with how any of these functions work. If new functions are added to the program at some later date, this routine is the only one that will have to be changed. The new functions would be added to the program as additional subroutines.

Now let's see how the routine will be structured. The entire process of making a selection and calling the proper subroutine is in a loop so the major part of the routine will be a DO-LOOP, DO-WHILE, or DO-UNTIL structure. The rest of the instructions will be contained within this loop. Execution of the loop will continue until the player says to quit. Since that means an undetermined number of passes, the primary structure will be a DO-UNTIL. Note that the condition being tested is directly set by the player; when the player gets tired, he will choose to quit. Therefore we will not need a secondary check to prevent an endless loop.

According to Appendix C there are six activities the player can choose:

1. Show instructions for the game.
2. Deal with the bank.
3. Report the game's current status.
4. Shuffle the deck of cards.
5. Play a hand of Blackjack.
6. Quit the game.

It will be easier to deal with a numeric choice from one to six than with a descriptive string such as DEAL WITH BANK. We can do this by using the variable CHOICE from the data dictionary. And once we are choosing from a list of several possible values, the CASE statement will be more efficient than a series of IF-THEN statements using all of these considerations, the sketch code to select the next activity might look like this:

```
SELECTACTIV

REPEAT
    DISPLAY THE AVAILABLE SELECTIONS ON
    THE SCREEN
    CALL INPUTCHOICES
    IF CHOICE NOT 6 THEN
        CASE CHOICE OF
            1: CALL SHOWINSTRUCT
            2: CALL BANKER
            3: CALL RPTSTATUS
            4: CALL SHUFFLE
            5: CALL PLAYHAND
        END OF CASE
    UNTIL CHOICE = 6
RETURN
```

Astute readers will realize that there will probably have to be some sort of communication between this routine and INPUTCHOICES so that the input routine knows that it must allow a value of one through six as valid selections. We will worry about this after we know more about editing choices later in the program. It is quite likely, however, that we are going to have to make some changes or additions to this routine as the design progresses. In fact, most programs are developed by reworking and polishing the existing routines as more details become available. Don't feel that you have to get it right the first time.

The last routine at this level of the system structure is the termination routine. Here we wish to show some game statistics, then print a parting message. We already know there will be a routine which the player may use at will to report the current status of the game. The simplest way to show how we did as the game ends is to call this routine again. Eventually, we may find other things to report here, but this will give us a good start. The sketch code for the termination routine looks like this:

TERMINATE

    CALL RPTSTATUS
    PRINT THE PARTING MESSAGE TO THE PLAYER
    WAIT FOR A <RETURN> TO CONTINUE

RETURN

This completes the second level of the system structure. The modules that have been identified so far are shown in Figure 5.3.

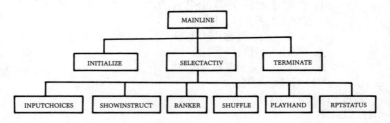

Figure 5.3. Expanded Detailed System Structure

This figure reflects the sketch code developed so far without designating any of the routines as utility subroutines. It is quite close to the general design structure, although we have made some changes.

This takes care of most of the high-level control routines in the program. What we have left are the routines that will be used to respond to the player's commands and a few utility subroutines. Let us proceed, therefore, more deeply into the heart of the program.

C. Developing the Third-Level Routines

According to the chart in Appendix C, the next routine to be developed is the one that shows the rules of the game when the player selects activity number one: SHOWINSTRUCT. If the instructions message will not fit on one screen, the program must stop at the end of each screen of text until the player has read the information. Since we do not know how long the message will be, we assume that we will need several screens to show it all. We will then indicate in the sketch code that there will be a pause between each screen. The actual number of pauses will depend on the final text that is to be printed. SHOWINSTRUCT will therefore look like this:

```
SHOWINSTRUCT
   PRINT INSTRUCTIONS
   WAIT FOR A <RETURN> TO CONTINUE
   PRINT INSTRUCTIONS
   WAIT FOR A <RETURN> TO CONTINUE
      •
      •
      •
RETURN
```

The next routine at this level is DEAL WITH THE BANK, which has been given the subroutine name BANKER. At this point things begin to get more complicated. (just as I promised).

C-1. Banking: A More Complex Procedure

The first thing to do is to define what transactions will be possible between the bank and the player. Let us allow for the two basic functions of buying or cashing in the chips used at the Blackjack table. When chips are bought, we must reduce the player's cash and increase the value of the player's chips. When they are cashed in, we must do just the opposite. We can use the player's credit limit (PLAYERLIMIT) as the player's current supply of cash. CHIPS will, of course, be the current value of the player's chips. At the first glance, this seems fairly straightforward. The possible operations are:

- Have the player choose between buying chips or cashing them in.
- Have the player indicate how many chips are to be bought or cashed in.
- If chips are being bought, decrease PLAYERLIMIT and increase CHIPS by the amount bought.
- If chips are being cashed in, increase PLAYERLIMIT and decrease CHIPS by the amount cashed in.

This is not much more complicated than some of the other routines that we have already developed.

The problem is that these operations will only work when the player has enough cash or chips to cover the entire transaction. Unfortunately, this may not always be the case. This leads us to one of programming's primary rules:

>>> YOU MUST ALWAYS TAKE CARE OF THE EXCEPTIONAL CONDITIONS <<<

In our daily lives, we spend most of our time dealing with the usual case, or the way things normally work. Most people, therefore, think in terms of "what is most likely to happen." We deal with "the unusual case" whenever it does happen and then we go back to life as usual. When we do plan ahead for unusual situations (for instance when we buy insurance), it often feels odd to spend so much time and money dealing with things that may never happen.

The computer, however, cannot handle an unusual situation when it occurs unless provisions have already been included in its programs. This means that you have to think up every possible thing that could go wrong and then develop the processing that will be required to take care of each of them. It is not uncommon for a program to spend most of its time executing a small part of its code on the usual conditions, while the great bulk of the code is waiting for truly bizarre, but possible, conditions to occur. The banking operations listed above will take care of the usual case but now we have to cover the exceptions.

You have probably heard of Murphy's Law which states that:

ANYTHING THAT CAN GO WRONG WILL
GO WRONG.

You may have even heard of O'Toole's commentary on Murphy's Law which states that

MURPHY WAS AN OPTIMIST

I have often felt that there is a nasty, Puckish little creature who becomes a part of each project that I have worked on. His job has always been to think up every possible way for things to go wrong and then cause them to happen. I think of him as 'Murphy's Demon.' A programmer must play the part of Murphy's Demon, think of all the problems that could occur, and develop solutions for them before they happen. (You can often pick the programmers out of a crowd of people because they immediately jump on the exceptions to the rule that the rest of the crowd ignores.) With this in mind, let's take another look at dealing with the bank in our program.

To start things off, it will help to understand the flow of money in the program. Money can be in either of two forms: cash or chips. Everything will be much easier if we deal in even dollars for the cash and make each chip worth one dollar. The money can belong to either of two parties: the player or the bank. The player has the ability to exchange money between cash and chips at the bank so the game will feel like a real game of Blackjack. Money flows back and forth between the player and the bank during the actual Blackjack game as bets are won and lost. No money changes hands at the bank itself. Because cash and chips are both accounted for in dollars, the bank need not differentiate between the two. The flow of money is shown in Figure 5.4.

PLAYER'S MONEY   BANK'S MONEY

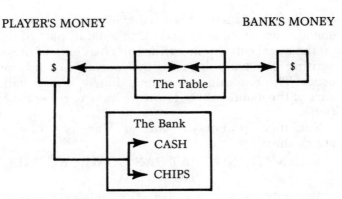

Figure 5.4. The Flow of Money in the Program

Now let us see if we can find where the odd conditions can occur when we change the form of the player's money at the bank.

When the game starts, the player and the bank both have plenty of money. The player will need to exchange some of it for chips. This does not affect the amount of money the bank has; only the amount that the player has in each form. Therefore, there will be no special conditions based on the amount of money currently in the bank. The player, on the other hand, must have cash to buy chips. What happens if the player wants to buy more chips than there is cash to pay for it? What happens in the extreme case when the player has no cash at all? Often, the odd conditions occur when a data value becomes a maximum, a minimum, negative, or zero.

In this case, if the player has no more cash, the program should display a message saying, "You are broke and no credit can be extended." No transaction can be made. If there is some cash available, but not as much as the player wants in chips, the program should display a message showing the maximum number of chips that the player can afford and allow another transaction.

Cashing chips in is just the opposite of buying new chips, the error conditions will be the same, except we must check the value of the player's chips rather than the amount of the player's cash. If there are no chips to be cashed in, the program should display a message saying, "You have no chips to cash." The program must also make sure that the player does not try to cash in more chips than he has.

The player's amount of money in cash and current chips are the only values affected by this routine, so there should be no other exceptional conditions. The next step is to develop the instructions that will check for each of these conditions and process the legal transactions.

When you develop a complex set of instructions such as these, there are several approaches that may be used. The point of any approach is to help clarify what a routine must do and how it should do it. In developing complex instructions, your own programing style will begin to emerge. Any method that allows you to develop accurate instructions is okay to use, regardless of how useful it may or may not be to others.

C-2. Flow Charts: An Aid To Program Development.

One common aid that has been widely used for many years is called a *flow chart*. This is a chart that shows the instructions used and the flow of control from one instruction to the next. Flow charts are introduced here because they have been widely used and are known to a great number of people. They are of limited value in a top-down structured design, however, and can lead to significant problems for the beginning designer. After this short introduction to flow charts, we will not use them for the remainder of the book. There will be some programmers who find flow charts very useful, so I will leave the reader to evaluate their usefulness. My personal opinion is that they are out of date and can be replaced by more effective methods of developing structured programs.

For this introduction we will consider just four of the basic symbols commonly used in flow charts:

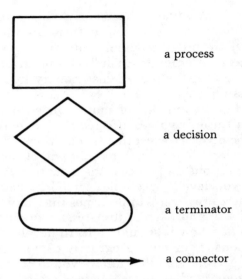

a process

a decision

a terminator

a connector

Figure 5.5 shows a flow chart of a simple routine that tests a condition and performs one of two procedures, depending on the outcome of the test.

The routine follows the connecting arrows from one procedure or test to another. At the point of the test, there will be an exit for TRUE and another for FALSE. There may also be three-way exits for conditions that result in a negative value, zero, or a positive value. This type of structure uses GOTO statements rather than the IF-THEN-ELSE statement. This use of GOTO as the primary control statement may, unfortunately, result in flow charts resembling Figure 5.6.

The problem with using such a program structure is that the programs usually come out looking a lot like the chart. They are the very thing we are trying to avoid through the design procedure we are using. If you find yourself compelled to use flow charts, try to draw them so they clarify the program logic rather than confuse it. For example, a good flow chart for the banking routine is shown in Figure 5.7.

Now that I have said all of these terrible things about flow charts, I must admit that I use them on rare occasions, usually to help clear up confusing logic before the sketch code is developed. If you want to learn more about

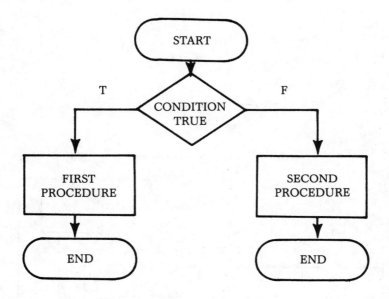

Figure 5.5. A Simple Flow Chart

flow charts, you can consult some of the books listed in the Bibliography. For now, let's return to the bank routine.

C-3. Back to the Banking Routine

This is the first routine we have developed from the general design that looks like it should be sub-divided into smaller functions. There should be one routine to buy chips and another to cash them in. There is no interaction between these two procedures which requires that they be combined into a single routine. Therefore BANKER might look like this:

```
BANKER

    DISPLAY A CHOICE FOR BUY OR CASH IN
    CALL INPUTCHOICES
    IF CHOICE = 1 THEN
      CALL BUY
    ELSE
      CALL CASHIN

RETURN
```

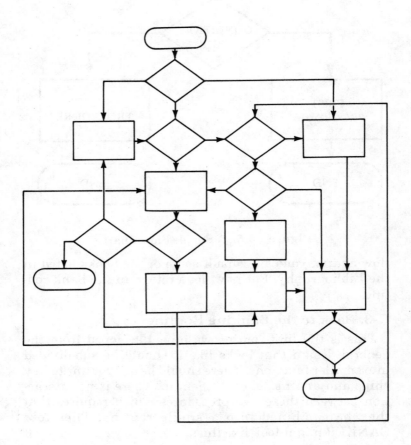

Figure 5.6. A Typical Flow Chart Configuration

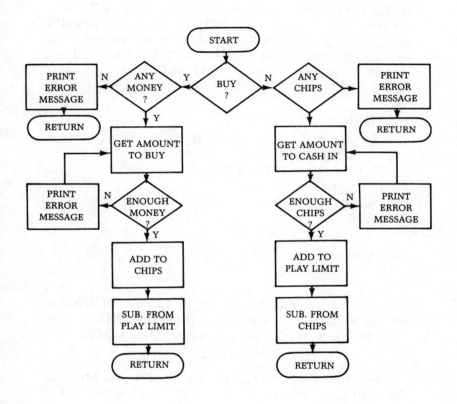

Figure 5.7. A Flow Chart for the Banking Routine

Remember that in SELECTACTIV the call to INPUT-CHOICES was to return a choice made from six options. In this case, there is a choice of only two options. To work for both these cases, INPUTCHOICES must know the number of options to allow as valid input. Therefore we will add the numerical variable OPTIONS to the Data Dictionary and improve BANKER as follows:

```
BANKER
    DISPLAY A CHOICE FOR BUY OR CASH IN
    OPTIONS = 2
    CALL INPUTCHOICES
    IF CHOICE = 1 THEN
        CALL BUY
    ELSE
        CALL CASHIN
RETURN
```

This does not mean that the variable OPTIONS is always equal to two, but rather that OPTIONS is to be set to the value two. This is sometimes indicated as:

$$OPTIONS := 2$$

Where the symbol := can be read "is set equal to." (In the example programs at the end of Chapter two, notice that Pascal uses this convention.)

Now that we have changed the way INPUTCHOICES is to work, all of the routines we have already developed that call INPUTCHOICES will have to be changed to set OPTIONS to the proper value.

We can guess that there will be similar problems involving the INPUTAMOUNT routine, so we add two other variables to the Data Dictionary: the maximum acceptable value, MAXVAL; and the minimum acceptable value, MINVAL.

Now each of the banking procedures can be developed as subroutines of BANKER. First the BUY routine is developed:

```
BUY
  IF PLAYLIMIT = 0 THEN
    DISPLAY "YOU HAVE NO MORE MONEY"
    RETURN
  MAXVAL = 10,000
  MINVAL = 0
  REPEAT
    DISPLAY "HOW MUCH DO YOU WANT TO
    BUY?"
    CALL INPUTAMOUNT
    IF AMOUNT > PLAYLIMIT THEN
      DISPLAY "YOU DO NOT HAVE ENOUGH
      MONEY FOR THAT"
      MAXVAL = PLAYLIMIT
  UNTIL AMOUNT <= PLAYLIMIT
  PLAYLIMIT = PLAYLIMIT - AMOUNT
  CHIPS = CHIPS + AMOUNT
RETURN
```

Notice that there are two exits from this routine: one in the first IF-THEN statement and one at the end of the routine. Logically, these are the same because a RETURN is the proper exit from a CALLED routine. Only one return can be used each time the routine is called. It does not matter that there is more than one RETURN statement in the routine.

The notations in our sketch code for comparing two numeric values and performing arithmetic operations are as follows:

$<$ less than	$>=$ greater than or equal to
$=$ equals	$+$ addition
$>$ greater than	$-$ subtraction
$<>$ not equal	$*$ multiplication
$<=$ less than or equal to	$/$ division

Note the two lines of sketch code in the BUY listing:

PLAYLIMIT = PLAYLIMIT-AMOUNT
CHIPS = CHIPS + AMOUNT

The second line, CHIPS=CHIPS+AMOUNT, does not mean that the variable CHIPS is equal to the variable

CHIPS plus the variable AMOUNT. This would mean that when the value of CHIPS is five and the value of AMOUNT is two you could write:

5=5+2   or   5=7

This is definitely not right. In the sketch code, the = symbol is an "assignment operator"; it really means "is set equal to," just as it did in the sketch code "options=2" for the BANKER routine. Here, for example, the new value of the variable CHIPS is to be set equal to the current value of CHIPS plus the current value of AMOUNT. This is the same as saying that the variable CHIPS is to be incremented by the current value of the variable AMOUNT.

One more comment about the syntax of the sketch code should be of particular interest to people who often use a typewriter. The character for zero must always be the numeral zero (0), not the upper case "oh" (o). The character for one must likewise be the numeral one (1), not the lower case "ell" (l). To a computer there is a vast difference between numerals and letters.

The routine for cashing in chips will be almost the same as buying chips except different variables will be tested or modified:

```
CASHIN
   IF CHIPS = 0 THEN
      DISPLAY "YOU HAVE NO MORE CHIPS"
      RETURN
   MAXVAL = 10,000
   MINVAL = 0
   REPEAT
      DISPLAY "HOW MUCH DO YOU WANT TO CASH
      IN?"
      CALL INPUTAMOUNT
      IF AMOUNT > CHIPS THEN
         DISPLAY "YOU DO NOT HAVE ENOUGH
         CHIPS FOR THAT"
         MAXVAL = CHIPS
   UNTIL AMOUNT<= CHIPS
   PLAYLIMIT = PLAYLIMIT + AMOUNT
   CHIPS = CHIPS - AMOUNT
RETURN
```

In both routines, the player is free to enter almost any value to be bought or cashed in the first time a value is requested. After being reminded of the current limit in funds or chips, however, the input routine will only accept a proper amount. This is because the maximum allowable value, MAXVAL, is changed when an invalid amount is entered.

This is the first routine that uses instructions of any significant complexity. If you are not sure how the routine is to work or how it was developed, re-read this section paying attention to the decisions that were made which lead to the final sketch code. If you try to continue while you are confusd, things will only get more confusing. If you understand most of what we have done here, then you can continue to a simpler routine which will report the current status of the game.

C-4. The Rest Of The Third Level Function

The program should keep track of various items of game information: the number of hands we have played, how many hands have been won or lost, the amount of money that is available, how much has been won or lost, and the average amount won or lost on each hand. This information is reported on demand or when the player quits by the routine RPTSTATUS. We will use the following report format:

NUMBER OF HANDS PLAYED:	XXX
NUMBER OF HANDS WON/LOST:	XXX
PERCENTAGE OF HANDS WON/LOST:	XXX
CURRENT VALUE OF CASH:	$XXXXX
CURRENT VALUE OF CHIPS:	$XXXXX
CURRENT FUNDS:	$XXXXX
TOTAL AMOUNT WON/LOST:	$XXXXX
AVERAGE WON/LOST PER HAND	$XXXXX

Here XXX indicates a number, $XXXX represents an amount of money, and WON/LOST is the word Won or LOST, depending on the current situation. The sketch code for RPTSTATUS will be:

```
RPTSTATUS
  DISPLAY "NUMBER OF HANDS PLAYED",
  HANDSPLAYD
  DISPLAY "NUMBER OF HANDS"
  IF HANDSWON >= 0 THEN
    DISPLAY "WON"
  ELSE
    DISPLAY "LOST"
  DISPLAY ABS(HANDSWON)
  DISPLAY "PERCENTAGE OF HANDS"
  IF HANDSWON >= 0 THEN
    DISPLAY "WON"
  ELSE
    DISPLAY "LOST"
  IF HANDSPLAYD = 0 THEN
    DISPLAY 0
  ELSE
    DISPLAY  (ABS(HANDSWON)/HANDSPLAYD)  *
    100, "%"
  DISPLAY "CURRENT VALUE OF CASH",
  PLAYLIMIT
  DISPLAY "CURRENT VALUE OF CHIPS", CHIPS
  DISPLAY "CURRENT  FUNDS", (PLAYLIMIT +
  CHIPS)
  DISPLAY "TOTAL AMOUNT"
  IF AMOUNTWON >= 0 THEN
    DISPLAY "WON"
  ELSE
    DISPLAY "LOST"
  DISPLAY ABS(AMOUNTWON)
  DISPLAY "AVERAGE"
  IF AMOUNTWON >= 0 THEN
    DISPLAY "WON"
  ELSE
    DISPLAY "LOST"
  DISPLAY "PER HAND"
  IF HANDSPLAYD = THEN
    DISPLAY 0
  ELSE
  DISPLAY (ABS(AMOUNTWON)/HANDSPLAYD)
  WAIT FOR <RETURN> TO CONTINUE
RETURN
```

This routine contains several new ideas that have not appeared in previous modules. Notice that when several items are to be displayed on the terminal, they can be presented as a list of constants and variables separated by commas. As usual, string constants are in quotes. The variables in this list can contain calculations that allow us to display values that are not stored in the program as variables. We can, therefore, delete AVERAGEWON and PERCNTWON from the data dictionary, since we can calculate these values whenever we wish to display them. Notice, too, that a single message may take several statements to print the values in the proper place on the proper line. The way this is done differs from one language to another, so refer to your particular programming manual for details.

Several statements that print the word "WON" or "LOST" are repeated and could be performed in a subroutine. The code that is repeated, however, is only a single IF-THEN-ELSE statement, and this would be a pretty small subroutine. Besides, each one would be replaced by a CALL statement so that the number of statements in RPTSTATUS would remain the same. In this case, then, the IF-THEN-ELSE statements are repeated to avoid cluttering the program.

Values that may be positive or negative, like HANDS-WON, are printed using an absolute value function, ABS(HANDSWON). This mathematical function gives the positive value of a variable; for example, ABS(–500) = 500. This is a convenient way to avoid printing the negative values. Most computer languages have an absolute value function, so this will probably translate without change into the final program.

There are not too many places for Murphy's Demon to cause problems here except when calculations are to be done using variables. Notice that the code has been developed so that the word WON is shown when the amount won or lost is zero. This could just as well say that nothing has been LOST, but the game will feel more friendly if it shows the zero as winnings.

A more serious consideration is that it is not possible to divide a number by zero. If a program tries to do so, an error results. Any time you use a variable as the divisor, you should check to see if the variable is equal to zero. If it is, an alternative calculation or procedure must be used. In the two examples above, a zero value is printed when the divisor would be zero.

This covers all of the functions at this level of the program except the actual playing of the Blackjack hands. The functions to shuffle the cards will be implemented later on as a utility subroutine, and the function to quit the game has been taken care of in previous routines. So, let's play cards!!

D. Playing the Actual Hand of Blackjack

A routine called PLAYHAND will control all the details required to play a hand of Blackjack. The functions to be used as subroutines are listed as the lowest level modules in Appendix C, in the order in which they will be used. PLAYHAND must call these routines using the following rules:

- Call the betting routine to place the bets.
- Call the deal routine to deal the cards.
- Call the routine that evaluates the dealer's hand for naturals.
- If the dealer has a natural, settle the bets with the players and return.
- If the player has a pair, call the routine that handles splitting of pairs.
- Call the routine that lets the player play his or her hand.
- If the player goes over twenty-one, settle the bets with the player and return.
- Call the routine that lets the dealer (computer) play its hand.
- Settle the bets for the hand.
- Return.

The only place where this might not work is when a player starts to play a hand but does not have enough chips to cover the amount of a minimum bet. Therefore, we must check at the end of the betting routine to see if a legal bet has been made and return if it has not. These steps can be converted to the following sketch code:

PLAYHAND

    CALL BETTING

```
        IF BET < MINBET THEN
            RETURN
        CALL DEAL
        CALL NATURALS
        IF HAND FINISHED THEN
            CALL SETTLE
            RETURN
        IF PLAYER HAS A PAIR THEN
            CALL SPLITPAIRS
        CALL PLAYER
        IF HAND FINISHED THEN
            CALL SETTLE
            RETURN
        CALL DEALER
        CALL SETTLE
RETURN
```

These instructions have added some new names to our system. Two new variables are required. The variable BET will contain the amount of the player's bet. Also, a flag is needed to see if the hand has been finished after evaluating naturals or after the player's hand is played. We will call this flag DONE. It must be set to false (or zero) at the beginning of the hand and changed to true (or non-zero) by any subroutine that concludes the hand. The names of the lowest level modules in Appendix C appear in the CALL statements.

Notice that the call to SPLITPAIRS follows IF HAND FINISHED, a condition that is not given as a mathematical operation. The condition description that is shown is quite specific, however, so the details may be worked out later. Sketch code should be written to identify exactly what must be done, but not necessarily how it is to be done.

One other improvement can be made in PLAYHAND to make the game run faster. As it is, the program will return to SELECTACTIV after each hand, forcing the player to select the proper activity from the screen to play another hand. In a real game, however, the player usually plays one hand after another in rapid succession. We can change this by writing PLAYHAND as a loop that ends each hand by simply asking if the player wants to play another hand. Only when the answer to this question is NO will the program return to SELECTACTIV.

A Yes/No question could be handled by INPUTCHOICES by numbering the two choices: 1. YES and 2. NO. The game will feel more natural, however, if the player can enter the words YES or NO, rather than the values one or two. We can do this by passing a special value of OPTIONS to INPUTCHOICES that will be interpreted as an instruction to get a YES or NO entry rather than choosing from a list of options. We are not very likely to choose from a list of zero or one options, so either of these values in OPTIONS could indicate a Yes/No question. There does not seem to be much reason to pick one over the other, so we will simply pick the value one. OPTIONS may now have the following values:

zero or negative number: invalid value
one: return YES or NO
number greater than one: return CHOICE of 1 to OPTIONS

To return a YES or NO answer, INPUTCHOICES will set CHOICE to one for YES and two for NO. Now we will not need another routine with another set of editing procedures to ask YES/NO questions.

All of these improvements in PLAYHAND are shown in the following sketch code:

PLAYHAND

```
    REPEAT
        DONE = FALSE
        CALL BETTING
        IF BET < MINBET THEN
            RETURN
        CALL DEAL
        CALL NATURALS
        IF DONE THEN
            CALL SETTLE
            RETURN
        IF PLAYER HAS A PAIR THEN
            CALL SPLITPAIRS
```

```
        CALL PLAYER
        IF DONE THEN
            CALL SETTLE
            RETURN
        CALL DEALER
        CALL SETTLE
        DISPLAY "PLAY AGAIN?"
        OPTIONS = 1
        CALL INPUTCHOICES
    UNTIL CHOICE = 2
RETURN
```

This seems to be a better way for this routine to work. There is no way to get into an endless loop because the player has control over CHOICE: the value tested by the loop. However, there is a problem with this routine. If the dealer has a natural or the player goes over twenty-one, a RETURN which will take us out of the loop we just created is executed. When the logic of a program is incorrect like this, it is referred to as a *bug*. This routine has a bug in it.

The logic must be reorganized so that any condition that ends the hand results in settling the hand and asking if another one should be played. This will also reduce the number of calls to SETTLE and simplify the routine. This can be done by having the parts of the routine that may or may not be used controlled by an IF-THEN statement. The RETURN after the call to BETTING should stay the way it is, however, because if there are not enough funds for a minimum bet, there is no reason to ask if another hand should be played. When the money runs out, we will return to SELECTACTIV.

PLAYHAND

    REPEAT

```
        DONE = FALSE
        CALL BETTING
        IF BET< MINBET THEN
            RETURN
        CALL DEAL
```

```
        CALL NATURALS
        IF NOT DONE THEN
            IF PLAYER HAS A PAIR THEN
                CALL SPLITPAIRS
            CALL PLAYER
            IF NOT DONE THEN
                CALL DEALER
        CALL SETTLE
        DISPLAY "PLAY AGAIN?"
        OPTIONS = 1
        CALL INPUTCHOICES
    UNTIL CHOICE = 2
RETURN
```

Now that we know how the program will run as a whole and how the hands will be controlled, it is time to move to the functions on the lowest level of the general design's structure chart: the details of a hand of cards.

E. The Detailed Routines For a Hand Of Cards

The first activity of a hand of Blackjack is for the player to place a bet for the hand. There are several conditions that must be checked to make sure the bet is valid: it cannot be more than the house limit, less than the house minimum, or more than the current value of the player's chips. (Remember, the player must have an escape route when there are not enough chips to make the minimum bet.)

For realism, we will allow the player to enter any reasonable amount before minimum and maximum conditions are checked. If a bad amount is entered, the program should report the error on the screen and adjust the limits on INPUTAMOUNT, so the same mistake will not be repeated.

The betting routine will have to be controlled by some sort of loop to allow corrections to be entered when errors are found. The best way to develop a routine controlled by a loop is the way we developed PLAYHAND: develop the logic within the loop and then develop the proper statements for the loop itself. A first approximation of the instructions for BETTING might look like this:

```
BETTING
    DISPLAY "HOW MUCH DO YOU WISH TO BET?"
    CALL INPUTAMOUNT
    IF AMOUNT > MAXBET THEN
        DISPLAY "THAT IS MORE THAN THE
        HOUSE LIMIT"
    ELSE
        IF AMOUNT < MINBET THEN
            DISPLAY "THAT IS UNDER THE HOUSE
            MINIMUM"
        ELSE
            IF AMOUNT > CHIPS THEN
                DISPLAY "YOU DO NOT HAVE THAT
                MUCH"
            ELSE
                BET = AMOUNT
RETURN
```

We are checking a series of conditions rather than selecting a condition from a list, so we shall use several IF-THEN-ELSE statements rather than a CASE statement. When one statement is controlled by (contained within) another statement of the same type, the statements are called *nested*. For example, the series of IF-THEN-ELSE statements used in BETTING to check the value of the bet are nested statements. Notice that the last ELSE clause, which changes the value of BET, will not be executed unless all of the other tests are passed.

The loop that controls BETTING will operate until a value from the player has been accepted. A more complete version of the routine would look like this:

```
BETTING
    BET = 0
    REPEAT
        DISPLAY "HOW MUCH DO YOU WISH TO BET?"
        CALL INPUTAMOUNT
        IF AMOUNT > MAXBET THEN
            DISPLAY "THAT IS MORE THAN THE HOUSE
            LIMIT"
        ELSE
            IF AMOUNT < MINBET THEN
```

```
        DISPLAY "THAT IS UNDER THE HOUSE
        MINIMUM"
      ELSE
      IF AMOUNT > CHIPS THEN
        DISPLAY "YOU DO NOT HAVE THAT MUCH"
      ELSE
        BET = AMOUNT
    UNTIL BET <> 0
RETURN
```

This looks pretty close to what we want. However, there are still a few problems. The most likely way for a player to indicate that there is not enough money for a bet is to enter a value of zero. Unfortunately, this loop will only end if BET is set to some value other than zero. A much better test can be made by setting the initial value of BET to something that can never be entered by a player. Then if the value of bet is changed, we know that an acceptable bet has been entered. In this case we can limit the input to positive numbers and set the original value of BET to minus one.

While we are considering the allowable numbers to be entered, we should add the logic that sets the minimum and maximum values for INPUTAMOUNT. The final version of BETTING will look like this:

```
BETTING
  BET = -1
  REPEAT
    DISPLAY "HOW MUCH DO YOU WISH TO BET?"
    MAXVAL = 10,000
    MINVAL = 0
    CALL INPUTAMOUNT
    IF AMOUNT > MAXBET THEN
      DISPLAY "THAT IS MORE THAN THE HOUSE
      LIMIT"
      MAXVAL = MAXBET
    ELSE
      IF (AMOUNT < MINBET) and
        (AMOUNT <> 0) THEN
        DISPLAY "THAT IS UNDER THE HOUSE
        MINIMUM"
        MINVAL = MINBET
```

```
    ELSE
       IF AMOUNT > CHIPS THEN
          DISPLAY "YOU DO NOT HAVE THAT
          MUCH"
          MAXVAL = CHIPS
       ELSE
          BET = AMOUNT
    UNTIL BET <> -1
RETURN
```

Notice that when we check to see if the bet is under the minimum bet, we must make an exception for a zero value which really means that no bet is being placed at all. This will not become an endless loop because the player can always enter a zero to return to PLAYHAND (which will itself return to SELECTACTIV).

The development of this routine is a good example of a step-by-step approach to a complex function. Start by developing the heart of the routine in a few simple statements. Then add any controlling loops that may be necessary. Once the form of the routine has been developed, add the detail that will make the whole thing work properly.

The routine to deal the cards should be easy enough to write once we know just how it should work. Methods of dealing vary, but in the common method explained in Appendix B, all but the dealer's first card are dealt face down with the dealers first card dealt face up. Since the computer can't turn the cards, we will modify this slightly by dealing the players cards face up. The first card goes to the player face up. The next card goes to the dealer face up. The third goes to the player face up. The fourth goes to the dealer face down.

The first problem we face is how to show the cards in each hand on the terminal screen. If each card is displayed on a new line as it is dealt, the hands will be interleaved with each other like this:

PLAYER CARD ONE
DEALER CARD ONE
PLAYER CARD TWO
DEALER CARD TWO

Perhaps it would be better to create two columns on the screen, one for each player. This way the first two cards can be shown on the first line and the next two on the next line like this:

PLAYER CARD ONE   DEALER CARD ONE
PLAYER CARD TWO   DEALER CARD TWO

The program can indicate whose hand a card is in by spacing over to the proper column before displaying it. All of the computer languages you will encounter will allow you to space over to a specific column by printing a series of blank (or space) characters. If your machine has more sophisticated terminal capabilities, you may wish to develop this part of the program in a more elegant way. We should leave enough room for three columns on the screen because the player may wish to split a pair of cards and play two hands at once. We can also print a heading over each column so the player can identify each hand.

The next thing to determine is what will happen when a card is dealt to a hand. This will happen four times, so it should probably be handled by a subroutine. First we must figure out what must be done with the deck. Then we must figure out what must be done with the hand. Finally, we must figure out what must be done to show this on the screen.

The deck of cards is stored in the program as an array of 104 numbers, with each of the numbers from one to fifty-two appearing twice. To simulate a real deck, the two sets of numbers from one to fifty-two should be randomly distributed throughout the 104 positions in the deck. The first card to be dealt will be the card value in the first position of the deck: DECK(1). As each next card is dealt, the program will use the card value stored in the next position of the array: DECK(2), DECK(3), . . .

This procedure can continue until we reach DECK(104). At this point the entire deck has been played and must be reshuffled. The positions of the card values are redistributed throughout the array, and we start over with DECK(1) as the next card. We will need a variable to keep track of how far we have dealt through the deck as the game progresses. Therefore, we will add DECKCOUNT to the data dictionary to use as the index in the array

DECK. The next card in the deck will always be DECK(DECKCOUNT).

As each card is added to a hand, it must be placed in the next available position in the array for that hand. We have an array HANDCOUNT which keeps track of how many cards that are currently in each hand. The value in HANDCOUNT will point to the last card added to the hand. As each card is added to a hand, the value of HANDCOUNT for that hand must first be incremented so that the card will go into the next empty position.

As each card is dealt, the program must display the result in the proper column on the terminal. To get to the proper column, the program can display blank characters until the appropriate position has been reached. Usually, there is a character on the terminal screen which shows where the next item will be printed. This character is called the *cursor*. Getting to the proper column on the screen is called *positioning the cursor*. Once the cursor has been positioned, the card can be displayed. If the card is dealt face down, the screen should show the characters XXXXX. If the card is dealt face up, the screen should show the value and suit of the card just as in the example programs at the end of Chapter Two.

We know that the first cards of the hand will be the first and second card for the player's primary hand and the dealer's hand. Therefore we can simplify this routine by using constant values to put the cards where we want them rather than setting variable values and then referring to the variables. We must take care, however, to see that all the variables are properly set at the end of the routine. The following sketch code will deal the cards.

DEAL

```
    DISPLAY"          PLAYER          DEALER"
    CALL GETCARD
    PLAYER1(1) = CARD
    MOVE CURSOR TO COLUMN ONE OF THE
       NEXT LINE
    CALL PRINTCARD

    CALL GETCARD
    DEALER(1) = CARD
```

```
          MOVE CURSOR TO COLUMN TWO OF THE
            SAME LINE
          DISPLAY "XXXXX"

        CALL GETCARD
          PLAYER1(2) = CARD
          MOVE CURSOR TO COLUMN ONE OF NEXT
            LINE
          CALL PRINTCARD

          CALL GETCARD
          DEALER(2) = CARD
          MOVE CURSOR TO COLUMN TWO OF THE
            SAME LINE
          CALL PRINTCARD

          MOVE CURSOR TO THE NEXT LINE
          HANDCOUNT(1) = 2
          HANDCOUNT(2) = 2
          HANDCOUNT(3) = 0
RETURN
```

We have to add a new variable, CARD, to keep track of the card currently being used. This will be filled in by GETCARD when a card is pulled from the deck, used here in DEAL to put the card in someone's hand, and used by PRINTCARD to display a card on the screen.

Notice that the values of the hands from previous games are not cleared out when a new hand is dealt. HANDCOUNT will keep track of all cards used in this hand so it does not matter what may be in the rest of the array from a previous hand. This is an easy place to make a mistake, however. You should always ask if Murphy's Demon will cause problems when data from previous processing is not cleared before a part of a program (the hands of cards in this case) is used again.

At the end of the routine, the cursor is moved to the beginning of the next line of the terminal so the next item displayed will not show up on the same line as the last card dealt.

The routine to retrieve the next card from the deck will use the variable DECKCOUNT in the same way DEAL uses HANDCOUNT: The counter always points to the next available card. When the counter is greater than 104 it is time to re-shuffle the deck.

GETCARD

```
IF DECKCOUNT > 104 THEN
    CALL SHUFFLE
CARD = DECK(DECKCOUNT)
DECKCOUNT = DECKCOUNT + 1
```

RETURN

The last routine required to deal the cards will be PRINTCARD. It will probably come as no surprise that we can use most of the logic developed in the demonstration program in Chapter Two for this function. We will have to add the array SUIT for the four names of the suits and the array VALUE for the values of the thirteen card values to the data dictionary. Recall from Chapter Two that the suit number can be calculated when it is needed by a single equation, so we can discard the variable CARDSUIT in the data dictionary. This will not work for the card value, however, so we will keep CARD-VALUE in the dictionary.

Looking ahead, we can see that calculating the value of a card (one through thirteen) from the card number (one through fifty-two) will be required when we evaluate a player's hand to see if it has gone over twenty-one or if it is less than, equal to, or greater than another hand. Therefore, we will define a new utility subroutine called GETCARDVALUE to calculate the current value of CARD and put in into CARDVALUE for us.

The final routine to display a card on the terminal looks like this:

PRINTCARD

```
CALL GETCARDVALUE
DISPLAY "THE", VALUE(CARDVALUE),
    "OF", SUIT(INT((CARD-1)/13) + 1)
```

RETURN

This looks reasonable enough except for the funny looking expression in the middle:

$$SUIT(INT((CARD-1)/13 + 1)$$

This can be rewritten as:

$$CARDSUIT = INT((CARD-1)/13) +1$$

What on earth does all this mean?

This is the equation that was shown at the end of Chapter Two to calculate the suit of a card from its card number (one through fifty-two). To understand how this works it will be easiest to start within the inner pair of parentheses and work outward until the whole equation has been analyzed. The innermost calculation is

$$(CARD-1)$$

This is simply the number of the card minus one. The next layer of the calculation is

$$((CARD-1)/13)$$

This divides the value of (CARD-1) by thirteen, the number of cards in each suit. If the current value of card is twenty-nine, for example, then ((CARD-1/13) will be equal to 28/13 or 2.1538461. Now we come to something more interesting: the final layer of the calculation performs a function called INT in ((CARD-1)/13), then adds the value one to the results:

$$INT((CARD-1/13)+1$$

The INT stands for INTEGER, a function common to BASIC, Pascal, and most other computer languages. A function is a mathematical* procedure which takes some value or values as input and calculates a result. The values that are used as input are called parameters or arguments and are passed to the expression in parentheses after the function name. The function returns the value that is calculated from the parameters it is given.

The INT function receives a single number as a parameter and returns the integer part of the number after any fractional or decimal part has been stripped off. Here are several numbers and the values returned by the INT function:

---

*Usually mathematical — it is possible in some languages to create functions that work with strings or entire processes that may be as complex as a major subroutine.

- Count all the cards, treating the aces as eleven.
- If the total is twenty-one or less, return.
- As long as the total is over twenty-one, subtract ten for each ace in the hand. This is the same as treating it as one instead of eleven.
- When the score drops below twenty-one or you run out of aces, return.

The first thing the evaluation routine will have to do is to make sure it is looking at the proper hand by using the variable HAND. It will be easier to write this routine to always evaluate the same hand rather than to evaluate any of the three possible hands in the game. This can be accomplished by creating a fourth "dummy" hand that is only used to evaluate a hand of cards. The routine will first load this extra hand with the values from the proper playing hand, then analyze the hand.

The sketch code for this evaluation routine will require that EXTRAHAND be added to the data dictionary as another array and that HANDCOUNT be expanded from a three to a four position array.

It appears that we may be required to calculate the value of a card, from the card's number, throughout the program. This is now done with the utility subroutine GETCARDVALUE which has yet to be developed. It would be much easier, however, if we could calculate the value of a card by a function like the integer value function that we have already used. This user-defined function will be called CARDVALUE and will require one value: the number of the card being evaluated. Using such a function we can display the value of card number one by writing:

DISPLAY CARDVALUE(1)

In like manner, the value of the card indicated by the value of the variable CARD may be displayed by writing:

DISPLAY CARDVALUE(CARD)

This time we will use the function, rather than the subroutine, for two reasons: The program will be easier to write using the function, and we will be able to see how user-defined functions are used. We will, of course, have to go back and change PRINTCARD and any other routine that has used GETCARDVALUE.

The sketch code to determine the value of a hand will look like this:

```
EVALUATE
  CASE HAND OF
    1: EXTRAHAND = DEALER
       HANDCOUNT(4) = HANDCOUNT(1)
    2: EXTRAHAND = PLAYER1
       HANDCOUNT(4) = HANDCOUNT(2)
    3: EXTRAHAND = PLAYER2
       HANDCOUNT(4) = HANDCOUNT(3)
  END CASE
  DO FOR COUNT = 1 TO HANDCOUNT(4)
    V = CARDVALUE(EXTRAHAND(COUNT))
    IF V > 10 THEN      {face cards = 10}
      V = 10
    IF V = 1 THEN       {aces = 11}
      V = 11
    HANDVALUE = HANDVALUE + V
  END LOOP
  COUNT = 1
  DO WHILE (HANDVALUE > 21) AND
    (COUNT <= HANDCOUNT(4) )
    IF CARDVALUE(EXTRAHAND(COUNT) )=1
    THEN
      HANDVALUE = HANDVALUE – 10     {adjust
                                      aces to = 1}
    COUNT = COUNT + 1
  END LOOP
RETURN
```

V is a temporary variable to hold the value of the card while it is checked for being a face card or an ace, and COUNT is a general counter used to control the loops in the routine. The case statement loads the array EXTRAHAND with the proper playing hand depending on whether the value of HAND is one, two, or three. It also loads HANDCOUNT(4) with the proper HAND-COUNT value to indicate how many cards are in the hand.

The first loop is executed once for each card in the hand. The function CARDVALUE is used to determine the value of each of the cards. The cards themselves are in the array EXTRAHAND which is indexed by the counter COUNT as it is incremented from one to the number of cards in the hand. There is a bug here, however, because we are adding the values of the cards to whatever HANDVALUE was when the routine started. Therefore, we must first initialize HANDVALUE to zero so we count only the card values in this hand.

The DO-WHILE loop to adjust the values of aces is controlled by two conditions — the value of the hand dropping (or starting out) below twenty-one and the value of COUNT going over the number of cards in the hand (HANDCOUNT(4)).

All this would be simpler if we did not have separate arrays for the three hands. Then we would not need the case statement at the start of the routine or the extra set of variables used only when hands are being evaluated. In fact, this is the perfect place for a two-dimensional array; the three hands can be combined into one array controlled by two indexes. The first index will indicate which hand is being used, and the second will indicate which card in the hand is being used. We call this new array HANDS. The first index will have a value of one for the dealer, two for the player's normal hand, and three for the player's second hand when a pair of cards has been split. These values will correspond to the three values in the HANDCOUNT array. The second index will have a value of one to fifteen to indicate one of the fifteen possible cards in a hand.

The arrays HANDS and HANDCOUNT are shown in Figure 5.8. Both arrays contain three columns, one for each possible hand. HANDS also contains room for fifteen rows of cards in each column. The first index in each array points to the proper column. The second index in the HAND array points to the appropriate row of cards. The two indexes together indicate a specific card by its location, row and column.

Figure 5.8 shows the values for these variables after the first four cards have been dealt. The very first card is dealt into the player's hand: CARD 1. This would be represented as:

HANDS(2,1)

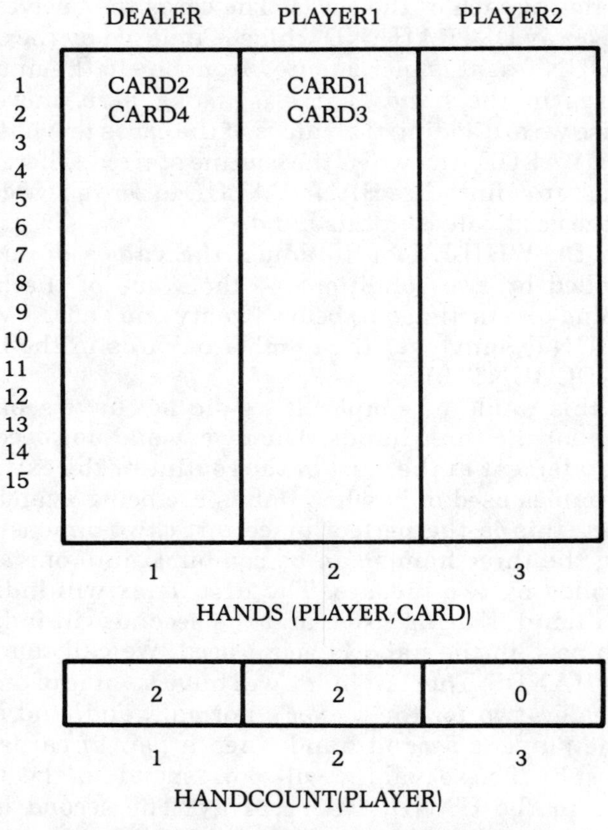

	DEALER	PLAYER1	PLAYER2
1	CARD2	CARD1	
2	CARD4	CARD3	
3			
4			
5			
6			
7			
8			
9			
10			
11			
12			
13			
14			
15			
	1	2	3

HANDS (PLAYER,CARD)

2	2	0
1	2	3

HANDCOUNT(PLAYER)

Figure 5.8. The Hands After the Deal

Notice that as the cards are dealt, they show up on the screen with the player's cards in the first one or two columns and the dealer's cards in the last column, since the dealer's cards are dealt last. In the array HANDS, however, the order has been changed to put the player's hand(s) last because usually, there will not be anything in the last column. This means that sometimes the dealer will be in the first position and sometimes in the last position. This is perfectly all right as long as we remember whether we are referring to columns on the screen or positions in the array HANDS.

In the EVALUATE routine, the hand to be evaluated will be indicated by the value of the variable HAND. This variable will always be used to indicate the player in our new arrays. Therefore, the first card in the hand to be evaluated will be:

HANDS(HAND,1)

As we count through the cards in a hand using COUNT to keep track of the cards, each card will be selected by the expression:

HANDS(HAND,COUNT)

The value of each of these cards will be obtained by using this card expression as the parameter in the CARDVALUE function. This can be expressed as:

CARDVALUE(HANDS(HAND,COUNT))

It may not be a good idea to use two variables with such similar names as HAND and HANDS because it can lead to confusion. We will leave them as they are for now to illustrate the fact that similar names in the Data Dictionary are possible, but they may be confusing. We can change one of these names before the project is done if they present too much of a problem.

The evaluation routine using the re-designed arrays will now look like this:

```
EVALUATE
  HANDVALUE = 0
  DO FOR COUNT = 1 TO HANDCOUNT(HAND)
    V = CARDVALUE(HANDS(HAND,COUNT))
    IF V > 10 THEN        {face cards = 10}
      V = 10
    IF V = 1 THEN
      V = 11                    {aces = 11}
    HANDVALUE = HANDVALUE + V
  END LOOP
  COUNT = 1
  DO WHILE (HANVALUE > 21) AND
      (COUNT <= HANDCOUNT(HAND)
    IF CARDVALUE(HANDS(HAND,COUNT))=1
    THEN
      HANDVALUE = HANDVALUE - 10    {adjust
                                 aces to = 1}
    COUNT = COUNT + 1
  END LOOP
RETURN
```

Now of course, we will have to go back to any routine that used the old DEALER, PLAYER1, or PLAYER2 arrays and update them to use the new two-dimensional array. It is a shame that we did not know how the arrays would work in the first place, but that is the whole idea of the detailed design. The design is continually improved whenever possible as more is learned about the processing that must take place. We are, after all, still working on the design of the program, and not on the program code itself. In the meantime, let's continue to the next routine.

The next routine will only be called if the player is dealt a pair of cards with matching values: a pair of fives, for example. We will ask the player if the pair is to be split into two hands. If the answer is no, we can return without making any other changes.

If the answer is yes, we must check to see if the player has enough chips to cover a double bet. If there is enough, we must move the player's second card out of hand number two and make it the first card of hand number three. Two more cards are then dealt, one for each of the player's new hands. HANDCOUNT must then be updated to reflect the changes in the number of cards in each hand.

Playing three hands will also change how cards are displayed on the terminal screen. We should, therefore, re-display all of the cards in three columns.

The sketch code for SPLITPAIRS looks like this:

```
SPLITPAIRS
   DISPLAY "DO YOU WISH TO SPLIT YOUR PAIR?"
   OPTIONS = 1
   CALL INPUTCHOICES
   IF CHOICE = 1 THEN
      IF CHIPS < (2 * BET) THEN
         DISPLAY "YOU CAN'T COVER THE BET"
      ELSE
         HANDS(3,1) = HANDS(2,2)
         DISPLAY " PLAYER-1 PLAYER-2 DEALER "
         MOVE CURSOR TO COLUMN ONE
         CARD = HAND(2,1)
         CALL PRINTCARD
         MOVE CURSOR TO COLUMN TWO OF THE
```

```
      SAME LINE
      CARD = HAND(3,1)
      CALL PRINTCARD
      MOVE CURSOR TO COLUMN THREE OF THE
      SAME LINE
      DISPLAY "XXXX"
      MOVE CURSOR TO COLUMN ONE OF THE
      NEXT LINE
      CALL GETCARD
      HAND(2,2) = CARD
      CALL PRINTCARD
      MOVE CURSOR TO COLUMN TWO OF THE
      SAME LINE
      CALL GETCARD
      HAND(3,2) = CARD
      CALL PRINTCARD
      MOVE CURSOR TO COLUMN THREE OF THE
      SAVE LINE
      CARD = HAND(1,2)
      CALL PRINTCARD
      MOVE CURSOR TO START OF NEXT LINE
RETURN
```

Now we come to the part of the program where the player actually plays a hand of Blackjack. The tricky part is that the player may actually be playing two hands of Blackjack if the original pair of cards was split. According to the rules, the player may draw a card for any available hand until he decides to stop or until the hand(s) go over twenty-one. When a card is drawn, it must be displayed on the terminal screen and the hand must be evaluated again.

All of this sounds quite complex so perhaps we had better break this routine into smaller functions. A high-level function called PLAYER will ask if another card is desired, decide which hand is to be played, and determine when the player has quit or gone over twenty-one. A lower-level function call PLAYERHAND will actually add the card to the hand, display it, and re-evaluate the hand. This routine can be written so that the variable HAND indicates which hand is having cards added to it. Therefore, we will need only one routine to play both of the player's hands.

The high-level function PLAYER will check to see if a second hand is being played. It will then ask if another card is to be drawn, and possibly, for which hand it is to be drawn. If no card is to be drawn, the player is done. To prevent the game from continuing after one or both hands have exceeded twenty-one, we will need a new variable to indicate when a hand is finished. We will use HANDONE, an array of three flags that will initially be set to FALSE but will be set to TRUE as each hand finishes. The number of cards in the third hand, HANDCOUNT(3), will be zero if one hand is being played, and greater than zero if the player has split a pair into two hands. We can test this value to see how many hands the player has. This PLAYER routine will contain a DO-UNTIL loop which will continue until the player requests no more cards or until all possible hands have been completed. The sketch code for PLAYER will be:

```
PLAYER
  HANDONE(2) = FALSE
  IF HANDCOUNT(3) = 0 THEN
    HANDONE(3) = TRUE
  ELSE
    HANDONE(3) = FALSE
  REPEAT
    DISPLAY "WHAT NEXT?"
    IF HANDCOUNT(3) = 0 THEN
      DISPLAY "DO YOU STAND ON THIS HAND?"
      OPTIONS = 1
    ELSE
      DISPLAY "1: DONE   2: CARD FOR 1   3: CARD
      FOR 2"
      OPTIONS = 3
    CALL INPUTCHOICES
    IF CHOICE <> 1 THEN
      HAND = CHOICE
      CALL PLAYERHAND
  UNTIL (CHOICE = 1) OR
    (HANDONE(2) = TRUE AND HANDONE(3) =
    TRUE)
RETURN
```

Notice we have been able to word the YES/NO questions, "DO YOU STAND ON THIS HAND?" so the value of CHOICE to stop for one hand (YES=1) will be the same as the value of CHOICE to stop when playing two hands (DONE=1). For most hands, the simple YES/NO question will be asked. When a pair has been split into two hands, a more complex question will be asked. Once the question has been answered, however, the rest of the routine does not need to know how many hands the player has in order to process CHOICE.

Even though the player may split a pair of cards into two hands only on rare occasions, the program has to be written as if this were always the case. As we said before, if something is only going to happen once, the program MUST be able to take care of it; remember the programmer's rule: we must cover the unusual situations. This routine will play one or two hands until the player is done or until both hands go over twenty-one.

Now we must develop the routine PLAYERHAND to add a card to the proper hand, display it on the screen, and check to see if the hand has gone over twenty-one. As in the EVALUATE routine, the hand being used will be indicated by HAND. Unlike the previous routines, however, we do not know how many cards are in each hand without using HANDCOUNT. The number of cards in the hand we are currently processing will be HAND-COUNT(HAND). The sketch code for PLAYERHAND will be:

```
PLAYERHAND
    IF HANDONE(HAND) = TRUE THEN
        DISPLAY "THAT HAND IS ALREADY OVER
            21"
        RETURN
    MOVE CURSOR TO COLUMN (HAND – 1)
    CALL GETCARD
    CALL PRINTCARD
    HANDCOUNT(HAND) = HANDCOUNT(HAND) + 1
    HANDS(HAND,HANDCOUNT(HAND)) = CARD
    CALL EVALUATE
    IF HANDVALUE > 21 THEN
        DISPLAY "TOO BAD, PLAYER GOES OVER
            21"
        HANDONE(HAND) = TRUE
RETURN
```

The player may be using hands number two or three, but they are shown on the screen as columns one and two. This is why we must use (HAND-1) as the column to which the cursor is moved.

Once the player has finished with this hand (or hands), a routine called DEALER will play the dealer's hand. This will be easier because the dealer can have only one hand. Furthermore, the dealer must draw another card if the value of the hand is under seventeen, and must stand if the value of the hand is seventeen or over.

We will start by turning over the dealer's card that was originally shown face down. By the time we get to the dealer's hand, however, we may have already filled the screen up with all sorts of messages and cards from the player's hand. We might as well re-display both the dealer's cards in the proper column before playing the rest of the hand.

The loop in DEALER will execute as long as the value of the hand is less than seventeen. We use a DO-WHILE here because the value of the first two cards may already be greater than seventeen; in that case, the loop should not be executed at all. The sketch code for DEALER will look like this:

```
DEALER
    IF HANDCOUNT(3) = 0 THEN
        DEALERCOLUMN = 2
    ELSE
        DEALERCOLUMN = 3
    MOVE CURSOR TO DEALERCOLUMN OF NEXT
        LINE
    CARD = HANDS(1,1)
    CALL PRINTCARD

    MOVE CURSOR TO DEALERCOLUMN OF NEXT
        LINE
    CARD = HANDS(1,2)
    CALL PRINTCARD

    HAND = 1
    CALL EVALUATE
    WHILE (HANDVALUE < 17) DO
        MOVE CURSOR TO DEALERCOLUMN OF
        NEXT LINE
```

```
        CALL GETCARD
        CALL PRINTCARD
        HANDCOUNT(1) = HANDCOUNT(1) + 1
        HANDS(1,HANDCOUNT(1)) = CARD
        CALL EVALUATE
    ENDLOOP

    IF HANDVALUE <= 17 THEN
        DISPLAY "THE DEALER STANDS AT",
            HANDVALUE
    ELSE
        DISPLAY "THE DEALER GOES OVER"
RETURN
```

We have used DEALERCOLUMN to indicate whether the dealer's cards should be shown in column two or column three. This way, we only have to test the number of columns once, when DEALERCOLUMN is set, rather than each time a card is displayed in the dealer's column.

The last routine at this level of the general design will settle the bets between the dealer and the player. First, we must determine what happened in the game, how many hands there were, who had naturals, and who won. Then, we must settle the bets by increasing or decreasing the chips for each possible condition.

There are three ways the game may end as viewed by the dealer: the dealer has a natural, the dealer goes over twenty-one, or the dealer stands. For each option there are several ways that a player's hand may be evaluated depending on what the player has done. The following list shows how the game may end:

- The dealer has a natural and every other hand either loses or stands off by also having a natural.
- The dealer goes over twenty-one ("breaks") and the other hands are treated as follows:
    - A hand that has a natural will be paid one and one-half times the player's bet.
    - A hand that has gone over twenty-one loses the player's bet.
    - A hand that has not gone over twenty-one wins the player's bet.
- The dealer stands between seventeen and twenty-one and the other hands are treated as follows.

- A hand that has a natural will be paid one and one-half times the player's bet.
- A hand that is under the value of the dealer's hand loses the player's bet.
- A hand that is equal to the value of the dealer's hand stands off and does not win or lose.
- A hand that is better than the value of the dealer's hand wins the player's bet.

The following sketch code for SETTLE will evaluate the dealer's hand to see how the game ends:

```
SETTLE

    HAND = 1
    CALL EVALUATE
    DEALERVALUE = HANDVALUE
    IF (HANDVALUE = 21) AND
        (HANDCOUNT(1) = 2) THEN
            CALL DEALERNATURAL
    ELSE
        IF HANDVALUE > 21 THEN
            CALL DEALEROVER
        ELSE
            CALL DEALERSTANDS

RETURN
```

DEALERVALUE must be established so the value of the player's hands can be compared to that of the dealer's hand when the dealer stands or goes over twenty-one.

Now we can develop each of the routines that actually settle the bets between the player and the dealer. Each routine will have to look at hands two and three to see if the player split a pair of cards into two hands. We will use a DO-FOR loop to look at the hands. For each hand that has cards in it, a separate settlement will be made with the dealer. If there is a second hand for the player, a special message will be displayed before it is settled to separate the two settlements on the screen.

Remember that when chips were being bought at the bank we checked to see that the player had enough money to cover them. We will now have to check to see that the bank has enough money to cover the bets that the dealer has to pay off. When the bank runs out of money, we will call a subroutine that informs the player that the bank is broken. At this point, we will do no more than display this information. It will be up to the player to end the game when the bank goes broke.

The three routines that settle bets will be DEALER NATURAL, DEALEROVER, and DEALERSTANDS. Here is the sketch code for each of these routines:

```
DEALERNATURAL

    DO FOR HAND = 2 TO 3
        IF HANDCOUNT(HAND) = 0 THEN
            RETURN
        IF HAND = 3 THEN
            DISPLAY "FOR THE PLAYER'S SECOND
                HAND:"
        CALL EVALUATE
        IF HANDVALUE = 21 THEN
            DISPLAY "STANDOFF WITH
                NATURALS"
        ELSE
            DISPLAY "DEALER WINS WITH A
                NATURAL"
            CHIPS = CHIPS - BET
            BANKLIMIT = BANKLIMIT + BET
    NEXT HAND

RETURN

DEALEROVER

    DO FOR HAND = 2 TO 3
        IF HANDCOUNT(HAND) = 0 THEN
            RETURN
        IF HAND = 3 THEN
            DISPLAY "FOR THE PLAYER'S SECOND
                HAND:"
        CALL EVALUATE
        IF (HANDVALUE = 21) AND
          (HANDCOUNT(HAND)) = 2) THEN
            DISPLAY "PLAYER WINS WITH A
                NATURAL"
```

```
                    CHIPS = CHIPS + (1.5 * BET)
                    BANKLIMIT = BANKLIMIT - (1.5 * BET)
               ELSE
                    IF HANDVALUE > 21 THEN
                         DISPLAY "PLAYER LOSES"
                         CHIPS = CHIPS - BET
                         BANKLIMIT = BANKLIMIT + BET
                    ELSE
                         DISPLAY "PLAYER WINS"
                         CHIPS = CHIPS + BET
                         BANKLIMIT = BANKLIMIT - BET
          NEXT HAND
          IF BANKLIMIT < 0 THEN
               CALL BROKENBANK

     RETURN

     DEALERSTANDS

          DO FOR HAND = 2 TO 3
               IF HANDCOUNT(HAND) = 0 THEN
                    RETURN
               IF HAND = 3 THEN
                    DISPLAY "FOR THE PLAYER'S SECOND
                    HAND:"
               CALL EVALUATE
               IF (HANDVALUE = 21) AND
                 (HANDCOUNT(HAND)) = 2) THEN
                    DISPLAY "PLAYER WINS WITH A
                    NATURAL"
                    CHIPS = CHIPS + (1.5 * BET)
                    BANKLIMIT = BANKLIMIT - (1.5 * BET)
               ELSE
                    IF HANDVALUE < DEALERVALUE
                    THEN
                         DISPLAY "PLAYER LOSES"
                         CHIPS = CHIPS - BET
                         BANKLIMIT = BANKLIMIT + BET
                    ELSE
                         IF HANDVALUE > DEALERVALUE
                         THEN
                              DISPLAY "PLAYER WINS"
                              CHIPS = CHIPS + BET
```

$$\text{BANKLIMIT} = \text{BANKLIMIT} - \text{BET}$$
ELSE
DISPLAY "STANDOFF WITH
DEALER"
NEXT HAND
IF BANKLIMIT < 0 THEN
CALL BROKENBANK

RETURN

We could combine the three routines with the SETTLE routine to make one long routine that would settle all bets. However, it is easier to deal with parts of a program that are about one page in length, so we will leave it the way we have it.

It also looks as if some of the processing in these subroutines could be combined into a more sophisticated single routine that would be able to settle any of the bets. This would reduce some of the code that is now duplicated, especially in DEALEROVER and DEALERSTANDS. However, such programming would be more complicated. It would also reduce the routine's level of internal strength, since it would be responsible for several individual functions. We mentioned before that structured programming is more efficient for the programmer than for the machine. This example of somewhat duplicated code is a good illustration of programmer efficiency:

The last routine we must develop for the basic system structure will handle the messages for breaking the bank:

BROKENBANK

DISPLAY "****** YOU HAVE BROKEN THE
BANK ******"
DISPLAY AN APPROPRIATE MESSAGE ABOUT
FURTHER BETS
BANKLIMIT = 0

RETURN

F. Developing the Utility Subroutines

We have now completed the detailed design of all of the modules in the program except the utility subroutines. By developing the rest of the system first, we have defined, in detail, the processing that these subroutines must do and the variables that they must use. We can now develop these functions knowing exactly how they must interact with the rest of the system.

We will start with the two modules that interact directly with the player: INPUTVALUES and INPUT-CHOICES. In both cases, we require that a variable be filled in with a value entered by the player. This is the place where Murphy's Demon will have the most fun. If a person can possibly enter something wrong, sooner or later somebody will.

The point, then, is to think of every type of wrong answer that can be entered and provide an appropriate response. As we have said before, if the information is edited correctly in this part of the system, it can be assumed to be correct in the rest of the system. As you may have noticed, we have not questioned the value requested from the player in any other routine. This means that we have to get it right here.

This idea of checking and correcting information, only when it is first received, is common to systems of all sizes. This is very important, for example, when information is stored on magnetic tape or disk for later processing. The editing must be done when the information is entered. When another program reads the information, it can assume that it has been edited and does not need further checking.

We shall proceed, therefore, to try to outsmart the player in the input routines. In general, we must check that the proper type of information has been entered and that the values are neither too large nor too small. For most applications the following checks should take care of editing the incoming information:

NUMERIC DATA
- There must be no characters except the digits zero through nine (0-9), the plus sign (+), the minus sign (-) and the period (.). In some cases data in scientific notation (or "Floating Point") must be entered. These cases require checking of both the number and its

exponent (i.e. 1.00E-5). This type of checking is more complex than checking simple numbers.

- The number must be no smaller than some minimum limit. This can also be used to check for negative values.
- The number must be no larger than some maximum limit.
- If the number is to be an integer, there should be no fractional or decimal portion to it.
- Perhaps the number must be one of a specific list of number values.

CHARACTER DATA

- There may usually be any printable character including numbers, upper or lower case letters, and punctuation marks in the data. There may be other characters that your keyboard can produce that you wish to exclude. This is often taken care of by the language being used, however, and is usually not a problem.
- The character string must be no longer than some maximum string size.
- The character string must be no shorter than some minimum string size.
- Perhaps the character string must be one of a specific set of strings.

The first thing an editing routine must do is to check for the conditions that apply to each particular data item. If an error is found, the program should display a specific message stating what is wrong and possibly how it should be corrected. It is no help to the user to see a message such as INVALID ENTRY when an error is found. Finally, the user must be given a chance to enter the correct value.

The following sketch code will make the proper checks on values and choices entered by the player in our game of Blackjack. The new variable DATAOK is used to make the loop continue until a proper value is entered. The string variable STRING has been added to INPUT CHOICES to cover the case of YES/NO questions. These will be answered by character strings that start with a

"Y" or an "N" which would not work with a numeric variable such as CHOICE.

```
INPUTAMOUNT
  DATAOK = FALSE
  REPEAT
    INPUT AMOUNT FROM THE TERMINAL
    IF AMOUNT IS NOT NUMERIC THEN
      DISPLAY "YOU MUST ENTER A NUMBER"
    ELSE
      IF AMOUNT < MINVALUE THEN
        DISPLAY "ENTER A NUMBER LESS THAN",
        MINVALUE
      ELSE
        IF AMOUNT > MAXVALUE THEN
          DISPLAY "ENTER A NUMBER GREATER
          THAN", MAXVALUE
        ELSE
          IF AMOUNT<> INT(AMOUNT) THEN
            DISPLAY "ENTER AN INTEGER
            NUMBER"
          ELSE
            DATAOK = TRUE
  UNTIL DATAOK = TRUE
RETURN

INPUTCHOICES
  DATAOK = FALSE
  REPEAT
    INPUT STRING FROM THE TERMINAL
    IF OPTIONS = 1 THEN
      IF LENGTH OF STRING = 0 THEN
        DISPLAY "PLEASE ENTER YES OR NO"
      ELSE
        IF (FIRST CHARACTER <> "Y") AND
        (FIRST CHARACTER <> "N") THEN
          DISPLAY "PLEASE ENTER YES OR NO"
        ELSE
          DATA = OK
          IF FIRST CHARACTER = "Y" THEN
            CHOICE = 1
          ELSE
            CHOICE = 2
```

```
    ELSE
      IF STRING IS NOT NUMERIC THEN
         DISPLAY "YOU MUST ENTER A NUMBER"
      ELSE
         CHOICE = VALUE OF STRING
         IF CHOICE < 1 THEN
            DISPLAY"ENTER A NUMBER FROM 1 TO",
            OPTIONS
         ELSE
            IF CHOICE > OPTIONS THEN
               DISPLAY"ENTER A NUMBER FROM 1 TO",
               OPTIONS
            ELSE
               IF CHOICE <> INT(CHOICE) THEN
                  DISPLAY "ENTER AN INTEGER
                  NUMBER"
               ELSE
                  DATAOK = TRUE
  UNTIL DATAOK = TRUE
RETURN
```

In both of these routines, DATAOK is set to TRUE only when all the tests in the nested IF-THEN-ELSE statements have been passed. Notice that we have again used the INT function to obtain the integer part of a variable.

The last regular subroutine that we need is the one that shuffles the deck of cards. This routine should randomly distribute two sets of numbers from one to fifty-two into the 104 available positions in the deck. It must then set DECKCOUNT to one so the system will start drawing cards from the top of the deck again.

To do this, we will first set all 104 values of DECK to zero. We will then go through two loops. The outer loop will be executed twice, once for each deck. The inner loop will be executed fifty-two times, once for each card in a deck. This will take us through the numbers one through fifty-two twice, the very numbers that must be stored in DECK. For each number we will pick a position in the deck by calculating a random number from one to 104. If this position of the deck contains a zero, meaning nothing has yet been put there, we will set it to the value of the current card (one through fifty-two). If the position in DECK is not zero, meaning a card has already been put there, we will search consecutive positions in DECK until an empty space can be found. The logic for this operation looks like this:

```
SHUFFLE
   DO FOR COUNT = 1 TO 104
      DECK(COUNT) = 0
   END LOOP
   DO FOR COUNT = 1 TO 2
      DO FOR CARD = 1 TO 52
         X = RANDOM NUMBER FROM 1 TO 104
         WHILE DECK(X) <> 0 DO       {look for an empty
            X = X + 1                               slot}
            IF X > 104 THEN
               X = 1
         END LOOP
         DECK (X) = CARD
      END LOOP
   END LOOP
RETURN
```

Notice that while we are searching for an empty slot, we check to see if we have run off the end of the array. If so, we simply start again at the beginning of the array with slot one.

The final routine that we need to define is called CARDVALUE. It will receive a card number from one to fifty-two and return the value of the card from one to thirteen. The logic of this function will be similar to that used in the programming examples at the end of Chapter Two. The parameter(s) passed to the function will be shown in parentheses after the name of the function. The value to be returned will be shown as part of the RETURN statement. The sketch code for the CARD-VALUE looks like this

```
CARDVALUE (X)
   DO WHILE X > 13
      X = X - 13
   END LOOP
RETURN X
```

Unfortunately, most versions of BASIC only allow one statement in a user-defined function. We will have to come up with a more compact way of calculating a card's value. We can find which suit a card is in by taking the integer value of the card's number (1 to 52), dividing it by thirteen (the number of cards in a suit), and then adding one. The integer value of cards in the first suit divided by thirteen will be zero. Likewise, the integer value of the cards in the second suit divided by thirteen will be one; in the third suit, two; and in the fourth suit, three. Adding one to these values, then, gives the proper suit value.

Finally, if we subtract the number of cards in the previous suits from the current card number, we should have the current card value. For example, for card fourteen, there is one previous suit. Subtracting the thirteen cards for the previous suit from fourteen yields one, the ace of the second suit. So the equation for the function is

CARDVALUE = CARDNUMBER − (INT(CARD-
                NUMBER/13) * 13)

This is more efficient than the CARDVALUE function previously shown because there is no loop. Only one calculation is required. The improved CARDVALUE function may be represented as

CARDVALUE (X)

RETURN X − (INT(X/13) × 13)

You may have noticed that this is exactly what the original loop was doing anyway. For every suit preceding the current card's suit (X>13), thirteen was subtracted from the present value.

There should be some way to distinguish subroutines from functions, so from now on we will precede the name of each routine with the name PROCEDURE or FUNCTION.

III. ANOTHER LOOK AT WHAT WE HAVE DONE

WE DID IT! We have now developed the whole system right down to the last little function and subroutine. For all practical purposes, the program has now been written. Of course, we still have to translate it into a computer language and try it in real life. There is always the out-side chance that we have made a little error here or there along the way. In fact, there will, no doubt, be some inter-esting and perhaps difficult problems yet to be resolved. The fact remains, however, that all of the logic for the program has been worked out and the only thing that remains to be done is to implement the program in the language of our choice.

Each previous step of this project has ended with a pause, which we have used to evaluate the project as a whole. This should also be done at the end of the detailed design. Of course, just completing the detailed design indicates that there are probably no major problems in the system design. This is particularly true if we are only developing programs to run on our computer. If we are also developing equipment or other details of a larger system, we may still have a long way to go. These items, which we called *other environmental requirements* in the general design, should all be worked out to the same level of detail that we have used for the program. For our cur-rent project, however, we can feel confident that the pro-gram we have just developed will be able to play Black-jack according to Hoyle as long as the memory of the computer is large enough to hold the program and all its variables.

Because we have been making changes to the data dic-tionary and finished routines throughout the detailed design, we should take a final look at our design after all of these changes have been recorded. First, however, this seems like a good place to see if any final changes are required in the design. Perhaps we could reduce the con-fusion between the similar names of the variable HAND and the array HANDS if we changed the name of one of them. We will, therefore, change the name of the variable HAND to CURRENTHAND to indicate that this is the hand that is currently being used.

The final system is shown in Appendix D. This in-cludes the data dictionary, a complete list of all of the sketch code, and the final structural diagram of the sys-tem as it exists at the end of detailed design. Notice that as more of the system's details were developed, the number of variables in the data dictionary, and the number of routines in the program, increased quite a bit. Thus, the general design was close but not complete.

IV. REVIEW OF MAJOR IDEAS

This chapter has dealt with the heart of any programming project: the development of the specific instructions required to make a program work. It has shown how decisions are made at each step of a program's development, mostly by examples taken from the Blackjack system. This approach was deliberate. We hope that by following the actual thought processes and rationale behind each step (including some backtracking and design changes), you have learned more than you would from a clean crisp theoretical discussion.

In listing the major ideas of the chapter, we can only touch upon those items which can be stated as general points and can therefore be listed as a simple idea or rule-of-thumb. Be sure that you know how each of these items was applied in the chapter so you can see how it can be applied to other programs as well.

- Start with the data dictionary listing all of the data that was developed in the general design.
- The dictionary can be organized any way you like. It is common to list data alphabetically by name, perhaps grouped within the data type. Each listing should include the following information:
  - Data name; avoid similar or confusing names.
  - Data type.
  - Allowable values, including the length requirements for strings.
  - Sub-element organization for data structures. All high level structures and all data elements should be in the dictionary. Assign sizes to arrays and be careful to make them big enough to hold the most elements that will ever be needed. An array any larger than this will only waste computer memory.
- Add to, or change, the dictionary as new data is developed in the program routines.

- There is no need to keep data dictionary entries or data elements for items that can be calculated as they are used.
- Develop a functional dictionary to include the sketch code for every routine in the system. Each routine will be given a name similar to (but different from) the data names.
- The level of detail for the sketch code should explain specifically what should be done, not necessarily how it is to be done. Make the syntax of the sketch code look similar to your programming language so the final translation into a computer program will be as easy as possible.
- Start by developing the program mainline routine.
- Develop each module working down from the top of the general design structure.
  - Ignore details that are not yet known, as we did with the initialization routine. These can be updated later on. Note that this is not working in a rigidly top-down fashion.
  - You may go down one branch of the structure at a time or you may go across one level of all branches at a time.
  - The utility subroutines should be saved until last so that you will know the exact requirements for them.
- New modules may be created whenever multiple functions are encountered (as in BANKER) or when a routine becomes too long and complex (as in SET-TLE).
- When splitting a routine into sub-elements, the basic routine becomes the controller for the new subroutines. This does not change the general design, it merely expands the detail of the design.
- Be sure you know what a routine is to do before you start to develop its logic. Start by listing general instructions you would use with a person unfamiliar with the task. For items that display information on a terminal screen or printed report, be sure you know how the output will look before you start developing the routine. The format of all input should be defined as well.

- Always take care of the unusual cases even if it means that most of the program exists to take care of things that may never happen. Play the part of Murphy's Demon to find out every possible thing that can go wrong because sooner or later, it will.
- When you work on a complex routine, it is easier to start with a simple sketch code that performs the routine's basic function. This can be refined step by step as more detail is added until the routine contains everything you need.
- Flow charts should generally be avoided. They can be used to show how a complex operation should work, but flow charts are based on GOTO's rather than structured statements. This can add confusion rather than clarity.
- It may be easiest to develop the logic for a loop by first working out the sketch code for the basic logic and then adding the controlling loop around it. Loops may be nested several deep. Be sure you know what type of loop should be used and don't create an endless loop with no escape provisions.
- Calculations can be nested within several layers of parentheses. They are easiest to develop and understand if you work with one level of parentheses at a time and build them up to the final result.
- Multiple conditions can be checked by using nesting IF-THEN-ELSE statements where the last condition of the innermost statement is only reached when all the previous conditions have been satisfied.
- If you use a variable's value as a processing flag (as BET was used in BETTING), be sure the initial value is not a possible final value, since then, the variable will not be recognized as a changed condition.
- Be familiar with the functions that your language provides like the absolute value and integer functions (ABS and INT) that we have used. Use them freely whenever they can simplify a module's logic.
- You may be able to develop your own functions which will work as easy-to-use subroutines. Do not worry if your language does not provide for user-defined functions, however, because you can always use a standard subroutine instead of a function.

- When a subroutine is used, be sure each item of information required by the subroutine or being returned by the subroutine (e.g., OPTIONS and CHOICE) is defined as a data element, and that it is set to the proper value before each subroutine call.
- Always edit any information that is entered by the user. This is where Murphy's Demon will have the most fun. If it is properly edited as it comes in, this information will not have to be checked by any other routine. You should usually check the following conditions:
  - The data must be the proper data type.
  - There may be upper or lower limits on a value or on the length of a string.
  - Special checks may be required for zero values or for strings that contain no characters (null strings).
  - Numbers may have to be integers (contain no fractional parts).
  - There may be a list of valid entry values, with any other entry in error.
- Error messages should be specific and, if possible, indicate how the error can be corrected. The user must then have another chance to enter a correct value.
- If there are any other environmental requirements in the system, they should be developed to the same level of detail that we have used in developing the routines for the Blackjack program.
- When all of the routines have been developed, make a final listing of the data dictionary, the functional dictionary, and the new detailed structure of the program. It is from these items that you will develop the final computer program.

Now that we have done all of this without encountering any serious problems, we can go on to the implementation of the program on the computer itself.

6

Implementing the Program (The Implementation)

"What I say is, patience, and shuffle the cards."
Miguel de Cervantes

So far we have designed, developed, and written (in a very high-level sketch form) a complete Blackjack program without so much as looking at an actual computer. In fact, we don't even know what type of computer we will be using. This may seem odd to many programmers, and it may have been downright frustrating if you have had a computer just sitting there all this time, begging to be used. Well, cheer up, because your patience is about to be rewarded.

Oddly enough, we still may not need to know what type of computer we will be using. We will, however, have to know which language we will be using before we can write code in that language. The first step of the implementation, therefore, is to determine which programming language to use.

I. SELECTING THE LANGUAGE

There have been hundreds of computer languages developed over the years. Many of these are specialized languages used only in the specific application for which they were developed. The most commonly used languages are called *general purpose languages* because they have been developed to work well with most computing applications.

One of the first general purpose computer languages was FORTRAN (from <u>FOR</u>mula <u>TRAN</u>slation). FORTRAN was developed in the early 1950's for engineering and mathematical applications in which the computer had to be very fast, very good at math, and able to use fairly simple forms of data input and output. So many programs have been written in FORTRAN that it will probably be with us for many years to come.

Programmers working with business applications, however, usually deal with large amounts of input data, long files of stored information, and voluminous piles of detailed reports. They complained about FORTRAN's limited ability to get information into and out of a program or to maintain the types of files that were required. In response to these problems, COBOL (an acronym for <u>CO</u>mmon <u>B</u>usiness <u>O</u>riented <u>L</u>anguage) was developed in 1960. COBOL offers tremendous flexibility in processing large amounts of data, but it can be difficult and slow to work with in operations which require complex calculations. One of COBOL's secondary goals was to make the language self-documenting. It is therefore a very wordy and cumbersome tool to use for a simple program.

Meanwhile, languages that were designed around the structured statements in Chapter One were being developed, primarily in Europe. The most successful of these languages, ALGOL, has become the basis for several more recent structured languages. This was one of the first languages that logically built up the structure of the language from well-defined building blocks, just as we have built up our system design from a well-defined set of instructions.

PL/1, which stands for Programming Language One, was developed in the late 1960's to bring together the speed and power of FORTRAN, the flexible data structures of COBOL, and the structural organization of ALGOL. Unfortunately it was so large and complex that many people decided it was not worth the overhead required to support it. It is, however, a very powerful language in the hands of a competent programmer.

Most commercial applications today are written in FORTRAN, COBOL, or PL/1. In the meantime, however, simpler languages have been developed that allow students to learn the fundamentals of computer programming but avoid the intricacies of a general purpose language. One of the first teaching languages, called BASIC, was developed at Dartmouth college. The original Dartmouth BASIC had very few instructions and used such simple words as INPUT, PRINT, and IF-THEN, as well as standard mathematical notation for representing calculations. Like most simple ideas it caught on well and was soon being used in applications that were far beyond the intent of the original design.

Pascal is another language that was developed as a teaching aid. It is a direct descendant of ALGOL and has the advantage that it teaches good structured programming. Like BASIC, it lacked the features required to make it a true general purpose language but was soon being used in applications that were far more complex than teaching programming classes.

When small computers were first developed, BASIC was about the only language simple enough to run in the small amount of memory that was usually available. Since that time, three trends have made more and more languages available to small system users. First, the major languages have developed well-defined subsets that maintain most of the features of the original language but can be implemented on the smaller machines. Second, the simple teaching languages have been expanded into more powerful languages by the addition of new features and by the expansion of the original features. And finally, improvements in computer technology increased the speed and capacity of small machines to the point where they can now handle more complex languages. The result has been that many of the general purpose languages are now available on small computers, and the simple teaching languages are now powerful enough to be truly called general purpose.

You may therefore find that you have a choice of several languages with which to develop your projects. Today a small single-user computer may support FOR-

TRAN, COBOL, PL/1, BASIC, PASCAL, FORTH, APL, as well as several more specialized languages. Let us then decide which of these languages we will use to write the Blackjack program.

The first requirement is to pick a language that is available for your computer. Many of the more powerful languages may need more memory space than you have available on your machine. They usually require that you have at least one, and perhaps two floppy disk units to hold all the support programs and data files. You must therefore choose among the languages that will work on your machine.

Among the languages that you can use on your computer, try to eliminate those that will not perform well for your specific project. BASIC may not be fast enough for some applications that are dependent on the computer's speed. FORTRAN may not provide a way for the system's data input and output to be handled easily. COBOL and PL/1 may be cumbersome to use on a small system. If you have existing programs that will be useful in your current project, you may want to use the same language for new programs so they will be compatible with the old ones. Different languages often use different methods of handling data or input and output, and may not work well with each other.

Some languages are quite expensive and may only be available from a few manufacturers. On the other hand, your own computer probably comes with a general purpose programming language along with the other programs needed to run the machine. Sometimes the language is built right into the memory of the computer. The most common language for small computers is BASIC, so that is probably the first language you will have to work with.

Finally, when you first start programming, you should use a language that you are familiar with, want to become familiar with, or plan to use for most of your other programming requirements. It is far easier to become skilled in the use of one language than it is to constantly move from one language to another trying to remember how things are done in each one. New languages can be fun to learn and should certainly be explored, but be sure you are quite familiar with one language before you start branching out into new areas.

We stated in the introduction that our example program would be developed in BASIC and Pascal*. BASIC is a natural choice because it is the most common language available on small computers. The Blackjack program will make no special demands on execution speed, and it will not require extensions that have been added to the original language. Pascal will serve as an excellent example of a structured programming language. It will be surprisingly easy to develop a Pascal program from our existing sketch code. It will also illustrate some of the deficiencies of BASIC and show how the design can be independent of the language used.

Now that we know what the program will do, how it will do it, and what language it will use, it is finally time to write the first lines of our computer program.

II. CREATING THE PROGRAM

The chart in Appendix A indicates that most of the work has been completed by the end of the detailed design. It should all be down-hill from here. Once you have mastered the techniques presented in the earlier chapters of this book, implementation is the easy part!

Our program will be based on the data dictionary and the sketch code developed in the detailed design. It will usually be necessary, however, to translate the variables and routine names into the proper form for the language that we are going to use.

For the simple versions of BASIC, a variable name must be a single upper case letter (A through Z), or a single letter followed by a number (A0 through Z9). Character string variables are indicated by placing a dollar sign ($) after the variable name (A0$ through Z9$). In the simple versions of BASIC there are no subroutine

_____

*Languages that are acronyms are spelled with all upper case letters. Pascal is not an acronym, but the name of the French mathematician-philosopher, Blaise Pascal who built one of the first pieces of computing equipment in 1644. BASIC, believe it or not, stands for Beginners' All-purpose Symbolic Instruction Code.

names; subroutines within the program will be identified
by the line number of the first line of code for each routine. The more advanced versions of BASIC will usually
work with these simple data names and line numbers.
The data dictionary for the BASIC program is shown in
Figure 6.1.

SKETCH CODE	BASIC
AMOUNT	A
AMOUNTWON	A1
BANKLIMIT	L1
BET	B
CARD	C
CHIPS	C1
CHOICE	C2
COUNT	C9
CURRENTHAND	H8
DATAOK	D8
DEALERCOLUMN	D7
DEALERVALUE	D2
DECK	D(204)
DECKCOUNT	D1
DONE	D9
HANDCOUNT	H1(3)
HANDONE	H9(3)
HANDS	H(3, 15)
HANDSPLAYD	H2
HANDSWON	H3
HANDVALUE	H4
MAXBET	M1
MAXVAL	M2
MINBET	M3
MINVAL	M4
OPTIONS	X9
PLAYLIMIT	L2
STRING	S1$
SUIT	S$(4)
V	V
VALUE	V$(13)
WONTHISHAND	W
X	X

Figure 6.1. Variable Names for the BASIC Program

We will generally use the first letter of the full name as the letter for the BASIC variable name. When there is more than one variable starting with a particular letter, we will use the numbers in the second position of the variable name to distinguish them. Variables that will be used often will be numbered from zero up, while flags and counters will be numbered from nine down. Notice that the variable name for OPTIONS is X9, not the upper case "oh" (O). This would look too much like a printed zero and could lead to confusion. It is a good idea to stay away from variable names starting with "oh". Also watch out for the letter "eye" (I). The variable I1 ("eye"-one) looks a lot like 11 (eleven).

In Pascal, variable and routine names may contain any number of characters. The first character must be a letter of the alphabet. The remaining characters may be letters, numbers, or (in some versions of the language) additional types of characters. All versions of Pascal use at least the first eight characters to differentiate between names. Beyond this there may be confusion. For example, the variable names:

THISisTHEvariable

and

THISisTHEsameVARIABLE

would be treated as the same variable name in many versions of Pascal because the first eight characters are the same, although both variables would be allowed in the program. We will therefore require that all of our names for data and parts of the program contain no similar groups of the first eight characters, start with a letter of the alphabet, and contain only letters and numbers. The data dictionary translated for the Pascal program will therefore appear as in Figure 6.2.

DATA NAMES

SKETCH CODE	PASCAL
AMOUNT	AMOUNT
AMOUNTWON	AMTWON
BANKLIMIT	BANKLMIT
BET	BET

CARD	CARD
CHIPS	CHIPS
CHOICE	CHOICE
COUNT	COUNT
CURRENTHAND	THISHAND
DATAOK	DATAOK
DELERCOLUMN	DLRCOLM
DEALERVALUE	DEALERV
DECK	DECK[204]
DECKCOUNT	DECKNEXT
DONE	DONE
HANDCOUNT	HANDCNT[3]
HANDONE	HANDONE[3]
HANDS	HANDS[3, 15]
HANDSPLAYD	HANDPLAD
HANDSWON	HANDSWON
HANDVALUE	HANDVALU
MAXBET	MAXBET
MAXVAL	MAXVAL
MINBET	MINBET
MINVAL	MINVAL
OPTIONS	OPTIONS
PLAYLIMIT	PLAYLMIT
STRING	INSTRING
SUIT	SUIT[4]
V	V
VALUE	VALUE[13]
WONTHISHAND	WONHAND
X	X

PROGRAM ROUTINE NAMES

BANKER	BANKER
BETTING	BETTING
BROKENBANK	BROKEN
BUY	BUY
CARDVALUE	CARDVAL
CASHIN	CASHIN
DEAL	DEAL
DEALER	DEALER
DEALERNATURAL	DEALERN
DEALEROVER	DEALERO
DEALERSTANDS	DEALERS
EVALUATE	EVALUATE

GETCARD	GETCARD
INITIALIZE	INIT
INPUTAMOUNT	AMOUNTIN
INPUTCHOICES	CHOICEIN
MAINLINE	BLAKJACK
NATURALS	NATURALS
PLAYER	PLAYER
PLAYERHAND	PLYRHAND
PLAYHAND	PLAYHAND
PRINTCARD	SHOWCARD
RPTSTATU	STATUS
SELECTACTIV	NEXTACTV
SETTLE	SETTLE
SHOWINSTRUCT	INSTRUCT
SHUFFLE	SHUFFLE
SPLITPAIRS	SPLIT
TERMINATE	TERM

Figure 6.2. Variable and Program Names for the Pascal Program

None of these names are the same in the first eight characters. They are enough like the original names used in the sketch code that it should be quite easy to remember what each Pascal name means.

We may now proceed to write the program. The first thing to do is to lay out the program's basic organization. All programs should start with a descriptive heading containing the following items:

- The program's name
- The date the program was written
- The author's name.
- A copyright notice if you ever expect any one else to use the program but you do not want to just give it away.
- A description of what the program will do.
- A list of all changes that have been made to the program since it was completed.
- A list of the variables used in the program if the list is not too long. This is quite helpful in BASIC where variable names may mean next to nothing. Our list of variables is long enough, however, that we will keep a separate dictionary instead.

The program will be developed in a top-down manner similar to the way the detailed design was developed. We will therefore start by writing the program's mainline routine. To get the program to work at all we will need to have some sort of routine for each of the three CALL statements in the mainline. We will therefore write a "dummy" subroutine that simply provides the program with a routine to CALL and immediately does a RETURN back to the mainline.

By developing the program one level at a time from the highest level down, we will have an excellent opportunity to test each level as it is written. Unfortunately, calling three subroutines that do nothing will not give us much information about how well the first level of the program will be working. Therefore each dummy subroutine will be expanded to display a message on the terminal screen stating which subroutine the program is now executing.

The mainline routine for our Blackjack program will look like Listing 6.1(B) in BASIC and Listing 6.1(P) in Pascal.

Here at last is a computer program! Before you continue, here are a few additional observations about BASIC and Pascal.

BASIC code will not look just like our sketch code because there are no DO-WHILE, DO-UNTIL, or CASE statements, and the IF-THEN-ELSE statement is not as powerful. You will notice as we develop our BASIC Blackjack program that some IF-THEN-ELSE procedures are made up from simple IF-THEN statements, while others use a form common to most extended versions of the language. This has been done to show that either form will work just fine. The order in which the program's routines are listed, however, will be almost the same as the order in which they were developed in Chapter Five. The highest levels of the program, starting with the mainline routine, will be at the beginning of the program; the utility subroutines are at the end. Each routine will usually come *after* all of the references made to it in the program.

Pascal code will look quite similar to our sketch code because the language was developed around the structured statements that we have used. The order of listing

```
10        REM  BLACKJACK    VERSION 1.0
20        REM      THIS PROGRAM WILL PLAY THE PART OF THE
30        REM      DEALER IN A GAME OF BLACKJACK PLAYED
40        REM      ACCORDING TO HOYLE'S RULES
50        REM
60        REM  WRITTEN BY JACK EMMERICHS,   1/1/82
70        REM  (COPYRIGHT MESSAGE GOES HERE IF YOU WANT ONE)
80        REM
90        REM  PROGRAM MAINLINE
100       REM
110  GOSUB 180
120  GOSUB 230
130  GOSUB 280
140  END
150       REM
160       REM  INITIALIZATION PROCEDURE
170       REM
180  PRINT "INITIALIZATION"
190  RETURN
200       REM
210       REM  SELECT THE NEXT ACTIVITY
220       REM
230  PRINT "SELECT ACTIVITY"
240  RETURN
250       REM
260       REM  TERMINATION PROCEDURE
270       REM
280  PRINT "TERMINATION"
290  RETURN
```

Listing 6.1(B). The Blackjack Program Mainline in BASIC

the program's routines, however, will be almost the opposite of the order in which they were developed in Chapter Five. Each routine must be defined in the program *before* the first reference to it is made. The utility subroutines will be at the beginning of the program and the mainline routine will be at the very end.

Now that we have an actual computer program that we can run on our computer, it is time to see if it will work.

A. Testing and Debugging the Mainline Routine

Testing and debugging are two separate operations. Testing is running a program to see if it performs the way it should. Debugging is trying to find out why a program

```
(*   BLACKJACK    VERSION 1.0
          THIS PROGRAM WILL PLAY THE PART OF THE
          DEALER IN A GAME OF BLACKJACK PLAYED
          ACCORDING TO HOYLE'S RULES

          WRITTEN BY JACK EMMERICHS,   1/1/82
          (COPYRIGHT MESSAGE GOES HERE IF YOU WANT ONE)   *)

PROGRAM BLAKJACK (INPUT, OUTPUT);


    PROCEDURE INIT;                    (* INIT ROUTINE *)
       BEGIN
          WRITELN (OUTPUT,'INITIALIZATION');
       END;


    PROCEDURE NEXTACTV;                (* NEXT ACTIV ROUTINE *)
       BEGIN
          WRITELN (OUTPUT,'SELECT ACTIVITY');
       END;


     PROCEDURE TERM;                   (* TERMINATION ROUTINE *)
       BEGIN
          WRITELN (OUTPUT,'TERMINATION');
       END;


BEGIN                                  (* PROGRAM MAINLINE *)
    INIT;
    NEXTACTV;
    TERM;
END.
```

Listing 6.1(P). The Blackjack Program Mainline in Pascal

does not run the way it should once the errors have been discovered, and fixing the bug so that the program will run correctly. Traditionally, most programs have been completely written before any testing is done. When an error occurs, the entire program must be examined to find the bug. This makes it very difficult to find bugs, or to ensure that correcting one problem does not create another problem someplace else in the program.

The top-down method of development allows us to test each level of the program as it is completed. At each level we can ignore the details that have not yet been coded because they do not exist. We can also ignore the levels that have previously been tested because they have already been debugged. This means that we will test and debug the program in small sections, which is clearly much easier than trying to test the whole thing at once. At this point we can test the Blackjack program's mainline routine.

When the mainline was first written we noted that it was pretty simple. There is almost nothing here to test. When the program that we have just written is run it should call each subroutine in the proper order. Each subroutine should display its message and then the mainline should end. A successful test of the mainline should display:

> INITIALIZATION
> SELECT ACTIVITY
> TERMINATION

This is exactly what the program displays when it is run, so the testing has been completed for the mainline routine. There is no need for any debugging because there are no bugs. Now it is time to go on to the next level of detail.

It was easy to write the mainline routine because none of the subroutines that were called had to actually perform their functions. This will not be the case for the remainder of the program, however, because we will start running into calls to the utility subroutines. By their very nature these subroutines will be called throughout the program. The routines that call them will not work correctly if the utility subroutines are not available, so we should write and complete these modules before we continue with the second level of the program.

B. The Utility Subroutines

These routines could be written directly into our existing Blackjack program but that would make them very difficult to test and debug. We will be able to test them much more easily if they are written as simple stand-alone programs that can be tested separately. After each routine has been tested and debugged, it can be added to the program.

To test each subroutine we will have to write a small program to set up all the conditions that the subroutine requires, call the subroutine, and then display information that tells us if the subroutine worked correctly. This type of testing program is called a *driver*. We shall therefore develop a driver program for each of the subroutines to be tested.

The subroutines themselves are shown in the last chart in Appendix D. The seven modules and their relationships to each other are shown in Figure 6.3.

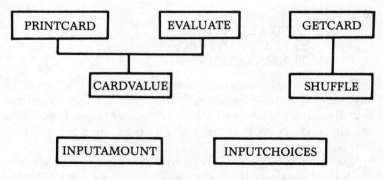

Figure 6.3. The Utility Subroutines for Blackjack

CARDVALUE should be developed first. It can then be used to help develop PRINTCARD and EVALUATE. SHUFFLE and GETCARD can be developed together because, while GETCARD is quite simple, it must be able to call SHUFFLE. Finally, INPUTCHOICES and INPUTAMOUNT can be developed separately.

Study the CARDVALUE driver programs listed below to see how they test the subroutine being developed. The operator can enter any valid card value to be tested or a special value (zero in this case) to end the test. Remember that the only reason we need the driver programs is because we are developing the utility subroutines from the bottom up instead of from the top down. The CARDVALUE driver is shown in BASIC (Listing 6.2(B)) and in Pascal (Listing 6.2(P)). Notice that the driver program

```
10        REM  DRIVER FOR CARDVALUE FUNCTION:  FNC(C)
20        REM
30        REM
40    DEF FNC(X)=X-(INT(X/13)*13)
50        REM
60        REM  DRIVER
70        REM
80    PRINT "ENTER A CARD NUMBER FROM 1 TO 52"
90    PRINT "OR ENTER A ZERO TO STOP THE TEST"
100   INPUT C
110   IF C=0 THEN GOTO 180
120   PRINT
130   PRINT "FOR CARD ";C;" THE FACE VALUE WILL BE ";FNC(C)
140   PRINT
150   GOTO 80
160       REM
170       REM
180   END
```

Listing 6.2(B). Driver Program for Cardvalue Function in
BASIC

```
        (*  DRIVER FOR CARDVALUE FUNCTION:  CARDVAL(CARD)  *)

PROGRAM DRIVER1 (INPUT, OUTPUT);

   VAR   CARD:  INTEGER;


   FUNCTION CARDVAL (CARD: INTEGER): INTEGER;
      BEGIN
         CARDVAL:=CARD-((CARD DIV 13) * 13);
      END;


BEGIN
   REPEAT
      WRITELN (OUTPUT,'ENTER A CARD NUMBER FROM 1 TO 52');
      WRITELN (OUTPUT,'OR ENTER A ZERO TO-STOP THE TEST');
      READLN  (INPUT,CARD);
      IF CARD<>0 THEN
         BEGIN
            WRITELN (OUTPUT);
            WRITELN (OUTPUT,'FOR CARD ',CARD,
               'THE FACE VALUE WILL BE ',CARDVAL(CARD));
            WRITELN (OUTPUT);
         END;
   UNTIL CARD=0;
END.
```

Listing 6.2(P). Driver Program for Cardvalue Function in
Pascal

does not have all the fancy input editing required for the final Blackjack program. The idea here is simply to see if the function works. Once the testing is done the driver will be discarded.

To test the function we must run the driver program and enter a value for each of the possible card numbers: one through fifty-two. We expect the following results:

CARD	VALUE	CARD	VALUE	CARD	VALUE	CARD	VALUE
1	- 1	14	- 1	27	- 1	40	- 1
2	- 2	15	- 2	28	- 2	41	- 2
3	- 3	16	- 3	29	- 3	42	- 3
4	- 4	17	- 4	30	- 4	43	- 4
5	- 5	18	- 5	31	- 5	44	- 5
6	- 6	19	- 6	32	- 6	45	- 6
7	- 7	20	- 7	33	- 7	46	- 7
8	- 8	21	- 8	34	- 8	47	- 8
9	- 9	22	- 9	35	- 9	48	- 9
10	- 10	23	- 10	36	- 10	49	- 10
11	- 11	24	- 11	37	- 11	50	- 11
12	- 12	25	- 12	38	- 12	51	- 12
13	- 13	26	- 13	39	- 13	52	- 13

When the program is run, the actual results are as follows:

CARD	VALUE	CARD	VALUE	CARD	VALUE	CARD	VALUE
1	- 1	14	- 1	27	- 1	40	- 1
2	- 2	15	- 2	28	- 2	41	- 2
3	- 3	16	- 3	29	- 3	42	- 3
4	- 4	17	- 4	30	- 4	43	- 4
5	- 5	18	- 5	31	- 5	44	- 5
6	- 6	19	- 6	32	- 6	45	- 6
7	- 7	20	- 7	33	- 7	46	- 7
8	- 8	21	- 8	34	- 8	47	- 8
9	- 9	22	- 9	35	- 9	48	- 9
10	- 10	23	- 10	36	- 10	49	- 10
11	- 11	24	- 11	37	- 11	50	- 11
12	- 12	25	- 12	38	- 12	51	- 12
13	- 0	26	- 0	39	- 0	52	- 0

Well, how about that! When we try it, it doesn't work. Rats! Now it is time to find out how a bug in a program can be located and corrected.

According to these tests, the function will work for any value except one that is an even multiple of thirteen: 13, 26, 39, and 52. All of these numbers yield a face value of zero. There seems to be something wrong with the calculation that resets the values to one (1) at the start of each new suit. It is resetting the value to zero at the last card of the previous suit.

The part of the calculation that identifies when card numbers go from one suit to the next is

$$INT(X/13)$$

where X is the number of the card. When X changes from 12 to 13, this value changes from 0 to 1. When X changes from 25 to 26, this value changes from 1 to 2, and so on. It changes just before the last card of the suit is reached rather than just after the last card of the suit has been reached. This is the problem.

Once the problem has been found, a correction must be made. Developing a correction that does not cause other problems is often more difficult than finding the problem in the first place. For example, if the suit is being changed one card too soon, it might seem correct to change the calculation to

$$INT((X+1)/13)$$

If you run the test program with this calculation, however, the problem becomes worse rather than better. The correct change is to see what suit the previous card was in by using the calculation

$$FNC(X)=X-(INT((X-1)/13*13)$$

The same change can be made in the Pascal program by changing the function to read

```
CARDVAL:=CARD-(((CARD-1) DIV 13) * 13);
```

Notice that the Pascal integer division operation, DIV, provides an integer answer so there is no need for an INT function.

Whenever a change is made to a program, any tests that were made before the changes must be repeated after the change to make sure we have not messed up something that was already working correctly. This is called *regression testing*. For the CARDVALUE function we must again enter all fifty-two card numbers to see that the right face value is being returned. When we do, the program works perfectly. The bug has been fixed.

Now that we have a working CARDVALUE function we can use it to update the example program shown at the end of Chapter Two to create a driver program for the PRINTCARD routine. The BASIC and Pascal programs shown in Listing 6.3 will test PRINTCARD.

```
10        REM   DRIVER FOR PRINTCARD ROUTINE
20        REM
30        REM
40     DEF FNC(X)=X-(INT((X-1)/13)*13)
50        REM
60        REM  LOAD ARRAYS
70        REM
80     DIM S$(4), V$(13)
90     DATA "SPADES","HEARTS","DIAMONDS","CLUBS"
100    DATA "ACE","2","3","4","5","6","7","8","9","10"
110    DATA "JACK","QUEEN","KING"
120    FOR X=1 TO 4
130      READ S$(X)
140    NEXT X
150    FOR X=1 TO 13
160      READ V$(X)
170    NEXT X
180        REM
190        REM  DRIVER
200        REM
210    PRINT "ENTER A CARD NUMBER FROM 1 TO 52"
220    PRINT "OR ENTER A ZERO TO STOP THE TEST"
230    INPUT C
240    IF C=0 THEN GOTO 340
250    GOSUB 300
260    GOTO 210
270        REM
280        REM  PRINTCARD SUBROUTINE
290        REM
300    PRINT "THE ";V$(FNC(C));" OF ";S$(INT((C-1)/13)+1)
310    RETURN
320        REM
330        REM
340    END
```

Listing 6.3(B). Test Program for Printcard Routine in BASIC

```
           (*  DRIVER FOR SHOWCARD  *)

PROGRAM DRIVER2 (INPUT, OUTPUT);

    VAR   CARD:  INTEGER;
          SUIT:  ARRAY [1..4] OF STRING [8];
          VALUE: ARRAY [1..13] OF STRING [5];


    FUNCTION CARDVAL (CARD: INTEGER): INTEGER;
       BEGIN
          CARDVAL:=CARD-(((CARD-1) DIV 13) * 13);
       END;


    PROCEDURE SHOWCARD;
       BEGIN
          WRITELN (OUTPUT,'THE ',VALUE[CARDVAL(CARD)],
                   ' OF ',SUIT[((CARD-1) DIV 13) + 1]);
       END;


BEGIN
    SUIT[1] := 'SPADES';          SUIT[2] := 'HEARTS';
    SUIT[3] := 'DIAMONDS';        SUIT[4] := 'CLUBS';
    VALUE[1] := 'ACE';    VALUE[2] := '2';      VALUE[3] := '3';
    VALUE[4] := '4';      VALUE[5] := '5';      VALUE[6] := '6';
    VALUE[7] := '7';      VALUE[8] := '8';      VALUE[9] := '9';
    VALUE[10] := '10';    VALUE[11] := 'JACK';
    VALUE[12] := 'QUEEN'; VALUE[13] := 'KING';
    REPEAT
       WRITELN (OUTPUT,'ENTER A CARD NUMBER FROM 1 TO 52');
       WRITELN (OUTPUT,'OR ENTER A ZERO TO STOP THE TEST');
       READLN  (INPUT,CARD);
       IF CARD<>0 THEN
           SHOWCARD
    UNTIL CARD=0;
END.
```

Listing 6.3(P). Test Program for Printcard Routine in Pascal

This time everything works correctly the first time. If the numbers one through fifty-two are entered, the names of all the cards in the deck are correctly printed. You may have noticed that the program to test CARDVALUE will work correctly for any positive whole number. The PRINTCARD driver, however, will not work for values over fifty-two because there is no fifth suit in the SUIT table. When a program fails with such an error, it is said to have *CRASHED*. This is a rather disastrous sounding term considering that nothing is really broken and no equipment has been damaged. The term is well established, however, so we can say that the PRINTCARD driver program will crash when given a value above fifty-two.

The second utility subroutine to use CARDVALUE is EVALUATE. A driver for this routine will require the arrays used to hold the hands of cards but will not require PRINTCARD. We must be able to test any combination of cards in any hand. The driver for EVALUATE is shown in BASIC and Pascal in Listing 6.4.

```
10        REM   DRIVER FOR EVALUATE ROUTINE
20        REM
30        REM
40   DEF FNC(X)=X-(INT((X-1)/13)*13)
50        REM
60        REM   DRIVER
70        REM
80   DIM H(3,15), H1(3)
90        REM   GET A HAND
100  PRINT "ENTER A HAND NUMBER FROM 1 TO 3"
110  PRINT "OR ENTER ZERO TO STOP THE TEST"
120  INPUT H8
130  IF H8=0 THEN GOTO 290
140      REM   GET CARDS FOR THE HAND
150    H1(H8)=0
160    PRINT "ENTER A CARD NUMBER FROM 1 TO 52"
170    PRINT "OR ENTER ZERO TO END THE HAND"
180    INPUT C
190    IF C=0 THEN GOTO 240
200        REM   ADD CARDS TO THE HAND
210      H1(H8)=H1(H8)+1
220      H(H8,H1(H8))=C
230      IF H1(H8)<=14 THEN GOTO 160
240    GOSUB 330
245    PRINT
250    PRINT "THE VALUE OF THE HAND IS ";H4
255    PRINT
260    GOTO 100
270      REM
280      REM
290  END
300      REM
```

```
310        REM  EVALUATE THE HAND
320        REM
330    H4=0
340    FOR C9=1 TO H1(H8)
350      V=FNC(H(H8,C9))
360      IF V>10 THEN V=10
370      IF V=1 THEN V=11
380      H4=H4+V
390    NEXT C9
400    C9=1
410    IF H4<=21 THEN GOTO 460
420    IF C9>H1(H8) THEN 460
430      IF FNC(H(H8,C9))=1 THEN H4=H4-10
440      C9=C9+1
450    GOTO 410
460    RETURN
```

Listing 6.4(B). Driver for Evaluation Routine in BASIC

```
(*  DRIVER FOR EVALUATE  *)

PROGRAM DRIVER3 (INPUT, OUTPUT);

    VAR   THISHAND,
          CARD,
          HANDVALU:     INTEGER;
          HANDS:        ARRAY [1..3, 1..15] OF INTEGER;
          HANDCNT:      ARRAY [1..3]        OF INTEGER;


    FUNCTION CARDVAL (CARD: INTEGER): INTEGER;
       BEGIN
          CARDVAL:=CARD-(((CARD-1) DIV 13) * 13);
       END;


    PROCEDURE EVALUATE;
       VAR V, COUNT: INTEGER;
       BEGIN
          HANDVALU:=0;
          FOR COUNT:=1 TO HANDCNT[THISHAND] DO
             BEGIN
                V:=CARDVAL(HANDS[THISHAND,COUNT]);
                IF V>10 THEN
                   V:=10;
                IF V=1 THEN
                   V:=11;
                HANDVALU:=HANDVALU+V;
             END;
          COUNT:=1;
          WHILE (HANDVALU>21) AND (COUNT<=HANDCNT[THISHAND]) DO
             BEGIN
```

```
                IF CARDVAL(HANDS[THISHAND,COUNT])=1 THEN
                    HANDVALU:=HANDVALU-10;
                COUNT:=COUNT+1;
            END;
    END;  (*  OF EVALUATE  *)


BEGIN   (*  START OF MAINLINE  *)
    REPEAT;
        WRITELN (OUTPUT,'ENTER A HAND NUMBER FROM 1 TO 3');
        WRITELN (OUTPUT,'OR ENTER ZERO TO STOP THE TEST');
        READLN  (INPUT, THISHAND);
        IF THISHAND<>0 THEN
            BEGIN
                HANDCNT[THISHAND]:=0;
                REPEAT;
                    WRITELN (OUTPUT,'ENTER A CARD NUMBER FROM 1 TO 52');
                    WRITELN (OUTPUT,'OR ENTER ZERO TO END THE HAND');
                    READLN  (INPUT,CARD);
                    IF CARD<>0 THEN
                        BEGIN
                            HANDCNT[THISHAND]:=HANDCNT[THISHAND] + 1;
                            HANDS[THISHAND,HANDCNT[THISHAND]]:=CARD;
                        END;
                UNTIL (CARD=0) OR (HANDCNT[THISHAND]=15);
                EVALUATE;
                WRITELN (OUTPUT);
                WRITELN (OUTPUT,'THE VALUE OF THE HAND IS ',
                                HANDVALU);
                WRITELN (OUTPUT);
            END;
    UNTIL THISHAND = 0;
END.    (*  OF PROGRAM  *)
```

Listing 6.4(P). Driver for Evaluation Routine in Pascal

Notice that the driver program is getting to be larger than the routine we are supposed to be testing. The only problem with a large driver program is that you may have to test and debug the driver before you can test and debug the routine. As the programs become more complex you will notice that the Pascal programs seem longer than the BASIC programs. This is because Pascal requires that all variables be defined before they are used, allows statements to be split into several lines, and uses structural statements like BEGIN and END on separate lines to improve program readability. BASIC programs can be much more compact, with each line containing a complete instruction. The Pascal programs could be written in a more compact form but they would be harder to read.

Listing 6.4 shows the final program used to test the EVALUATE routine after some minor bugs were corrected in the driver. Notice the two extra PRINT statements in lines 245 and 255 of the BASIC program. These were added to make the printed evaluation easier to see on the screen. Notice also that we created the hands being evaluated in this test by using the same logic (lines 200 to 220 in the BASIC program) that we will use to deal cards in the final program. The more program logic you can test before it is finally used, the easier the program will be to get running. Once the driver is running, the next question is: What constitutes a valid test of the evaluation routine?

There are far more possible Blackjack hands than we can test in a reasonable time. We must therefore try hands that will be most likely to find errors in the program. This type of test case is called a *pivot condition*. We should try to create pivot conditions that will exercise every instruction in the evaluation routine. These conditions will include hands with no cards, hands with fifteen cards, hands totaling less than twenty-one, and hands totaling more than twenty-one. All of these pivot conditions should be tried with aces in the hand to test the proper use of the one/eleven value of the ace, with face cards in the hand to test the proper evaluation of face cards as a value of ten, and with face cards and aces in the same hand. The following hands show some of the pivot conditions that were actually tested:

CARDS IN THE HAND	VALUE OF THE HAND
(no cards)	0
A	11
2 3	5
A 2 3	16
2 3 4	9
A 2 3 4 Q	20
2 3 4 Q	19
2 3 Q K	25
A A 2 3 Q K	27
A A 2 3 4 5	16
A A A 2 3 4	12
A A A A A A A A A A A A A A A	15

```
A A A A A A A A A A A A A A 9 . . . . . . . . . . . . . . .  23
2 3 4 5 6 7 . . . . . . . . . . . . . . . . . . . . . . . . . . . . . . . . . . . .  27
A 2 3 4 5 6 7  . . . . . . . . . . . . . . . . . . . . . . . . . . . . . . . . .  28
```

The program actually assigned each of these card combinations, as well as every other combination tested, the correct value. Various combinations of cards were tested on each of the three hands in the system with equal success. Selecting the proper pivot conditions for testing allows us to be confident that the EVALUATE routine will work correctly without testing every possible Blackjack hand.

There are several things about this test that should be emphasized. Every line of code in the subroutine was tested at least once. This required using face cards and aces to test their special face values. All possible combinations of program parts were tested without trying all possible card combinations. This included hands without aces or face cards, hands with aces, hands with face cards, and hands with both aces and face cards. Furthermore, multiple occurrences of both aces and face cards were tried. Limiting conditions, including no cards present and fifteen cards present were tested. Finally, simple hands with no special problems were tested. We also managed to test the card dealing logic at the same time.

Next we will test the subroutines that shuffle the two decks of cards together (SHUFFLE) and get the next card from the shuffled decks (GETCARD). We can test the two routines together with the programs shown in Listing 6.5.

```
10       REM   DRIVER FOR SHUFFLE AND GETCARD ROUTINES
20       REM
30       REM   DRIVER
40       REM
50    DIM D(204)
55       REM   SOME BASICS REQUIRE A RANDOMIZE STATEMENT
56    RANDOMIZE
60    GOSUB 295
70       REM   LOOK THROUGH THE CARDS
80    PRINT "ENTER ANY CHARACTER TO GET A CARD"
90    PRINT "OR ENTER ZERO TO STOP THE TEST"
100   INPUT S1$
110   IF S1$="0" THEN GOTO 190
120      GOSUB 230
```

```
130      PRINT
140      PRINT "POSITION NUMBER ";D1-1;" CONTAINS A CARD NUMBER ";C
150      PRINT
160 GOTO 80
170      REM
180      REM
190 END
200      REM
210      REM  GET A CARD
220      REM
230 IF D1>104 THEN GOSUB 295
240 C=D(D1)
250 D1=D1+1
260 RETURN
270      REM
280      REM  SHUFFLE
290      REM
295 PRINT "RESHUFFLE THE CARDS"
300 FOR C9=1 TO 104
310    D(C9)=0
320 NEXT C9
330 FOR C9=1 TO 2
340    FOR C=1 TO 52
350      X=INT(RND(1)*104)+1
360      IF D(X)=0 THEN GOTO 400
370        X=X+1
380        IF X>104 THEN X=1
390        GOTO 360
400      D(X)=C
410    NEXT C
420 NEXT C9
430 D1=1
440 RETURN
```

Listing 6.5(B). BASIC Driver for Getcard and Shuffle
Routines

```
    (*  DRIVER FOR GETCARD AND SHUFFLE  *)

PROGRAM DRIVER4 (INPUT, OUTPUT);

   VAR  CARD, SEED,
        DECKNEXT:       INTEGER;
        INSTRING:       STRING;
        DECK:           ARRAY [1..104] OF INTEGER;


   FUNCTION RAND (MAX: INTEGER): INTEGER;
      BEGIN
         SEED:=SEED*((SEED DIV 2)-1)+21845;
         RAND:=(SEED MOD MAX)+1;
      END;  (*  OF RANDOM NUMBER GENERATOR  *)
```

```
PROCEDURE SHUFFLE;
   VAR COUNT, X: INTEGER;
   BEGIN
      WRITELN (OUTPUT,'RESHUFFLE THE CARDS');
      FOR COUNT:=1 TO 104 DO
         DECK[COUNT]:=0;
      FOR COUNT:=1 TO 2 DO
         BEGIN
            FOR CARD:=1 TO 52 DO
               BEGIN
                  X:=RAND(104);
                  WHILE DECK[X]<>0 DO
                     BEGIN
                        X:=X+1;
                        IF X>104 THEN
                           X:=1;
                     END;
                  DECK[X]:=CARD;
               END;
         END;
      DECKNEXT:=1;
   END;   (* OF SHUFFLE *)


PROCEDURE GETCARD;
   BEGIN
      IF DECKNEXT>104 THEN                         RAM
         SHUFFLE;
      CARD:=DECK[DECKNEXT];
      DECKNEXT:=DECKNEXT+1;                        GRAM
   END;   (* OF GETCARD *)


BEGIN   (* DRIVER *)
   SHUFFLE;
   REPEAT
      WRITELN (OUTPUT,'ENTER ANY CHARACTER TO GET A CARD');
      WRITELN (OUTPUT,'OR ENTER ZERO TO STOP THE TEST');
      READLN  (INPUT,INSTRING);
      IF INSTRING<>'0' THEN
         BEGIN
            GETCARD;
            WRITELN (OUTPUT);
            WRITELN (OUTPUT,'POSITION NUMBER ',DECKNEXT-1,
                     ' CONTAINS A CARD NUMBER ',CARD);
            WRITELN (OUTPUT);
         END;
   UNTIL INSTRING='0';
END.
```

Listing 6.5(P). Pascal Driver for Getcard and Shuffle
Routines

And now a word or two about random numbers in computer programs. There is no such thing as a truly random number from a computer program. The best that we can do is to calculate a number that appears to be random, called a "pseudo-random number." The calculations are based on the initial value of a variable called the "seed." The sequence of "random numbers" calculated from a given seed value will always be the same. With luck, however, the calculation will be so obscure that the results will look random to the user.

Most versions of BASIC have a pseudo-random number function, usually called RND, that will return a number between zero and one, or between zero and some other number. This function varies greatly between different versions of BASIC, so be sure you check the manual for your BASIC to see how it works. The driver in Listing 6.5(B) used a version of RND that returns a value between zero and one. Line 350 converts this value into a number from one to 104. The RANDOMIZE statement at the beginning of the program will ask the operator to set the initial value of the seed.

Most versions of Pascal do not have a pseudo-random number function, so the function RAND has been written to generate "random" numbers. RAND(MAX) will return a number from one to MAX rather than from zero to one, so no further calculations are required upon this value. The seed for RAND is not set to anything by this program so it will contain whatever value was already in the computer's memory at the location where the seed is stored at the time the program started to run.*

This is a very simple program to test. Each time the <RETURN> is pressed we will be shown a position in the deck from one to 104 and a card value from one to fifty-two. All we need to do is to press <RETURN> 104 times and keep track of the card values that are shown. Each value should appear twice. The next time <RETURN> is pressed the deck should be reshuffled and we should be back to the first position in the deck. When this is tried,

_____

*Pascal does not automatically initialize any variable value. Most versions of BASIC do.

the program works correctly. As a point of interest, we can compare the performance of the two languages by timing the shuffling operation on the computer that ran these programs. Pascal, which is semicompiled, took 1.8 seconds to shuffle the cards. BASIC, which is interpreted, took 11.5 seconds to do the same thing.

The only utility subroutines remaining to be tested are the ones that receive data from the terminal: INPUT-AMOUNT and INPUTCHOICES. These are shown in Listings 6.6 and 6.7, respectively, along with their drivers.

```
10         REM   DRIVER FOR INPUTAMOUNT ROUTINES
20         REM
30         REM   DRIVER
40         REM
50     PRINT "ENTER ZERO TO END THE TEST"
60     INPUT X9$
70     IF X9$="0" THEN GOTO 220
80       PRINT "ENTER THE MIN VALUE"
90       INPUT M4
100      PRINT "ENTER THE MAX VALUE"
110      INPUT M2
120      PRINT
130      PRINT
140      PRINT "THE ITEM TO ENTER IS PRINTED HERE"
150      GOSUB 260
160      PRINT
170      PRINT "THE AMOUNT ENTERED WAS ";A
180      PRINT
190      GOTO 50
200         REM
210         REM
220    END
230         REM
240         REM   INPUT AND EDIT AN AMOUNT
250         REM
260    PRINT
270    PRINT "YOUR AMOUNT: ";
280    INPUT S1$
290    A=VAL(S1$)
300    IF STR$(A)=" "+S1$ THEN GOTO 330
310      PRINT "PLEASE ENTER A NUMBER"
320      GOTO 270
330    IF A>=M4 THEN GOTO 360
340      PRINT "PLEASE ENTER AN AMOUNT NO LESS THAN ";M4
```

```
350     GOTO 270
360   IF A<=M2 THEN GOTO 390
370     PRINT "PLEASE ENTER AN AMOUNT NO GREATER THAN ";M2
380     GOTO 270
390   IF A=INT(A) THEN GOTO 420
400     PRINT "PLEASE ENTER AN INTEGER NUMBER"
410     GOTO 270
420   RETURN
```

Listing 6.6(B). Driver for Inputamount Routine in
BASIC

```
(*  DRIVER FOR AMOUNTIN  *)

PROGRAM DRIVER5 (INPUT, OUTPUT);

  VAR  MINVAL,
       MAXVAL,
       AMOUNT:         INTEGER;
       INSTRING,
       STOPTEST:       STRING;


  FUNCTION VALUE (INSTRING: STRING): INTEGER;
     VAR  COUNT, VAL: INTEGER;
          NUMBER:     BOOLEAN;
     BEGIN
        VAL:=0;
        NUMBER:=TRUE;
        FOR COUNT:=1 TO LENGTH(INSTRING) DO
           IF INSTRING[COUNT] IN ['0'..'9'] THEN
              VAL:=VAL*10+ORD(INSTRING[COUNT])-ORD('0')
           ELSE
              NUMBER:=FALSE;
        IF NUMBER THEN
           VALUE:=VAL
        ELSE
           VALUE:=-1;
     END;   (*  OF VALUE FUNCTION  *)


  PROCEDURE AMOUNTIN;
     VAR  DATAOK:     BOOLEAN;
     BEGIN
        DATAOK:=FALSE;
        WRITELN (OUTPUT);
        REPEAT
           WRITE (OUTPUT,'YOUR AMOUNT: ');
           READLN (INPUT,INSTRING);
           AMOUNT:=VALUE(INSTRING);
           IF AMOUNT=-1 THEN
              WRITELN (OUTPUT,'PLEASE ENTER A NUMBER')
```

```
       ELSE
          IF AMOUNT<MINVAL THEN
             WRITELN (OUTPUT,
             'PLEASE ENTER AN AMOUNT NO LESS THAN ',MINVAL)
          ELSE
             IF AMOUNT>MAXVAL THEN
                WRITELN (OUTPUT,
                'PLEASE ENTER AN AMOUNT NO MORE THAN ',MAXVAL)
             ELSE
                DATAOK:=TRUE;
    UNTIL DATAOK
END;   (* OF AMOUNTIN *)


BEGIN   (* DRIVER *)
   REPEAT
       WRITELN (OUTPUT,'ENTER ZERO TO STOP THE TEST');
       READLN  (INPUT,STOPTEST);
       IF STOPTEST<>'0' THEN
          BEGIN
             WRITELN (OUTPUT,'ENTER THE MIN VALUE');
             READLN  (INPUT,MINVAL);
             WRITELN (OUTPUT,'ENTER THE MAX VALUE');
             READLN  (INPUT,MAXVAL);
             WRITELN (OUTPUT);
             WRITELN (OUTPUT);
             WRITELN (OUTPUT,'THE ITEM TO ENTER IS PRINTED HERE');
             AMOUNTIN;
             WRITELN (OUTPUT);
             WRITELN (OUTPUT,'THE AMOUNT ENTERED WAS ',AMOUNT);
             WRITELN (OUTPUT);
          END;
   UNTIL STOPTEST='0';
END.
```

Listing 6.6(P). Driver for Inputamount Routine in Pascal

```
10        REM   DRIVER FOR INPUTCHOICES ROUTINES
20        REM
30        REM   DRIVER
40        REM
50     PRINT "ENTER A VALUE FOR OPTIONS"
60     PRINT "OR ENTER ZERO TO END THE TEST"
70     INPUT X9
80     IF X9=0 THEN GOTO 190
90        PRINT
100       PRINT
110       PRINT "THE CHOICES ARE PRINTED HERE"
120       GOSUB 230
130       PRINT
140       PRINT "THE CHOICE ENTERED WAS ";C2
150       PRINT
160       GOTO 50
```

```
170       REM
180       REM
190  END
200       REM
210       REM   INPUT AND EDIT A CHOICE
220       REM
230  E1$="PLEASE ENTER YES OR NO"
240  E2$="PLEASE ENTER A NUMBER FROM 1 TO "
250  PRINT
260  PRINT "YOUR CHOICE: ";
270  INPUT S1$
280  IF X9<>1 THEN GOTO 390
290       REM   EDIT YES/NO
300    IF LEN(S1$)>0 THEN GOTO 330
310      PRINT E1$
320      GOTO 260
330    IF LEFT$(S1$,1)="Y" OR LEFT$(S1$,1)="N" THEN GOTO 360
340      PRINT E1$
350      GOTO 260
360    IF LEFT$(S1$,1)="Y" THEN C2=1 ELSE C2=2
370  RETURN
380       REM   EDIT CHOICES
390  C2=VAL(S1$)
400  IF STR$(C2)=" "+S1$ THEN GOTO 430
410    PRINT E2$;X9
420    GOTO 260
430  IF C2>=1 AND C2<=X9 THEN GOTO 460
440    PRINT E2$;X9
450    GOTO 260
460  IF C2=INT(C2) THEN GOTO 490
470    PRINT "PLEASE ENTER AN INTEGER NUMBER"
480    GOTO 260
490  RETURN
```

Listing 6.7(B). Driver for Inputchoices Routine in
BASIC

```
    (*  DRIVER FOR CHOICEIN  *)

PROGRAM DRIVER6 (INPUT, OUTPUT);

    VAR  OPTIONS,
         CHOICE:        INTEGER;
         INSTRING,
         ERROR1,
         ERROR2:        STRING;


    FUNCTION VALUE (INSTRING: STRING): INTEGER;
       VAR  COUNT, VAL:  INTEGER;
            NUMBER:      BOOLEAN;
```

```
    BEGIN
       VAL:=0;
       NUMBER:=TRUE;
       FOR COUNT:=1 TO LENGTH(INSTRING) DO
           IF INSTRING[COUNT] IN ['0'..'9'] THEN
               VAL:=VAL*10+ORD(INSTRING[COUNT])-ORD('0')
           ELSE
               NUMBER:=FALSE;
       IF NUMBER THEN
           VALUE:=VAL
       ELSE
           VALUE:=-1;
    END;   (* OF VALUE FUNCTION *)


PROCEDURE CHOICEIN;
    VAR  DATAOK:    BOOLEAN;
    BEGIN
       ERROR1:='PLEASE ENTER YES OR NO';
       ERROR2:='PLEASE ENTER A NUMBER FROM 1 TO ';
       DATAOK:=FALSE;
       WRITELN (OUTPUT);
       REPEAT
           WRITE  (OUTPUT,'YOUR CHOICE: ');
           READLN (INPUT,INSTRING);
           IF OPTIONS=1 THEN
               IF LENGTH(INSTRING)=0 THEN
                   WRITELN (OUTPUT,ERROR1)
               ELSE
                   IF NOT (INSTRING[1] IN ['Y','N']) THEN
                       WRITELN (OUTPUT,ERROR1)
                   ELSE
                       BEGIN
                           DATAOK:=TRUE;
                           IF INSTRING[1]='Y' THEN
                               CHOICE:=1
                           ELSE
                               CHOICE:=2
                       END
           ELSE
               BEGIN
                   CHOICE:=VALUE(INSTRING);
                   IF (CHOICE<1) OR (CHOICE>OPTIONS) THEN
                       WRITELN (OUTPUT,ERROR2,OPTIONS)
                   ELSE
                       DATAOK:=TRUE;
               END;
       UNTIL DATAOK
    END;   (* OF CHOICEIN *)
```

```
BEGIN    (* DRIVER *)
   REPEAT
      WRITELN (OUTPUT,'ENTER A VALUE FOR OPTIONS');
      WRITELN (OUTPUT,'OR ENTER ZERO TO STOP THE TEST');
      READLN  (INPUT,OPTIONS);
      IF OPTIONS<>0 THEN
         BEGIN
            WRITELN (OUTPUT);
            WRITELN (OUTPUT);
            WRITELN (OUTPUT,'THE CHOICES ARE PRINTED HERE');
            CHOICEIN;
            WRITELN (OUTPUT);
            WRITELN (OUTPUT,'THE CHOICE ENTERED WAS ',CHOICE);
            WRITELN (OUTPUT);
         END;
   UNTIL OPTIONS=0;
END.
```

Listing 6.7(P). Driver for Inputchoices Routine in
Pascal

These drivers are quite straightforward and should be
easy to understand by now. We should test these routines
in the same manner we tested the EVALUATE routine:
try end conditions, combinations, empty entries, and
every other pivot condition that we can think of. The
entries that were found that could cause a problem were
special keys like the combination of <CONTROL> and
<C> in BASIC which interrupts the current program.
The programs correctly handle all other errors.

You may have noticed that the routines in these programs are not quite the same as the sketch code developed in Chapter Five. Just as we expanded and improved
the design during each previous step of our project, we
can also improve and expand the design during the
implementation. Major changes to the system's structure
would require that we return to an earlier step of our project, but minor improvements should be made whenever
possible. In this case, improvements in each of these
input routines have been made to take advantage of the
language being used.

The BASIC programs reflect the most significant
change: we have departed from the form of the structured

statements which we spent the first five chapters developing and defending. Furthermore, we have done so by using the lowly GOTO statement! The reason for doing this, oddly enough, is because to make the BASIC program simpler and easier to understand. To construct a nested IF-THEN-ELSE statement in simple versions of BASIC, you must use GOTO statements to get from the inner IF statements to the outer IF statement, like this:

```
100 IF not condition 1 THEN      GOTO 120
110      condition 1 was met,    GOTO 200
120 IF not condition 2 THEN      GOTO 140
130      condition 2 was met,    GOTO 200
140      IF not condition 3 THEN GOTO 160
150         condition 3 was met,    GOTO 200
160      no conditions were met,    GOTO 200
170      condition 3 was not met,   GOTO 200
180   condition 2 was not met,   GOTO 200
190 condition 1 was not met
200 next statement
```

At the end of each simple IF-THEN statement we know the results of the tests so far and have printed any appropriate error message. At this point, however, we must execute a GOTO 200. This takes us to a point in the program where we no longer know exactly what happened, since processing any of the conditions sends us to line 200. This is why we originally required DATAOK to indicate what happened within the nested IF statements. If the data were not okay, another GOTO would be needed to return to the INPUT statement and let the user retype the entry. This structure requires that errors be handled in the following manner:

- The error is handled by printing the appropriate error message.
- GOTO a location where we no longer know if an error occurred.
- Make another test to see that the error occurred.
- GOTO the INPUT statement to allow re-entry of the data.

In BASIC it is much less confusing to simply go back to the input statement at the time the error is known to occur. This eliminates the need for DATAOK and an additional GOTO for errors at the end of the nested IF statements.

The objective of our design philosophy is to write simple code that is easy to understand. In this case it is easier to understand a straightforward use of GOTO than to understand a complicated use of GOTO that simulates an IF-THEN-ELSE or DO-UNTIL statement.

When and how you bend the rules of structured programming is a matter of personal taste. Some programmers never break such a rule, no matter how convoluted the program becomes. Others are much more flexible in their approach, especially in a non-structured language such as BASIC. The point is that the program should be easy to understand and it should work correctly. In this case we will bend the rules a bit for our BASIC versions of Blackjack.

In the version of BASIC used for these examples we can test a string variable to see if it contains a number by using VAL, a function that returns the numeric value of a string. If the string is not a number, the value zero will be returned. This value can be converted back into a string using the BASIC function STR$. If the string can be converted to a number and back to a string without being changed, it must have been a number to start with. VAL and STR$ work differently in different versions of BASIC, so be sure you know how they work for your system before you try this numeric check. Notice that in this program, STR$ adds a blank character to the front of the string it creates, so another blank must be added to the original string to see if any changes were made.

The Pascal version of these routines has been changed in a different way. Pascal allows nested IF-THEN-ELSE statements of any complexity you wish without requiring special tricks like the GOTO statements in BASIC. In this case we can simplify the error handling by having each IF statement test as many conditions as possible. This results in fewer tests and therefore fewer conditions to handle.

Pascal does not have the VAR and STR$ functions, so we will have to write our own function to see if a string is a number and return the value of the string. In our Blackjack program the player will never need to enter a negative number, so we can use a value of negative one to indicate that the input was not a number.

In both versions of these routines, a check is made to see if any characters were entered before the first character of the input string is examined. In most languages a program will crash if you try to look at a character that is beyond the end of a string.

Throughout the rest of our implementation, minor changes will be made to the sketch code to take advantage of the facilities of the language being used. You should be able to understand why each change is made and how it will work.

C. Developing the Next Level of the Program's Structure

Now that we have developed each of our utility subroutines, they may be added to the existing Blackjack program. They will appear at the end of the BASIC program so they will be numbered high enough to allow the rest of the program to fall between the mainline routine and the first utility subroutine. In the Pascal program they will go at the very beginning of the program. As long as we now have these routines available, we may as well add the detail for the current dummy subroutines: INITIALIZATION, SELECTACTIVITY, and TERMINATION. Notice that new dummy routines will be required for the subroutines called from SELECTACTIVITY. Our program, which is getting fairly complicated, now looks like Listing 6.8.

```
10      REM  BLACKJACK   VERSION 1.0
20      REM      THIS PROGRAM WILL PLAY THE PART OF THE
30      REM      DEALER IN A GAME OF BLACKJACK PLAYED
40      REM      ACCORDING TO HOYLE'S RULES
50      REM
60      REM  WRITTEN BY JACK EMMERICHS,   1/1/82
70      REM  (COPYRIGHT MESSAGE GOES HERE IF YOU WANT ONE)
80      REM
90      REM  CARDVALUE FUNCTION AND ARRAYS
100     REM
110 DEF FNC(X)=X-(INT((X-1)/13)*13)
120     REM
130 DIM D(204), H(3,15), H1(3), H9(3), S$(4), V$(13)
```

```
140     REM
150     REM   PROGRAM MAINLINE
160     REM
170 GOSUB 240
180 GOSUB 610
190 GOSUB 900
200 END
210     REM
220     REM   INITIALIZATION PROCEDURE
230     REM
240 RANDOMIZE
250 DATA "SPADES","HEARTS","DIAMONDS","CLUBS"
260 DATA "ACE","2","3","4","5","6","7","8","9","10"
270 DATA "JACK","QUEEN","KING"
280 FOR X=1 TO 4
290   READ S$(X)
300 NEXT X
310 FOR X=1 TO 13
320   READ V$(X)
330 NEXT X
340 GOSUB 64320
350 L1=10000
360 L2=2000
370 M1=500
380 M2=10
390 C1=0
400 H2=0
410 H3=0
420 E1$="Please enter YES or NO"
430 E2$="please enter a number from 1 to "
440 PRINT
450 PRINT "Welcome to the Blackjack table.  We will be playing"
460 PRINT "   by the rules of Blackjack according to Hoyle."
470 PRINT "   the house limits on bets are:"
480 PRINT "        minimum bet: $";M2
490 PRINT "        maximum bet: $";M1
500 PRINT "   The house currently has $";L1;" in the bank"
510 PRINT "   You currently have $";L2;" in cash."
520 PRINT "   You may exchange cash and chips at the bank."
530 PRINT
540 PRINT "   Please sit down and play for a while."
550 PRINT "        (press RETURN to continue)"
560 INPUT "",S1$
570 RETURN
580     REM
590     REM   SELECT THE NEXT ACTIVITY
600     REM
610 PRINT
620 PRINT "   You may do any of the following things:"
630 PRINT
640 PRINT "        1.  Display the rules of the game."
650 PRINT "        2.  Visit the bank."
660 PRINT "        3.  Display the current status of the game."
670 PRINT "        4.  Shuffle the deck."
```

```
680    PRINT "         5.  Play a hand of cards."
690    PRINT "         6.  Quit the game."
700    X9=6
710    GOSUB 64710
720    IF C2=6 THEN RETURN
730    IF C2<>1 THEN GOTO 760
740      GOSUB 1000
750      GOTO 610
760    IF C2<>2 THEN GOTO 790
770      GOSUB 1050
780      GOTO 610
790    IF C2<>3 THEN GOTO 820
800      GOSUB 1100
810      GOTO 610
820    IF C2<>4 THEN GOTO 850
830      GOSUB 64320
840      GOTO 610
850    GOSUB 1150
860    GOTO 610
870        REM
880        REM   TERMINATION PROCEDURE
890        REM
900    GOSUB 1100
910    PRINT
920    PRINT "Thank you for the game, please come again sometime."
930    PRINT "  (Press RETURN to continue)"
940    INPUT "",S1$
950    RETURN
960        REM
970        REM   SHOW INSTRUCTIONS
980        REM
1000   PRINT "SHOW INSTRUCTIONS"
1010   RETURN
1020       REM
1030       REM   BANKER
1040       REM
1050   PRINT "YOU ARE IN THE BANK"
1060   RETURN
1070       REM
1080       REM   REPORT GAME STATUS
1090       REM
1100   PRINT "REPORT GAME STATUS"
1110   RETURN
1120       REM
1130       REM   PLAY A HAND OF CARDS
1140       REM
1150   PRINT "PLAY A HAND OF CARDS"
1160   RETURN
64000      REM
64010      REM   PRINTCARD
64020      REM
64030  PRINT "THE ";V$(FNC(C));" OF ";S$(INT((C-1)/13)+1)
64040  RETURN
64050      REM
```

```
64060      REM   EVALUATE
64070      REM
64080 H4=0
64090 FOR C9=1 TO H1(H8)
64100   V=FNC(H(H8,C9))
64110   IF V>10 THEN V=10
64120   IF V=1 THEN V=11
64130   H4=H4+V
64140 NEXT C9
64150 C9=1
64160 IF H4<=21 THEN GOTO 64210
64170 IF C9>H1(H8) THEN 64210
64180   IF FNC(H(H8,C9))=1 THEN H4=H4-10
64190   C9=C9+1
64200 GOTO 64160
64210 RETURN
64220      REM
64230      REM   GET A CARD
64240      REM
64250 IF D1>104 THEN GOSUB 64320
64260 C=D(D1)
64270 D1=D1+1
64280 RETURN
64290      REM
64300      REM   SHUFFLE
64310      REM
64320 PRINT "Reshuffle the cards."
64330 FOR C9=1 TO 104
64340   D(C9)=0
64350 NEXT C9
64360 FOR C9=1 TO 2
64370   FOR C=1 TO 52
64380     X=INT(RND(1)*104)+1
64390     IF D(X)=0 THEN GOTO 64430
64400       X=X+1
64410       IF X>104 THEN X=1
64420       GOTO 64390
64430     D(X)=C
64440   NEXT C
64450 NEXT C9
64460 D1=1
64470 RETURN
64480      REM
64490      REM   INPUT AND EDIT AN AMOUNT
64500      REM
64510 PRINT
64520 PRINT "Your amount: ";
64530 INPUT S1$
64540 A=VAL(S1$)
64550 IF STR$(A)=" "+S1$ THEN GOTO 64580
64560   PRINT "Please enter a number"
64570   GOTO 64520
64580 IF A>=M4 THEN GOTO 64610
64590   PRINT "Please enter an amount no less than ";M4
```

```
64600   GOTO 64520
64610 IF A<=M2 THEN GOTO 64640
64620   PRINT "Please enter an amount no greater than ";M2
64630   GOTO 64520
64640 IF A=INT(A) THEN GOTO 46470
64650   PRINT "Please enter an integer number"
64660   GOTO 64520
64670 RETURN
64680     REM
64690     REM  INPUT AND EDIT A CHOICE
64700     REM
64710 PRINT
64720 PRINT "Your choice: ";
64730 INPUT S1$
64740 IF X9<>1 THEN GOTO 64850
64750     REM  EDIT YES/NO
64760   IF LEN(S1$)>0 THEN GOTO 64790
64770     PRINT E1$
64780     GOTO 64720
64790   IF LEFT$(S1$,1)="Y" OR LEFT$(S1$,1)="N" THEN GOTO 64820
64800     PRINT E1$
64810     GOTO 64720
64820   IF LEFT$(S1$,1)="Y" THEN C2=1 ELSE C2=2
64830   RETURN
64840     REM  EDIT CHOICES
64850 C2=VAL(S1$)
64860 IF STR$(C2)=" "+S1$ THEN GOTO 64890
64870   PRINT E2$;X9
64880   GOTO 64720
64890 IF C2>=1 AND C2<=X9 THEN GOTO 64920
64900   PRINT E2$;X9
64910   GOTO 64720
64920 IF C2=INT(C2) THEN GOTO 64950
64930   PRINT "Please enter an integer number"
64940   GOTO 64720
64950 RETURN
```

Listing 6.8(B). An Expanded BASIC version of Blackjack

```
(*  BLACKJACK    VERSION 1.0
         THIS PROGRAM WILL PLAY THE PART OF THE
         DEALER IN A GAME OF BLACKJACK PLAYED
         ACCORDING TO HOYLE'S RULES

         WRITTEN BY JACK EMMERICHS,   1/1/82
         (COPYRIGHT MESSAGE GOES HERE IF YOU WANT ONE)   *)

PROGRAM BLAKJACK (INPUT, OUTPUT);

   VAR   AMOUNT,       CARD,
         CHOICE,       DECKNEXT,
```

```
          HANDVALU,       MAXVAL,
          MINVAL,         OPTIONS,
          THISHAND,       PLAYLIMT,
          BANKLIMT,       MINBET,
          MAXBET,         CHIPS,
          HANDPLAD,       HANDSWON,
          SEED:           INTEGER;

          DECK:           ARRAY [1..104]    OF INTEGER;
          HANDCNT:        ARRAY [1..3]      OF INTEGER;
          HANDS:          ARRAY [1..3, 1..15] OF INTEGER;
          SUIT:           ARRAY [1..4]      OF STRING [8];
          VALUE:          ARRAY [1..13]     OF STRING [5];

          INSTRING,
          ERROR1,
          ERROR2:         STRING;


FUNCTION RAND (MAX: INTEGER): INTEGER;
   BEGIN
      SEED:=SEED*((SEED DIV 2)-1)+21845;
      RAND:=(SEED MOD MAX)+1;
   END;   (*  OF RANDOM NUMBER GENERATOR  *)


FUNCTION CARDVAL (CARD: INTEGER): INTEGER;
   BEGIN
      CARDVAL:=CARD-(((CARD-1) DIV 13) * 13);
   END;   (*  OF CARDVAL  *)


FUNCTION VAL (INSTRING: STRING): INTEGER;
   VAR  COUNT, VALUE: INTEGER;
        NUMBER:        BOOLEAN;
   BEGIN
      VALUE:=0;
      NUMBER:=TRUE;
      FOR COUNT:=1 TO LENGTH(INSTRING) DO
         IF INSTRING[COUNT] IN ['0'..'9'] THEN
            VALUE:=VALUE*10+ORD(INSTRING[COUNT])-ORD('0')
         ELSE
            NUMBER:=FALSE;
      IF NUMBER THEN
         VAL:=VALUE
      ELSE
         VAL:=-1;
   END;   (*  OF VAL  *)


PROCEDURE SHOWCARD;
   BEGIN
      WRITELN (OUTPUT,'THE ',VALUE[CARDVAL(CARD)],
               ' OF ',SUIT[((CARD-1) DIV 13) + 1]);
   END;   (*  OF SHOWCARD  *)
```

```
PROCEDURE EVALUATE;
    VAR  V, COUNT: INTEGER;
    BEGIN
        HANDVALU:=0;
        FOR COUNT:=1 TO HANDCNT[THISHAND] DO
            BEGIN
                V:=CARDVAL(HANDS[THISHAND,COUNT]);
                IF V>10 THEN
                    V:=10;
                IF V=1 THEN
                    V:=11;
                HANDVALU:=HANDVALU+V;
            END;
        COUNT:=1;
        WHILE (HANDVALU>21) AND (COUNT<=HANDCNT[THISHAND]) DO
            BEGIN
                IF CARDVAL(HANDS[THISHAND,COUNT])=1 THEN
                    HANDVALU:=HANDVALU-10;
                COUNT:=COUNT+1;
            END;
    END;   (*  OF EVALUATE  *)



PROCEDURE SHUFFLE;
    VAR  COUNT, X:  INTEGER;
    BEGIN
        WRITELN (OUTPUT,'Reshuffle the cards');
        FOR COUNT:=1 TO 104 DO
            DECK[COUNT]:=0;
        FOR COUNT:=1 TO 2 DO
            BEGIN
                FOR CARD:=1 TO 52 DO
                    BEGIN
                        X:=RAND(104);
                        WHILE DECK[X]<>0 DO
                            BEGIN
                                X:=X+1;
                                IF X>104 THEN
                                    X:=1;
                            END;
                        DECK[X]:=CARD;
                    END;
            END;
        DECKNEXT:=1;
    END;   (*  OF SHUFFLE  *)



PROCEDURE GETCARD;
    BEGIN
        IF DECKNEXT>104 THEN
            SHUFFLE;
        CARD:=DECK[DECKNEXT];
        DECKNEXT:=DECKNEXT+1;
    END;   (*  OF GETCARD  *)
```

```
PROCEDURE AMOUNTIN;
    VAR  DATAOK:      BOOLEAN;
    BEGIN
        DATAOK:=FALSE;
        WRITELN (OUTPUT);
        REPEAT
            WRITE  (OUTPUT,'Your amount: ');
            READLN (INPUT,INSTRING);
            AMOUNT:=VAL(INSTRING);
            IF AMOUNT=-1 THEN
                WRITELN (OUTPUT,'Please enter a number')
            ELSE
                IF AMOUNT<MINVAL THEN
                    WRITELN (OUTPUT,
                    'Please enter an amount no less than ',MINVAL)
                ELSE
                    IF AMOUNT>MAXVAL THEN
                        WRITELN (OUTPUT,
                        'Please enter an amount no more than ',MAXVAL)
                    ELSE
                        DATAOK:=TRUE;
        UNTIL DATAOK
    END;    (* OF AMOUNTIN *)

PROCEDURE CHOICEIN;
    VAR  DATAOK:      BOOLEAN;
    BEGIN
        DATAOK:=FALSE;
        WRITELN (OUTPUT);
        REPEAT
            WRITE  (OUTPUT,'Your choice: ');
            READLN (INPUT,INSTRING);
            IF OPTIONS=1 THEN
                IF LENGTH(INSTRING)=0 THEN
                    WRITELN (OUTPUT,ERROR1)
                ELSE
                    IF NOT (INSTRING[1] IN ['Y','N']) THEN
                        WRITELN (OUTPUT,ERROR1)
                    ELSE
                        BEGIN
                            DATAOK:=TRUE;
                            IF INSTRING[1]='Y' THEN
                                CHOICE:=1
                            ELSE
                                CHOICE:=2
                        END
            ELSE
                BEGIN
                    CHOICE:=VAL(INSTRING);
                    IF (CHOICE<1) OR (CHOICE>OPTIONS) THEN
                        WRITELN (OUTPUT,ERROR2,OPTIONS)
                    ELSE
                        DATAOK:=TRUE;
                END;
        UNTIL DATAOK
    END;    (* OF CHOICEIN *)
```

```
PROCEDURE INSTRUCT;
   BEGIN
      WRITELN (OUTPUT,'SHOW INSTRUCTIONS');
   END;
PROCEDURE BANKER;
   BEGIN
      WRITELN (OUTPUT,'YOU ARE IN THE BANK');
   END;


PROCEDURE STATUS;
   BEGIN
      WRITELN (OUTPUT,'REPORT GAME STATUS');
   END;


PROCEDURE PLAYHAND;
   BEGIN
      WRITELN (OUTPUT,'PLAY A HAND OF CARDS');
   END;


PROCEDURE INIT;                    (* INIT ROUTINE *)
   BEGIN
      SUIT[1] := 'SPADES';         SUIT[2] := 'HEARTS';
      SUIT[3] := 'DIAMONDS';       SUIT[4] := 'CLUBS';
      VALUE[1] := 'ACE';    VALUE[2] := '2';    VALUE[3] := '3';
      VALUE[4] := '4';      VALUE[5] := '5';    VALUE[6] := '6';
      VALUE[7] := '7';      VALUE[8] := '8';    VALUE[9] := '9';
      VALUE[10] := '10';    VALUE[11] := 'JACK';
      VALUE[12] := 'QUEEN'; VALUE[13] := 'KING';
      SHUFFLE;
      PLAYLIMT:=2000;
      BANKLIMT:=10000;
      MINBET:=10;
      MAXBET:=500;
      CHIPS:=0;
      HANDPLAD:=0;
      HANDSWON:=0;
      ERROR1:='Please enter YES or NO';
      ERROR2:='Please enter a number from 1 to ';
      WRITELN (OUTPUT);
      WRITELN (OUTPUT,
      'Welcome to the Blackjack table.  We will be playing');
      WRITELN (OUTPUT,
      '   by the rules of Blackjack according to Hoyle.');
      WRITELN (OUTPUT,'   the house limits on bets are:');
      WRITELN (OUTPUT,'      minimum bet: $',MINBET);
      WRITELN (OUTPUT,'      maximum bet: $',MAXBET);
      WRITELN (OUTPUT,'   the house currently has $',
         BANKLIMT,' in the bank.');
      WRITELN (OUTPUT,'   You currently have $',
         PLAYLIMT,' in cash');
      WRITELN (OUTPUT);
      WRITELN (OUTPUT,
         '   Please sit down and play for a while.');
```

```
      WRITELN (OUTPUT, '            Press RETURN to continue');
      READLN  (INPUT,INSTRING);
   END;


PROCEDURE NEXTACTV;                   (* NEXT ACTIV ROUTINE *)
   BEGIN
      REPEAT
         WRITELN (OUTPUT);
         WRITELN (OUTPUT,
            '   You may do any of the following things:');
         WRITELN (OUTPUT);
         WRITELN (OUTPUT,
            '         1.  Display the rules of the game.');
         WRITELN (OUTPUT,
            '         2.  Visit the bank.');
         WRITELN (OUTPUT,
            '         3.  Display the current status of the game.');
         WRITELN (OUTPUT,
            '         4.  Shuffle the deck.');
         WRITELN (OUTPUT,
            '         5.  Play a hand of cards.');
         WRITELN (OUTPUT,
            '         6.  Quit the game.');
         OPTIONS:=6;
         CHOICEIN;
         IF CHOICE<>6 THEN
            CASE CHOICE OF
               1:  INSTRUCT;
               2:  BANKER;
               3:  STATUS;
               4:  SHUFFLE;
               5:  PLAYHAND;
            END;  (* OF CASE STATEMENT  *)
      UNTIL CHOICE=6;
   END;


PROCEDURE TERM;                      (* TERMINATION ROUTINE *)
   BEGIN
      STATUS;
      WRITELN (OUTPUT);
      WRITELN (OUTPUT,
         'Thank you for the game, please come again sometime.');
      WRITELN (OUTPUT,
         '   (Press RETURN to continue)');
      READLN  (INPUT,INSTRING);
   END;

BEGIN                                (* PROGRAM MAINLINE *)
   INIT;
   NEXTACTV;
   TERM;
END.
```

Listing 6.8(P). An Expanded Pascal version of Blackjack

As usual, things have continued to change a bit. Setting up the error messages is now done in the initialization routine. The details of the greeting message, goodbye message, and the activity selection screen have been completed. For the most part, however, there are no major changes from the original sketch code to the final routines.

Notice that some of the line numbers in the BASIC program had to change as the program expanded. This is a great source of bugs because it is quite easy to mistype a line number or to forget to change one when a module is moved from a driver program to the final program. Most versions of BASIC allow line numbers up to about 65000 so we have numbered the utility subroutines starting at 64000.

The program can now be completed by adding modules one level at a time. Each level should be thoroughly tested as it is added.

To make sure that each module is working properly, you may want to include temporary instructions to show you what is going on. For example, the BUY and CASH-IN routine for BANKER can be made to print the current value for the player's chips and credit limit at the start and end of the routine until you are sure they are working correctly. Of course you must be sure to remove these temporary statements when the routines have been completely tested. If you are an optimist you can simply take these statements out of the program. If you feel that you may need them later, you can remove them by turning them into comments. These statements can be reactivated by removing the comment indicators. In larger systems the testing statements are often written as IF-THEN statements that only operate if a testing variable is non-zero. By changing the value of one variable at the beginning of the program, you can turn all the testing statements on or off at once.

You may also need dummy routines that are more complex than the single display instruction that we have used so far. For example, the dummy module for BETTING can ask the terminal for the value of a bet so that we can test the reaction of its parent routine.

Now that we know how modules are to be developed for our program we can apply our efforts to one module at a time until the entire program has been completed.

III. THE FINAL PRODUCT

When all of the modules have been completed and all of the temporary code that was used for testing has been removed, the program is finally finished. This program is shown in BASIC and Pascal in Appendix E.

Once again, things have changed during development. Several modules are significantly different from the sketch code in Chapter Five. This is because of bugs that were found and corrected as the program was being finished. As one might suspect, we did not think of every possible situation during the detailed design, nor did we correctly develop all of the situations that we did consider. Here is a summary of the corrections that have been made:

- AMOUNTWON must be initialized in the INITIAL-IZE routine.
- Several messages have been made more explicit to help the player. See the error messages in BUY and CASHIN as examples.
- The number of games won has been changed from the net number of wins or losses to the actual number of wins.
- BETTING now sets the initial values of MAXVAL and MINVAL before the REPEAT loop. Furthermore, if MINVAL had been set to the house minimum it would become impossible to enter a zero bet when there are not enough chips to cover the house minimum. This has been fixed.
- All places in the program that position the cursor on the terminal screen must do so just before the next item is to be printed. Otherwise it is possible for some other output, such as "RESHUFFLING THE CARDS," to mess up the screen again.
- The dealer's cards are now displayed when the dealer wins with a natural.

- SPLITPAIRS must set the value of HAND-COUNT(3) to 2 after the two new cards are dealt to the new hand.
- PLAYER must set the DONE flag to true if all of the player's hands have gone over 21.
- DEALER must compare the dealer's hand to 21, not 17, to indicate when the "DEALER GOES OVER".
- The routines called by SETTLE must increment HAND-COUNT for each player hand that is evaluated. Furthermore, AMOUNTWON must be incremented or decremented when the player has won or lost, and HANDSWON must be incremented whenever the player has won.
- The combination of both the player and the dealer going over 21 is not possible, so the processing of this situation has been changed to print an error message.
- The logic to decide when the player wins in DEAL-ERSTANDS must exclude hands where the player loses by going over 21.
- BROKENBANK must restore the values of the player's funds and the bank's funds so that the player cannot win more than the bank had at the beginning of the game.

This may seem like quite a long list of problems for the few remaining modules that needed development. Furthermore, several of these items appear pretty obvious and look like they should have been developed correctly in the first place. Well, don't ever be surprised by bugs in a program. Bugs, like death and taxes, are inevitable.

Actually, we did rather well for a program of this complexity. As a general rule, you should expect to find bugs as you implement any program. Then, when they do show up you will be ready for them. If you manage to create a program with no discernible bugs in it, you have accomplished a feat worth celebrating. (Actually, you have probably overlooked something.) The most that an honest programmer will usually admit to is developing a program with no *known* bugs in it.

You will also notice that several minor changes have been made in the program. Perhaps the most obvious change is in the detailed rules display. It did not seem reasonable to expand the size of the program by including a complete set of Blackjack rules in the program's code. It is much easier to simply refer to the book which contains the original set of rules.

The Pascal program has been reorganized so that the order of the procedures, listed backwards from the main-line routine, more closely matches the order of the routines in the BASIC program. You may also notice that the BUY and CASHIN procedures are nested within BANKER and the evaluation procedures are nested within EVALUATE. The whole program could be structured in this way to match the system's structural diagram. Each level of the diagram from the top down would match a level of nested procedures within the program. All functions and procedures that must be called from more than one place in the program would then be gathered together as utility routines at the beginning of the program.

This has not been done because the Pascal compiler requires additional memory for each level of nested procedures. When Pascal is run on a small computer, the number of nested procedures should usually be held to a minimum to save memory space. The way we have structured the Blackjack program shows that it can be written as a series of separate procedures, as a hierarchy of nested procedures, or as a combination of both.

There is no RETURN statement in Pascal. Therefore, even though UCSD Pascal does have an EXIT statement, the logic of each routine has been changed so that a RETURN statement is not needed.

IV. TESTING THE FINAL PROGRAM

Now that the program is finished it may be tempting to show it off to anyone who may be within shouting distance. There may even be someone nearby who would really be interested in it. Unfortunately, the first person who looks at it is likely to say:

"What happens if I push this key over here?"

and thus crash the system within the first thirty seconds. The best way to avoid this problem is to do some additional testing by running the finished program. This is called *acceptance testing* or *integration testing*. It will be fairly easy to do with our program because the individual parts of it have all been tested before.

The first thing to do when testing the entire program is to try to make it fail. If you can crash the program then you have found an error to be corrected. There should be no way for the player to crash the system. A possible exception is a program interrupt (usually the combination of <CONTROL> and <C>) that is built into the language, although even this can be disabled in many versions of BASIC and other languages. Try things that no "reasonable" player would — like try random banging on the keyboard, an empty entry (just type <RETURN>), or a string of 300 X's. Try anything that you can think of that may make the program misbehave.

When you are unable to crash the system by yourself, invite someone else to play "Crash the System." You may be surprised to find how eager people will be to bring your elegant system to its humble knees. You may also be surprised that other people try things you never considered. The more people that you can get to test the program, the better your chances are of finding all (or at least most) of the bugs. When you have a program that nobody can crash, or ever confuse, it will be ready for public display.

If you find a truly bizarre error that would be very difficult to correct, you may want to simply note it and let it go. At some point you must strike a balance between the complexity of the program and the obscurity of the error. In some versions of BASIC, for example, it is almost impossible to prevent a crash when entering 300 X's.

The final test for any program is actual use. Testing that exercises a program or system with a large volume of information is called *Volume Testing*. This is usually the last acceptance test. For the Blackjack program, reasonable volume testing involves playing a large number of games. As you find and correct bugs, it becomes harder and harder to crash the system. Remember, however,that Murphy's Demon will usually leave at least one subtle bug buried deep within any complex program. It will surface and surprise you when you least expect it.

A safety measure against such *latent* bugs is to keep the design documentation for all your programs up to date as the programs are changed. We have included fewer comments within our program listings than some programmers would use because we have developed so much documentation outside of the listings. Most of the comments within the program itself are to identify each module rather than to explain how the module works. The data dictionary, structural network chart, and sketch code will help you remember what each instruction is supposed to be doing when you have to fix a bug in the program six months from now. This will be of limited usefulness, however, if the documentation is out of date.

The documentation shown in the appendices of this book chronicles the development of the project through each step of its development. Therefore the sketch code shown in Appendix D has been updated to show the program's logic as it stood at the end of the Detailed Design but it has not been updated with the changes developed during the implementation. The logic shown in this appendix has bugs in it because it is a snapshot of the development process rather than documentation for the finished project.

Now that we have completed the program that we set out to develop, we should sit down and have a game of Blackjack.

V. REVIEW OF MAJOR IDEAS

This chapter has dealt with the writing, testing, and debugging of our Blackjack program. As in Chapter Five, most of the information was contained in the examples used to develop the program one step at a time. Again we can only list major ideas within the chapter that can be stated as general rules-of-thumb:

- If you have not already done so, you must select the language that you will be using. Choose one that:
    - is available on your computer and is affordable.
    - will be compatible with related programs in your system.

- will meet your requirements for processing speed, memory space, and language functions.
- is familiar to you or which you are interested in learning.
- Translate the data dictionary (and possibly the program module names) into valid names for your language.
- Start the program by developing the heading information and the mainline routine.
- Build the program's major modules from the top down as they were developed in the Detailed Design.
- Build the program's common subroutines from the bottom up. Group them together in one part of the program.
- Use dummy subroutines or driver programs to help develop each module.
- Test each module before (or as) it is added to the program. A complete test should:
  - exercise all of the instructions in the module, including those which handle error conditions.
  - exercise all possible combinations of the module's parts. There may be no need, however, to test every possible way of creating each combination.
  - test normal entries as well as extreme or limiting pivot conditions like maximum values, minimum values, zero values, negative values, and null entries.
- When a module fails a test, debug it before you continue with other parts of the program. If there is a significant change or if the change affects other modules, be sure to re-test conditions that were already working to be sure the correction did not change another part of the system.
- Use temporary statements to display or accept questionable values during testing and debugging. Remember to remove these statements or to change them to comments when the module is finished.
- Do not be surprised when bugs are found and changes must be made.

- It is reasonable to bend the rules of structural programming if the result is a program that is easier to understand or use. This will usually depend on the language you are using.
- Be very careful about changing line numbers in BASIC programs as dummy subroutines are replaced with larger finished modules. This is a common source of bugs.
- Clean up the program when the last module has been added. Add missing comments, remove unused test statements, and leave the program so that it will be easy to work with.
- When the whole program is running, put it through a final series of "acceptance" tests by:
    - trying to crash the system in any way possible.
    - letting other people play "Crash the System."
    - simply running the system as much as possible.
- Try to strike a balance between eliminating every possible way to cause errors and creating a program that is far more complex than it really needs to be. In some languages there are some errors that cannot be avoided.
- Using the system will be its ultimate test.
- Now that we have completed the program that we set out to write, *let's use it!*

7

How Can the Program Be Changed?

". . . we may polish it at leisure."
John Dryden

The objective of our example project was to develop a program that would play the part of the dealer in a game of Blackjack according to Hoyle. The program presented at the end of Chapter six is a perfectly good example of just such a program. Why, then, are we here in another chapter instead of being at the end of the book? The answer is that the objective we set out to achieve, as in most programming projects, was a bit different from what we really needed.

When a project is finally done there are usually unforeseen details that did not come out quite right. Usually these may be remedied by making minor modifications to the new system. In some cases, where the user's real requirements only became apparent after the new system is finished, a whole new project may be required to solve the real problem. This would be an unusual case, however, and should not happen if the early steps of the project did a proper job of defining what must be done. In the case of our example project there are simply a few things that we could do to make the Blackjack program easier to use. We will therefore make a few changes to the original design.

I. IDENTIFYING THE CHANGES TO BE MADE

The usual reasons for changing a program are to fix parts of it that do not work, to remove parts of it that are not needed, or to add new parts to it so that it can do more than it does now. If we have done a good job on the program's development these should all be very minor items, especially the corrections for things that do not work.

The Blackjack program seems to work fine by now. Several people have played it for hours on end and found no bugs. Careful reading of the original instructions, however, reveals that during the deal, the dealer's *first* card should be dealt face up and the *second* one should be dealt face down. Oddly enough, the program does it just the other way around! A minor oversight on the part of the programmer no doubt. This will be fixed.

A second item that does not seem quite right is the way the program asks the player if another card is desired. The usual practice is to ask if the player wants another card. Our program asks if the player wants to stand with the current hand. You may recall that the question was worded this way to make the program easier to write. A general rule of good programming, however, is that the program should be modified to fit the user's needs, not the other way around. Therefore we should change this question to be what most players will expect: "Do you want another card?".

Now consider the elimination of some unnecessary parts of the program. We really have not implemented the function that allows the player to display the rules of the game. The function is there, but it only tells the reader to go look somewhere else. If we are not going to use this function properly we should take it out. Also, the pause at the end of the TERMINATION routine seems unnecessary. In actual use it becomes a nuisance and should be removed.

Finally, consider a new addition to the program. As the program stands, several parts of the game may clutter up the screen at one time. This does not affect how the game is played, but it keeps the program from looking as neat as it might. Things would look much better if we could control where items were printed on the terminal's screen. To some extent this has been purposely avoided so that we could write a program that will work on almost any small computer. The problem with using fancy terminal screen handling routines is that they will be different for almost every different computer or terminal.

The most common screen control, however, is to clear the screen and leave the cursor in the upper left hand corner. Almost any terminal will allow you to clear the screen with a single command, so we can create a simple utility subroutine CLEAR SCREEN which we can call from various places throughout the program. To implement this change on your computer you will have to put the appropriate command for your terminal in this one line subroutine. As we shall see, just clearing the screen from time to time will make a significant improvement in the appearance of the game.

The need for all of these changes will be apparent to anyone using the program. It is also possible to make improvements in the structure of a program that the user will never see. Such improvements usually make the program more efficient. Often a function can be rewritten so that it requires less memory, runs faster, requires fewer variables, or is a better function in some other way even though it is still doing the same thing.

A common problem with small computers is lack of memory space. One way to reduce the amount of memory used by a program is to remove any unused or duplicated parts of the program. We will do some of this by eliminating the routine that almost displays the rules of the game. In the case of our Blackjack program we could also remove routines that are not essential to the playing of the game. All of the banking functions, for example, could be removed if we assumed that the player started the game with chips instead of money.

A program may also contain long string constants that are used in several places — for example, the error messages for the input/editing routines. If a string constant is used more than two or three times, it will probably save memory to define it as a string variable which can be used throughout the program. In the Blackjack program such strings are used to ask the player to press <RE-TURN> to continue, to report the status of hands that are being evaluated, etc. These could be consolidated into a few string variables.

In BASIC you can also save memory space by removing comments. This makes a program harder to read, however, so you might want to keep a version that still has comments in it even if it is too large to run in your computer. The version you actually use can be the same program with all the comments removed. Most compiled languages, like Pascal, remove the comments when compiling the final program so no memory space is saved by removing comments from the original listing.

It is also possible to make the program easier to modify in the future. As we have seen, we can save memory space by placing repeated strings into string variables. A side effect of this change is that it becomes easier to change the message because now it only has to be changed in one place: where the variable's value is established. This improvement can be extended to most other constants in the program. For example, suppose we wanted to play with a single deck, or even three, four, or five decks shuffled together. As the program is currently written, we would have to change each statement in the whole program that depends on the size of the deck. If the number of decks and cards being used (currently two decks or 104 cards) were represented throughout the program by variables that are set at the beginning of the program, only that variable's value would have to be changed.

What we wish to do in this chapter is to polish the program, to put it into a more finished form. In actual practice this polishing may go on as long as the program is in use. This is one of the advantages of writing your own programs. For the purposes of this project, however, we will only follow the program's development through the changes we have just discussed. Now we must decide how the changes should be made.

II. IDENTIFYING HOW THE CHANGES SHOULD BE MADE

We indicated throughout the development of this program that we would appreciate its modular structure when it came time to make changes to it. Well, here we are about to make changes, so let's see how the modular structure works.

The cards dealt to the dealer are shown in two routines: DEAL and SPLITPAIRS. These are easy to change so that the first dealer card is shown face up and the second is shown face down.

The question "DO YOU STAND ON THIS HAND?" is controlled by PLAYER. We can change both the form of the question and the processing of the answer in this routine without affecting the input routine that actually gets the answer from the player.

To delete the rule printing function we just remove SHOWINSTRUCT, then modify SELECTACTIV to display and process the remaining five options correctly.

As we indicated above, we can write a new utility subroutine to clear the terminal screen. This routine can be called whenever a fresh screen would improve the appearance of the game.

It will be more difficult to replace constants with variables because we must search through the program to find the present occurrences of each constant. Keep this in mind, because it is easier to work with programs that are initially written using variables rather than constant values. We will use constants for the initial house and player credit limits as well as for the number of decks and cards being used.

In the case of the PRESS RETURN TO CONTINUE message, there is always an associated pause until the player presses <RETURN>. It makes more sense to gather the entire function of printing a message and pausing for a <RETURN> into another utility subroutine.

If reasonably large changes are required, it is a good idea to develop them using the same techniques used to develop the original program: define exactly what should be changed, develop a general design showing how these changes will fit into the existing program, develop a detailed design of how each change will be written, and finally make the changes one step at a time testing each step as it is completed.

The program will be easy to modify in the future only if the documentation is kept up to date as changes are made. Therefore, we must note all of our changes on the appropriate sketch code listings, structural diagrams, and data dictionaries. All changes should also be noted at the top of the program. This way, if you find several versions of the program lying about, you will know which one has the latest changes in it.

Now that we know what we want to do and how we are going to do it, the programs can be changed to incorporate our improvements.

III. MAKING THE CHANGES AND REVIEWING THE MAJOR IDEAS

Appendix F shows the final versions of the BASIC and Pascal Blackjack programs. All parts of the programs that were changed are marked by being underlined. Notice that even though many parts of the programs were changed, each change was largely independent of other changes.

Notice that once again we have a line number problem in the BASIC program. When you CALL a subroutine you can refer to the number of the first line of the subroutine or you can refer to the number of a comment line that comes before the subroutine. The advantage of using the first line of the subroutine is that no reference is ever made to a comment line. This makes it easy to shrink the program by removing comments. The advantage of using a comment line before the subroutine is that you can add new lines to the front of the subroutine without changing the subroutine's "line number". The BASIC examples in this book always refer to a subroutine's first line number so the comments can be changed at will. This means, however, to add a new line to the front of a subroutine (e.g., a call to the CLEAR SCREEN routine), you must renumber the current first line and then create the new line with the old first line's number. See the start of SELECTACTIV, lines 610 to 620, as an example.

This covers the entire development of our Blackjack project from its inception through final polishing as a completed computer program. We have followed all of the bright ideas, wrong turns, corrections, and triumphs that go along with any real programming project. You can imagine the final program being used on and off by family and friends as a standard part of a library of game programs. To make this example truly accurate, however, there is (at least) one more incident that should be brought to your attention.

Two years after the Blackjack program is finished, it is shown to some new friends one night as an example of an early program that was developed when the computer was still quite new. One of the crowd decides to try a few hands and becomes absorbed in the progress of the game. In playing a hand which is dealt two aces of spades*, the message:

Reshuffle the cards

appears on the screen. The player is then dealt a *third* ace of spades! Apparently there are still some bugs in our wonderful program. As a matter of practice, you might try to figure out why this happened, and how to change the program so it won't happen again.

The following ideas summarize the major ideas of this final chapter:

- Many projects which meet their original goals may not solve the real problem because the real problem may not have been well understood at the beginning of the project.
- When the real problem has not been solved, you may have to make changes in the final programs, redesign and rebuild parts of the project, or start a whole new project to solve the real problem as it is now understood.
- Most corrections are to fix bugs in the programs, to eliminate parts of the programs that are not needed, or to add new functions that were not originally included.
- Screen controls may be different for each terminal but using them (even if only the simple clear screen) usually results in a much more attractive program.

---

*Remember that we are using a double deck of cards.

- Changes may also be made to improve the efficiency of a program so that it uses less space, runs faster, or is easier to modify.
- A program will be easier to modify if variables are used instead of constants.
- If a complex change is required, it can be treated as a small project in itself with a general design, specific detailed design, and a step-by-step implementation that is tested as it progresses.
- Be sure to update any documentation when you change the program. This includes comments at the front of the program itself.
- Always keep your eye open for improvements that may be made in your programs or bugs that may show up even after you think everything has ben completely worked out.

Appendix A

The Steps in a Project's Life Cycle

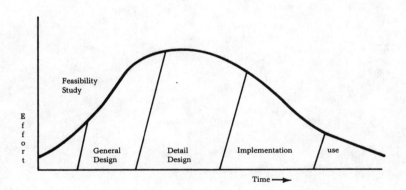

A SIMPLE PROJECT LIFE CYCLE

The primary steps of a programming project. The chart shows how the steps relate to each other and the relative amount of effort usually required for each step. Each step is described in a separate chapter as follows:

FEASIBILITY STUDY	CHAPTER THREE
GENERAL DESIGN	CHAPTER FOUR
DETAILED DESIGN	CHAPTER FIVE
IMPLEMENTATION	CHAPTER SIX
USE	CHAPTER SEVEN

See Chapter Three for additional details.

Appendix B

The Rules of Blackjack According to Hoyle

Blackjack is one of the most widely played games in homes and clubs (it traditionally rivals Poker for popularity in the United States Army). It has two main forms: *With a permanent bank,* the same player always deals and all bets are placed against this player; *with a changing bank,* every player in the game has a chance to be dealer. The latter form is the one most often played in homes.

BLACKJACK WITH A PERMANENT BANK

Number of players — As many as can sit at the table; but usually seats are provided for no more than seven or eight players besides the dealer.

The pack — 104 cards (two 52-card packs shuffled together). In addition, the dealer uses a joker or blank card which is never dealt, but is faced up at the bottom of the pack to mark the location of the last of the shuffled cards.

The shuffle and cut — Dealer and any other player who wishes to may shuffle portions of the pack until all cards have been shuffled and combined. Any player may cut the pack. The extra card is placed face up at the bottom.

Betting — Before the deal begins, each player places a bet, in chips, in front of him on the table; usually minimum and maximum limits are placed upon betting, so that, for example, no player may bet less than one chip nor more than ten.

The deal — When all players have placed their bets, dealer gives one card face down to each other player in rotation; then one card face up to himself; then another card face down to each player including himself. Thus each player except the dealer receives two cards face down, and the dealer receives one card face up and one card face down.

Object of the game — Counting any ace as 1 or 11, as he wishes, any face card as 10, and any other card as its pip value, each player attempts to get a count of 21, or as near to 21 as possible without going over 21.

Naturals — If a player's first two cards are an ace and a face card or ten, giving him a count of 21 in two cards, he has a *natural* or *blackjack*. If any player has a natural and dealer does not have a natural, dealer immediately pays that player one and one-half times the amount of his bet. If dealer has a natural, he immediately collects the bets of all players who do not have naturals, but no player need pay any more than he bet originally. If dealer and any other player both have naturals, the bet of that player is a stand-off (he takes back his chips, and neither pays nor collects).

If dealer's face-up card is a ten, face-card or ace, he may look at his face-down card to see if he has a natural; if his face-up card is anything else, he may not look at his face-down card until his turn comes to draw.

Drawing — If dealer did not have a natural, when he has settled all bets involving naturals he turns to the player nearest his left. That player may *stand* on the two cards originally dealt him, or may require the dealer to give him additional cards, one at a time, until after receiving any such card he stands on the total already dealt to him if it is 21 or under; or *busts* (goes over 21), in which case he immediately pays the amount of his bet to the dealer. Dealer then turns to the next player in turn to his left and serves him in the same manner.

When dealer has thus served every player, he turns up his own face-down card. If his total is 17 or more, he must stand. If his total is 16 or under, he must take a card and must continue to take cards until his total is 17 or more, at which point he must stand. If dealer has an ace, and counting it as 11 would bring his total to 17 or more (but not over 21), he must count the ace as 11 and stand.

Settlement — A bet once paid and collected is never returned. If dealer goes over 21, he pays to each player who has stood the amount of that player's bet. If dealer stands at 21 or less, he pays the bet of any player having a higher total; collects the bet of any player having a lower total; and is at a stand-off with any player having the same total.

Reshuffling — As each player's bet is settled, dealer gathers in that player's cards and places them face up on the bottom of the pack. Dealer continues to use the originally shuffled pack until he comes to the face-up blank card, which signifies the end of the shuffled cards. At this point he interrupts the deal, shuffles all cards not in play, has them cut by any player or players, again places the blank card face up on the bottom, and continues the deal. Before any deal, if the dealer does not think there are enough cards to go around in the next deal, he may gather up all cards for a new shuffle and cut.

Splitting pairs — If a player's two first cards are of the same denomination — as two jacks, or two sixes — he may choose to treat them as two separate hands. The amount of his original bet then goes on one of the cards, and he must place an equal amount as a bet on the other card. When this player's turn to draw comes, dealer first gives him one card face up to each hand. The player may then require dealer to give an additional card or cards to either hand, in whatever order he wishes, until he has gone over or stood on both hands. The two hands are treated separately, dealer settling with each on its own merits.

Irregularities — Since all player's cards are dealt face up, there is no penalty for any irregularity, but an irregularity must be corrected if discovered before the bet has been settled; after the bet has been settled, there can be no correction. If dealer has a natural, but fails to announce it before dealing an additional card to any player, his hand constitutes a count of 21, but can be tied by the hand of any other player whose total is 21 in 3 or more cards.

Appendix C

Results of the General Design

THE GENERAL DESIGN DATA STRUCTURE

Choice prompt messages.
- "What next" question.
- "Buy or cash in" question.
- "Split your pair" question.
- "Take another card" question.

Amount prompt messages.
- "How much to buy or cash in" question.
- 'How much to bet" question.

General messages.
- "Welcome to the game" message.
- "The following choices are available" message.
- Standard rules message.
- "The cards have been shuffled" message.
- "Dealer has a natural" message.
- "You won" message.
- "You lost" message.
- "Good bye" message.
- The back of the dealer's first card.
- Error messages.

Static variables.
- Player's credit limit.
- Bank's credit limit.
- Minimum bet.
- Maximum bet.

Dynamic variables.
- Total amount of money won (+-).
- Total number of hands played.
- Total number of hands won (+-).
- Current value of player's chips.
- The remaining deck. (an array)
- The dealer's hand. (an array)
- The player's regular hand. (an array)
- The player's second (split) hand. (an array)
- Amount won during this hand (+-).
- Answers to choice questions.
- Answers to amount questions.
- The number of cards in each hand. (an array)

Transient variables.
- Percentage of hands won (+-).
- Average amount won per hand (+-).
- The value of a card.
- The suit of a card.

THE GENERAL DESIGN SYSTEM STRUCTURE

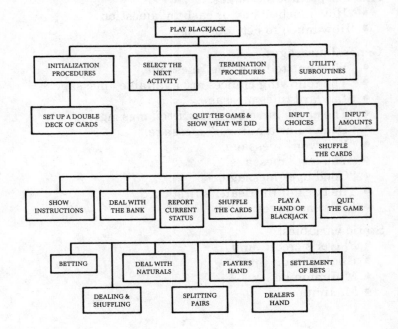

Appendix D

Results of the Detailed Design

THE DETAILED DESIGN DATA DICTIONARY

AMOUNT   NUMBER FROM –10,000 TO +10,000
  answer to amount questions

AMOUNTWON NUMBER FROM –2,000 TO +10,000
  amount won during this hand

BANKLIMIT   NUMBER FROM 0   TO 10,000
  bank's credit limit

BET   NUMBER FROM 10   TO 500
  amount of the current bet

CARD   NUMBER FROM 1   TO 52
  the value of a card

CHIPS   NUMBER FROM 0   TO 12,000
  current value of player's chips

CHOICE   NUMBER FROM 1   TO 10
  answers to choice questions

COUNT   NUMBER FROM 1   TO 12,000
  general purpose counter

CURRENTHAND NUMBER FROM 1   TO 3
  indicates whose hand is currently being used

DATAOK   FLAG
  indicates when incoming data passes all edit checks

DEALERCOLUMN NUMBER FROM 1   TO 80
  the terminal screen column where the dealer's cards are shown

DEALERVALUE NUMBER FROM 2   TO 30
  the value of the dealer's hand

DECK   NUMERIC ARRAY (1 to 104) FROM 1 TO 52
   the remaining deck

DECKCOUNT   NUMBER FROM   1   TO 104
   the number of the next card to be dealt from the deck

DONE   FLAG
   indicates when a hand is done and bets should be settled

HANDCOUNT   NUMERIC ARRAY (1 TO 3) FROM 1 TO 15
   number of cards in each hand

HANDONE   ARRAY OF FLAGS (1 TO 3)
   indicates when each hand goes over twenty-one

HANDS   NUMERIC ARRAY (1 TO 3 BY 1 TO 15) FROM 1 TO 52
   the cards in each of the player's hand

HANDSPLAYD   NUMBER FROM   0   TO 1,000
   total number of hands played

HANDSWON   NUMBER FROM   -1000   TO +1000
   total number of hands won

HANDVALUE   NUMBER FROM   0   TO 30
   the value of the current hand

MAXBET   NUMBER FROM   0   TO 500
   maximum bet

MAXVAL   NUMBER FROM   0   TO 10,000
   maximum allowed value for editing input

MINBET   NUMBER FROM   0   TO 10
   minimum bet

MINVAL   NUMBER FROM   0   TO 10,000
   minimum allowed value for editing input

OPTIONS   NUMBER FROM   1   TO 6
   controls the allowable entries for editing choice input

PLAYLMIT   NUMBER FROM   0   TO 2,000
   player's credit limit

STRING   CHARACTER STRING (20 LONG)
   used to check YES/NO entries in INPUTCHOICES

SUIT   CHARACTER STRING ARRAY (1 TO 4) (8 LONG)
   contains the names of the card suits

V   NUMBER FROM   1   TO 30
   temporary variable used to evaluate a hand

VALUE   CHARACTER STRING ARRAY (1 TO 13) (5 LONG)
   contains the names of the card values

WONTHISHAND   NUMBER FROM   -500   TO +500
    amount won during this hand

X   NUMBER FROM   -10,000   TO +10,000
    general purpose work variable

THE DETAILED DESIGN FUNCTIONAL DICTIONARY

```
PROGRAM: BLACKJACK

    START (MAINLINE)

        CALL INITIALIZE
        CALL SELECTACTIV
        CALL TERMINATE

    END MAINLINE

END PROGRAM



PROCEDURE INITIALIZE

        SET UP THE VALUES IN THE SUIT ARRAY
        SET UP THE VALUES IN THE VALUE ARRAY
        CALL SHUFFLE
        PLAYLIMIT  = 2,000
        BANKLIMIT  = 10,000
        MINBET     = 10
        MAXBET     = 500
        CHIPS      = 0
        HANDSPLAYD = 0
        HANDSWON   = 0
        PRINT THE GREETING TO THE PLAYER
        WAIT FOR A <RETURN> TO CONTINUE

    RETURN
```

```
PROCEDURE SELECTACTIV

    REPEAT
        DISPLAY THE AVAILABLE SELECTIONS ON THE SCREEN
        OPTIONS = 6
        CALL INPUTCHOICES
        IF CHOICE NOT 6 THEN
            CASE CHOICE OF
                1:  CALL SHOWINSTRUCT
                2:  CALL BANKER
                3:  CALL RPTSTATUS
                4:  CALL SHUFFLE
                5:  CALL PLAYHAND
            END OF CASE
    UNTIL CHOICE = 6

RETURN




PROCEDURE TERMINATE

    CALL RPTSTATUS
    PRINT THE PARTING MESSAGE TO THE PLAYER
    WAIT FOR A <RETURN> TO CONTINUE

RETURN




PROCEDURE SHOWINSTRUCT

    PRINT INSTRUCTIONS
    WAIT FOR A <RETURN> TO CONTINUE
    PRINT INSTRUCTIONS
    WAIT FOR A <RETURN> TO CONTINUE

        .
        .
        .

RETURN
```

```
PROCEDURE BANKER

     DISPLAY A CHOICE FOR BUY OR CASH IN
     OPTIONS = 2
     CALL INPUTCHOICES
     IF CHOICE = 1 THEN
          CALL BUY
     ELSE
          CALL CASHIN

RETURN


PROCEDURE BUY

     IF PLAYLIMIT = 0 THEN
         DISPLAY "YOU HAVE NO MORE MONEY"
         RETURN
     MAXVAL = 10,000
     MINVAL = 0
     REPEAT
         DISPLAY "HOW MUCH DO YOU WANT TO BUY?"
         CALL INPUTAMOUNT
         IF AMOUNT > PLAYLIMIT THEN
              DISPLAY "YOU DO NOT HAVE ENOUGH MONEY FOR THAT"
              MAXVAL = PLAYLIMIT
     UNTIL AMOUNT <= PLAYLIMIT
     PLAYLIMIT = PLAYLIMIT - AMOUNT
     CHIPS     = CHIPS     + AMOUNT

RETURN

PROCEDURE CASHIN

     IF CHIPS = 0 THEN
         DISPLAY "YOU HAVE NO MORE CHIPS"
         RETURN
     MAXVAL = 10,000
     MINVAL = 0
     REPEAT
         DISPLAY "HOW MUCH DO YOU WANT TO CASH IN?"
         CALL INPUTAMOUNT
         IF AMOUNT > CHIPS THEN
              DISPLAY "YOU DO NOT HAVE ENOUGH CHIPS FOR THAT"
              MAXVAL = CHIPS
     UNTIL AMOUNT <= CHIPS
     PLAYLIMIT = PLAYLIMIT + AMOUNT
     CHIPS     = CHIPS     - AMOUNT

RETURN
```

```
PROCEDURE RPTSTATUS

     DISPLAY "NUMBER OF HANDS PLAYED",HANDSPLAYD
     DISPLAY "NUMBER OF HANDS"
     IF HANDSWON >= 0 THEN
         DISPLAY "WON"
     ELSE
         DISPLAY "LOST"
     DISPLAY ABS(HANDSWON)
     DISPLAY "PERCENTAGE OF HANDS"
     IF HANDSWON >= 0 THEN
         DISPLAY "WON"
     ELSE
         DISPLAY "LOST"
     IF HANDSPLAYD = 0 THEN
         DISPLAY 0
     ELSE
         DISPLAY (ABS(HANDSWON)/HANDSPLAYD) * 100, "%"
     DISPLAY "CURRENT VALUE OF CASH",PLAYLIMIT
     DISPLAY "CURRENT VALUE OF CHIPS",CHIPS
     DISPLAY "CURRENT FUNDS", (PLAYLIMIT + CHIPS)
     DISPLAY "TOTAL AMOUNT"
     IF AMOUNTWON >= 0 THEN
         DISPLAY "WON"
     ELSE
         DISPLAY "LOST"
     DISPLAY ABS(AMOUNTWON)
     DISPLAY "AVERAGE"
     IF AMOUNTWON >= 0 THEN
         DISPLAY "WON"
     ELSE
         DISPLAY "LOST"
     DISPLAY "PER HAND"
     IF HANDSPLAYD = 0 THEN
         DISPLAY 0
     ELSE
     DISPLAY (ABS(AMOUNTWON) / HANDSPLAYD)

     WAIT FOR <RETURN> TO CONTINUE

RETURN


PROCEDURE PLAYHAND

     REPEAT
         DONE = FALSE
         CALL BETTING
         IF BET < MINBET THEN
             RETURN
```

```
            CALL DEAL
            CALL NATURALS
            IF NOT DONE THEN
                    IF PLAYER HAS A PAIR THEN
                            CALL SPLITPAIRS
                    CALL PLAYER
                    IF NOT DONE THEN
                            CALL DEALER
            CALL SETTLE
            DISPLAY "PLAY AGAIN?"
            OPTIONS = 1
            CALL INPUTCHOICES
        UNTIL CHOICE = 2

RETURN

PROCEDURE BETTING

        BET = -1
        REPEAT
            DISPLAY "HOW MUCH DO YOU WISH TO BET?"
            MAXVAL = 10,000
            MINVAL = 0
            CALL INPUTAMOUNT
            IF AMOUNT > MAXBET THEN
                    DISPLAY "THAT IS MORE THAN THE HOUSE LIMIT"
                    MAXVAL = MAXBET
            ELSE
                    IF (AMOUNT < MINBET) AND
                       (AMOUNT <> 0) THEN
                            DISPLAY "THAT IS UNDER THE HOUSE MINIMUM"
                            MINVAL = MINBET
                    ELSE
                            IF AMOUNT > CHIPS THEN
                                    DISPLAY "YOU DO NOT HAVE THAT MUCH"
                                    MAXVAL = CHIPS
                            ELSE
                                    BET = AMOUNT
        UNTIL BET <> -1

RETURN


PROCEDURE DEAL

        DISPLAY "   PLAYER           DEALER   "

        CALL GETCARD
        HANDS(2,1) = CARD
        MOVE CURSOR TO COLUMN ONE OF THE NEXT LINE
        CALL PRINTCARD
```

```
        CALL GETCARD
        HANDS(1,1) = CARD
        MOVE CURSOR TO COLUMN TWO OF THE SAME LINE
        DISPLAY "XXXXX"

        CALL GETCARD
        HANDS(2,2) = CARD
        MOVE CURSON TO COLUMN ONE OF NEXT LINE
        CALL PRINTCARD

        CALL GETCARD
        HANDS(1,2) = CARD
        MOVE CURSOR TO COLUMN TWO OF THE SAME LINE
        CALL PRINTCARD

        MOVE CURSOR TO THE NEXT LINE
        HANDCOUNT(1) = 2
        HANDCOUNT(2) = 2
        HANDCOUNT(3) = 0
RETURN




PROCEDURE NATURALS

        CURRENTHAND = 1
        CALL EVALUATE
        IF HANDVALUE = 21 THEN
            DONE = TRUE
RETURN




PROCEDURE SPLITPAIRS

        DISPLAY "DO YOU WISH TO SPLIT YOUR PAIR?"
        OPTIONS = 1
        CALL INPUTCHOICES
        IF CHOICE = 1 THEN
            IF CHIPS < (2 * BET) THEN
                DISPLAY "YOU CAN'T COVER THE BET"
            ELSE
                HANDS(3,1) = HANDS(2,2)
                DISPLAY " PLAYER-1    PLAYER-2    DEALER  "
                MOVE CURSOR TO COLUMN ONE
                CARD = HANDS(2,1)
```

```
                CALL PRINTCARD
                MOVE CURSOR TO COLUMN TWO OF THE SAME LINE
                CARD = HANDS(3,1)
                CALL PRINTCARD
                MOVE CURSOR TO COLUMN THREE OF THE SAME LINE
                DISPLAY "XXXX"
                MOVE CURSOR TO COLUMN ONE OF THE NEXT LINE
                CALL GETCARD
                HANDS(2,2) = CARD
                CALL PRINTCARD
                MOVE CURSOR TO COLUMN TWO OF THE SAME LINE
                CALL GETCARD
                HANDS(3,2) = CARD
                CALL PRINTCARD
                MOVE CURSOR TO COLUMN THREE OF THE SAVE LINE
                CARD = HANDS(1,2)
                CALL PRINTCARD
                MOVE CURSOR TO START OF NEXT LINE

RETURN




PROCEDURE PLAYER

        HANDONE(2) = FALSE
        IF HANDCOUNT(3) = 0 THEN
                HANDONE(3) = TRUE
        ELSE
                HANDONE(3) = FALSE

        REPEAT
                DISPLAY "WHAT NEXT?"
                IF HANDCOUNT(3) = 0 THEN
                        DISPLAY "DO YOU STAND ON THIS HAND?"
                        OPTIONS = 1
                ELSE
                        DISPLAY "1: DONE  2: CARD FOR 1  3: CARD FOR 2"
                        OPTIONS = 3
                CALL INPUTCHOICES
                IF CHOICE <> 1 THEN
                        CURRENTHAND = CHOICE
                        CALL PLAYERHAND
        UNTIL (CHOICE = 1) OR
                (HANDONE(2) = TRUE  AND  HANDONE(3) = TRUE)

RETURN
```

```
PROCEDURE PLAYERHAND

    IF HANDONE(CURRENTHAND) = TRUE THEN
        DISPLAY "THAT HAND IS ALREADY OVER 21"
        RETURN
    MOVE CURSOR TO COLUMN (CURRENTHAND - 1)
    CALL GETCARD
    CALL PRINTCARD
    HANDCOUNT(CURRENTHAND) = HANDCOUNT(CURRENTHAND) + 1
    HANDS(CURRENTHAND,HANDCOUNT(CURRENTHAND)) = CARD
    CALL EVALUATE
    IF HANDVALUE > 21 THEN
        DISPLAY "TOO BAD, PLAYER GOES OVER 21"
        HANDONE(CURRENTHAND) = TRUE

RETURN




PROCEDURE DEALER

    IF HANDCOUNT(3) = 0 THEN
        DEALERCOLUMN = 2
    ELSE
        DEALERCOLUMN = 3
    MOVE CURSOR TO DEALERCOLUMN OF NEXT LINE
    CARD = HANDS(1,1)
    CALL PRINTCARD
    MOVE CURSOR TO DEALERCOLUMN OF NEXT LINE
    CARD = HANDS(1,2)
    CALL PRINTCARD

    CURRENTHAND = 1
    CALL EVALUATE
    WHILE (HANDVALUE < 17) DO
        MOVE CURSOR TO DEALERCOLUMN OF NEXT LINE
        CALL GETCARD
        CALL PRINTCARD
        HANDCOUNT(1) = HANDCOUNT(1) + 1
        HANDS(1,HANDCOUNT(1)) = CARD
        CALL EVALUATE
    ENDLOOP

    IF HANDVALUE <= 17 THEN
        DISPLAY "THE DEALER STANDS AT",HANDVALUE
    ELSE
        DISPLAY "THE DEALER GOES OVER"

RETURN
```

```
PROCEDURE SETTLE

     CURRENTHAND = 1
     CALL EVALUATE
     DEALERVALUE = HANDVALUE
     IF (HANDVALUE = 21) AND
        (HANDCOUNT(1) = 2) THEN
             CALL DEALERNATURAL
     ELSE
             IF HANDVALUE > 21 THEN
                     CALL DEALEROVER
             ELSE
                     CALL DEALERSTANDS

RETURN




PROCEDURE DEALERNATURAL

     DO FOR CURRENTHAND = 2 TO 3
             IF HANDCOUNT(CURRENTHAND) = 0 THEN
                     RETURN
             IF CURRENTHAND = 3 THEN
                     DISPLAY "FOR THE PLAYER'S SECOND HAND:"
             CALL EVALUATE
             IF HANDVALUE = 21 THEN
                     DISPLAY "STANDOFF WITH NATURALS"
             ELSE
                     DISPLAY "DEALER WINS WITH A NATURAL"
                     CHIPS = CHIPS - BET
                     BANKLIMIT = BANKLIMIT + BET
     NEXT CURRENTHAND

RETURN

PROCEDURE DEALEROVER

     DO FOR CURRENTHAND = 2 TO 3
             IF HANDCOUNT(CURRENTHAND) = 0 THEN
                     RETURN
             IF CURRENTHAND = 3 THEN
                     DISPLAY "FOR THE PLAYER'S SECOND HAND:"
             CALL EVALUATE
             IF (HANDVALUE = 21) AND
                (HANDCOUNT(CURRENTHAND)) = 2) THEN
                     DISPLAY "PLAYER WINS WITH A NATURAL"
                     CHIPS = CHIPS + (1.5 * BET)
                     BANKLIMIT = BANKLIMIT - (1.5 * BET)
```

```
        ELSE
            IF HANDVALUE > 21 THEN
                DISPLAY "PLAYER LOSES"
                CHIPS = CHIPS - BET
                BANKLIMIT = BANKLIMIT + BET
            ELSE
                DISPLAY "PLAYER WINS"
                CHIPS = CHIPS + BET
                BANKLIMIT = BANKLIMIT - BET
    NEXT CURRENTHAND
    IF BANKLIMIT < 0 THEN
        CALL BROKENBANK

RETURN




PROCEDURE DEALERSTANDS

    DO FOR CURRENTHAND = 2 TO 3
        IF HANDCOUNT(CURRENTHAND) = 0 THEN
            RETURN
        IF CURRENTHAND = 3 THEN
            DISPLAY "FOR THE PLAYER'S SECOND HAND:"
        CALL EVALUATE
        IF (HANDVALUE = 21) AND
            (HANDCOUNT(CURRENTHAND)) = 2) THEN
                DISPLAY "PLAYER WINS WITH A NATURAL"
                CHIPS = CHIPS + (1.5 * BET)
                BANKLIMIT = BANKLIMIT - (1.5 * BET)
        ELSE
            IF HANDVALUE < DEALERVALUE THEN
                DISPLAY "PLAYER LOSES"
                CHIPS = CHIPS - BET
                BANKLIMIT = BANKLIMIT + BET
            ELSE
                IF HANDVALUE > DEALERVALUE THEN
                    DISPLAY "PLAYER WINS"
                    CHIPS = CHIPS + BET
                    BANKLIMIT = BANKLIMIT - BET
                ELSE
                    DISPLAY "STANDOFF WITH DEALER"
    NEXT CURRENTHAND
    IF BANKLIMIT < 0 THEN
        CALL BROKENBANK

RETURN
```

```
PROCEDURE BROKENBANK

     DISPLAY "****** YOU HAVE BROKEN THE BANK ******"
     DISPLAY AN APPROPRIATE MESSAGE ABOUT FURTHER BETS
     BANKLIMIT = 0

RETURN




FUNCTION CARDVALUE (X)

RETURN:  X - (INT(X / 13) * 13)




PROCEDURE PRINTCARD

     DISPLAY "THE", VALUE(CARDVALUE(CARD)),
             "OF",  SUIT(INT((CARD-1)/13) + 1)

RETURN




PROCEDURE EVALUATE

     HANDVALUE = 0
     DO FOR COUNT = 1 TO HANDCOUNT(CURRENTHAND)
          V = CARDVALUE(HANDS(CURRENTHAND,COUNT))
          IF V > 10 THEN
               V = 10
          IF V = 1 THEN
               V = 11
          HANDVALUE = HANDVALUE + V
     END LOOP

     COUNT = 1
     DO WHILE (HANDVALUE > 21) AND
             (COUNT <= HANDCOUNT(CURRENTHAND))
          IF CARDVALUE(HANDS(CURRENTHAND,COUNT))=1 THEN
               HANDVALUE = HANDVALUE - 10
          COUNT = COUNT + 1
     END LOOP

RETURN
```

```
GETCARD

    IF DECKCOUNT > 104 THEN
        CALL SHUFFLE
    CARD = DECK(DECKCOUNT)
    DECKCOUNT = DECKCOUNT + 1

RETURN




PROCEDURE SHUFFLE

    DO FOR COUNT = 1 TO 104
        DECK(COUNT) = 0
    END LOOP

    DO FOR COUNT = 1 TO 2
        DO FOR CARD = 1 TO 52
            X = RANDOM NUMBER FROM 1 TO 104
            WHILE DECK(X) <> 0 DO
                X = X + 1
                IF X > 104 THEN
                    X = 1
            END LOOP
            DECK (X) = CARD
        END LOOP
    END LOOP

RETURN




PROCEDURE INPUTAMOUNT

    DATAOK = FALSE
    REPEAT
        INPUT AMOUNT FROM THE TERMINAL
        IF AMOUNT IS NOT NUMERIC THEN
            DISPLAY "YOU MUST ENTER A NUMBER"
        ELSE
            IF AMOUNT < MINVALUE THEN
                DISPLAY "ENTER A NUMBER GREATER THAN",
                        MINVALUE
            ELSE
                IF AMOUNT > MAXVALUE THEN
                    DISPLAY "ENTER A NUMBER LESS THAN",
                            MAXVALUE
```

```
                    ELSE
                        IF AMOUNT <> INT(AMOUNT) THEN
                              DISPLAY "ENTER AN INTEGER NUMBER"
                        ELSE
                              DATAOK = TRUE
        UNTIL DATAOK = TRUE

RETURN




PROCEDURE INPUTCHOICES

    DATAOK = FALSE
    REPEAT
        INPUT STRING FROM THE TERMINAL
        IF OPTIONS = 1 THEN
            IF LENGTH OF STRING = 0 THEN
                DISPLAY "PLEASE ENTER YES OR NO"
            ELSE
                IF (FIRST CHARACTER <> "Y") AND
                   (FIRST CHARACTER <> "N") THEN
                    DISPLAY "PLEASE ENTER YES OR NO"
                ELSE
                    DATA = OK
                    IF FIRST CHARACTER = "Y" THEN
                        CHOICE = 1
                    ELSE
                        CHOICE = 2
        ELSE
            IF STRING IS NOT NUMERIC THEN
                DISPLAY "YOU MUST ENTER A NUMBER"
            ELSE
                CHOICE = VALUE OF STRING
                IF CHOICE < 1 THEN
                    DISPLAY "ENTER A NUMBER FROM 1 TO",
                            OPTIONS
                ELSE
                    IF CHOICE > OPTIONS THEN
                        DISPLAY "ENTER A NUMBER FROM 1 TO",
                                OPTIONS
                    ELSE
                        IF CHOICE <> INT(CHOICE) THEN
                              DISPLAY "ENTER AN INTEGER NUMBER"
                        ELSE
                              DATAOK = TRUE
        UNTIL DATAOK = TRUE

RETURN
```

SYSTEM STRUCTURE

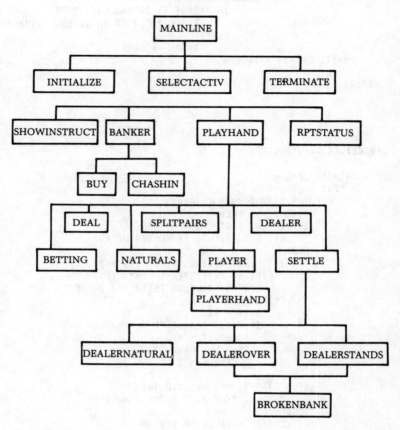

UTILITY SUBROUTINES

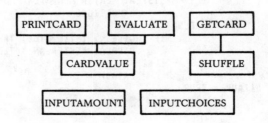

Appendix E

Results of the Implementation

VARIABLE NAMES FOR THE BASIC PROGRAM

AMOUNT	A
AMOUNTWON	A1
BANKLIMIT	L1
BET	B
CARD	C
CHIPS	C1
CHOICE	C2
COUNT	C9
CURRENTHAND	H8
DATAOK	D8
DEALERCOLUMN	D7
DEALERVALUE	D2
DECK	D(204)
DECKCOUNT	D1
DONE	D9
HANDCOUNT	H1(3)
HANDONE	H9(3)
HANDS	H(3,15)
HANDSPLAYD	H2
HANDSWON	H3
HANDVALUE	H4
MAXBET	M1
MAXVAL	M2
MINBET	M3
MINVAL	M4
OPTIONS	X9

PLAYLIMIT	L2
STRING	S1$
SUIT	S$(4)
V	V
VALUE	V$(13)
WONTHISHAND	W
X	X

BLACKJACK AS IMPLEMENTED IN BASIC

```
10       REM  BLACKJACK    VERSION 1.0
20       REM      THIS PROGRAM WILL PLAY THE PART OF THE
30       REM      DEALER IN A GAME OF BLACKJACK PLAYED
40       REM      ACCORDING TO HOYLE'S RULES
50       REM
60       REM  WRITTEN BY JACK EMMERICHS,   1/1/82
70       REM  (COPYRIGHT MESSAGE GOES HERE IF YOU WANT ONE)
80       REM
90       REM  CARDVALUE FUNCTION AND ARRAYS
100      REM
110 DEF FNC(X)=X-(INT((X-1)/13)*13)
120      REM
130 DIM D(204), H(3,15), H1(3), H9(3), S$(4), V$(13)
140      REM
150      REM  PROGRAM MAINLINE
160      REM
170 GOSUB 240
180 GOSUB 610
190 GOSUB 900
195      REM
200 END
210      REM
220      REM  INITIALIZATION PROCEDURE
230      REM
240 RANDOMIZE
245      REM  INITIALIZE ARRAYS
250 DATA "SPADES","HEARTS","DIAMONDS","CLUBS"
260 DATA "ACE","2","3","4","5","6","7","8","9","10"
270 DATA "JACK","QUEEN","KING"
280 FOR X=1 TO 4
290   READ S$(X)
300 NEXT X
310 FOR X=1 TO 13
320   READ V$(X)
330 NEXT X
340 GOSUB 64320
345      REM  INITIALIZE VARIABLES
```

```
350   L1=10000
360   L2=2000
370   M1=500
380   M3=10
390   C1=0
400   H2=0
410   H3=0
420   E1$="Please enter YES or NO"
430   E2$="please enter a number from 1 to "
435      REM   PRINT WELCOME MESSAGE
440   PRINT
450   PRINT "Welcome to the Blackjack table. We will be playing"
460   PRINT "    by the rules of Blackjack according to Hoyle."
470   PRINT "    the house limits on bets are:"
480   PRINT "         minimum bet: $";M3
490   PRINT "         maximum bet: $";M1
500   PRINT "    The house currently has $";L1;" in the bank."
510   PRINT "    You currently have $";L2;" in cash."
520   PRINT "    You may exchange cash and chips at the bank."
530   PRINT
540   PRINT "    Please sit down and play for a while."
550   PRINT "         (Press RETURN to continue)"
560   INPUT "",S1$
570   RETURN
580      REM
590      REM  SELECT THE NEXT ACTIVITY
600      REM
610   PRINT
620   PRINT "    You may do any of the following things:"
630   PRINT
640   PRINT "         1.  Display the rules of the game."
650   PRINT "         2.  Visit the bank."
660   PRINT "         3.  Display the current status of the game."
670   PRINT "         4.  Shuffle the deck."
680   PRINT "         5.  Play a hand of cards."
690   PRINT "         6.  Quit the game."
700   X9=6
710   GOSUB 64710
720   IF C2=6 THEN RETURN
730   IF C2<>1 THEN GOTO 760
740      GOSUB 1000
750      GOTO 610
760   IF C2<>2 THEN GOTO 790
770      GOSUB 1130
780      GOTO 610
790   IF C2<>3 THEN GOTO 820
800      GOSUB 1600
810      GOTO 610
820   IF C2<>4 THEN GOTO 850
830      GOSUB 64320
840      GOTO 610
850   GOSUB 1880
860   GOTO 610
```

```
870      REM
880      REM   TERMINATION PROCEDURE
890      REM
900   GOSUB 1600
910   PRINT
920   PRINT "Thank you for the game, please come again sometime."
930   PRINT "   (Press RETURN to continue)"
940   INPUT "",S1$
950   RETURN
960      REM
970      REM   SHOW INSTRUCTIONS
980      REM
1000  PRINT
1010  PRINT
1020  PRINT "The rules for this game are in the book:"
1030  PRINT
1040  PRINT "         HOYLE UP-TO-DATE"
1050  PRINT "   OFFICIAL RULES OF CARD GAMES"
1060  PRINT
1070  PRINT "Please read the rules there.
1080  PRINT
1085  PRINT "         Press RETURN to continue"
1086  INPUT "",S1$
1090  RETURN
1100     REM
1110     REM   BANKER
1120     REM
1130  PRINT
1140  PRINT "   You may do either of the following:"
1150  PRINT
1160  PRINT "      1. Buy more chips"
1170  PRINT "      2. Cash in your chips"
1180  X9=2
1190  GOSUB 64710
1200  IF C2=1 THEN GOSUB 1260 ELSE GOSUB 1430
1220  RETURN
1230     REM
1240     REM   BUY CHIPS
1250     REM
1260  IF L2>0 THEN GOTO 1290
1270    PRINT "You have no more money."
1280    RETURN
1290  M2=10000
1300  M4=0
1310  PRINT "How much do you wish to buy?"
1320  GOSUB 64510
1330  IF A<=L2 THEN GOTO 1370
1340    PRINT "You only have $";L2
1350    M2=L2
1360    GOTO 1310
1370  L2=L2-A
1380  C1=C1+A
1390  RETURN
```

```
1400      REM
1410      REM   CASH IN CHIPS
1420      REM
1430 IF C1>0 THEN 1460
1440   PRINT "You have no more chips."
1450   RETURN
1460 M2=10000
1470 M4=0
1480 PRINT "How many chips do you wish to cash in?"
1490 GOSUB 64510
1500 IF A<=C1 THEN GOTO 1540
1510   PRINT "You only have";C1;" chips."
1520   M2=C1
1530   GOTO 1480
1540 L2=L2+A
1550 C1=C1-A
1560 RETURN
1570      REM
1580      REM   REPORT GAME STATUS
1590      REM
1600 PRINT
1610 PRINT "Number of hands played:";H2
1620 PRINT "Number of hands won:";ABS(H3)
1650 PRINT "Percentage of hands won:";
1670 IF H2=0 THEN PRINT 0;"%" ELSE PRINT (ABS(H3)/H2)*100;"%"
1690 PRINT
1700 PRINT "Current value of your cash: $";L2
1710 PRINT "Current value of your chips: $";C1
1720 PRINT "Your current funds: $";L2+C1
1730 PRINT
1740 PRINT "Total amount ";
1750 IF A1>=0 THEN PRINT "won: $"; ELSE PRINT "lost: $";
1760 PRINT ABS(A1)
1770 PRINT "Average amount ";
1780 IF A1>=0 THEN PRINT "won"; ELSE PRINT "lost";
1790 PRINT " per hand: $";
1800 IF H2=0 THEN PRINT 0 ELSE PRINT ABS(A1)/H2
1810 PRINT
1820 PRINT "     Press RETURN to continue"
1830 INPUT "",S1$
1840 RETURN
1850      REM
1860      REM   PLAY A HAND OF CARDS
1870      REM
1880 D9=0
1890 GOSUB 2050
1900 IF B<H3 THEN RETURN
1910 GOSUB 2270
1920 GOSUB 2510
1930 IF D9<>0 THEN GOTO 1970
1940   IF FNC(H(2,1))=FNC(H(2,2)) THEN GOSUB 2580
1950   GOSUB 2910
1960   IF D9=0 THEN GOSUB 3260
```

```
1970 GOSUB 3540
1980 PRINT "Play again?"
1990 X9=1
2000 GOSUB 64710
2010 IF C2=1 THEN GOTO 1880 ELSE RETURN
2020      REM
2030      REM   BETTING
2040      REM
2050 M2=10000
2060 M4=0
2070 PRINT "How much do yo wish to bet?"
2080 GOSUB 64510
2090 IF A<=M1 THEN GOTO 2130
2100   PRINT "That is more than the $";M1;" house limit."
2110   M2=M1
2120   GOTO 2070
2130 IF A=0 THEN GOTO 2180
2140 IF A>=M3 THEN GOTO 2180
2150   PRINT "That is below the $";M3;" house minimum."
2170   GOTO 2070
2180 IF A<=C1 THEN GOTO 2220
2190   PRINT "You only have $";C1;" in chips."
2200   M2=C1
2210   GOTO 2070
2220 B=A
2230 RETURN
2240      REM
2250      REM   DEAL THE CARDS
2260      REM
2270 PRINT
2280 PRINT "PLAYER";TAB(21);"DEALER"
2290 PRINT
2300 GOSUB 64250
2310 H(2,1)=C
2320 GOSUB 64030
2330 GOSUB 64250
2340 H(1,1)=C
2350 PRINT TAB(21);"XXXXX"
2360 GOSUB 64250
2370 H(2,2)=C
2380 GOSUB 64030
2390 GOSUB 64250
2400 H(1,2)=C
2410 PRINT TAB(21);
2420 GOSUB 64030
2430 PRINT
2440 H1(1)=2
2450 H1(2)=2
2460 H1(3)=0
2470 RETURN
2480      REM
2490      REM   HANDLE DEALER NATURALS
2500      REM
```

```
2510 H8=1
2520 GOSUB 64080
2530 IF H4=21 THEN D9=-1
2540 RETURN
2550      REM
2560      REM   SPLIT A PAIR OF CARDS
2570      REM
2580 PRINT "Do you wish to split your pair?"
2590 X9=1
2600 GOSUB 64710
2610 IF C2=2 THEN RETURN
2620 IF C1>=2*B THEN GOTO 2650
2630    PRINT "You cannot cover the bet."
2640    RETURN
2650 H(3,1)=H(2,2)
2660 PRINT
2670 PRINT "PLAYER-1";TAB(21);"PLAYER-2";TAB(42);"DEALER"
2680 PRINT
2690 C=H(2,1)
2700 GOSUB 64030
2710 PRINT TAB(21);
2720 C=H(3,1)
2730 GOSUB 64030
2740 PRINT TAB(42);"XXXXX"
2750 GOSUB 64250
2760 H(2,2)=C
2770 GOSUB 64030
2780 GOSUB 64250
2790 H(3,2)=C
2800 PRINT TAB(21);
2810 GOSUB 64030
2820 C=H(1,2)
2830 PRINT TAB(42);
2840 GOSUB 64030
2850 PRINT
2860 H1(3)=2
2870 RETURN
2880      REM
2890      REM   PLAY THE PLAYER'S CARDS
2900      REM
2910 H9(2)=0
2920 IF H1(3)=0 THEN H9(3)=-1 ELSE H9(3)=0
2930 PRINT "What next?"
2940 IF H1(3)<>0 THEN GOTO 2980
2950    PRINT "Stand on this hand?"
2960    X9=1
2970    GOTO 3000
2980 PRINT "1: Done.  2: Card for 1.  3: Card for 2."
2990 X9=3
3000 GOSUB 64710
3010 IF C2=1 THEN RETURN
3020 H8=C2
3030 GOSUB 3090
```

```
3040 IF H9(2)=0 OR H9(3)=0 THEN GOTO 2930
3045 D9=-1
3050 RETURN
3060     REM
3070     REM     PLAY A PLAYER'S CARD
3080     REM
3090 IF H9(H8)=0 THEN GOTO 3120
3100   PRINT "That hand is already over 21."
3110   RETURN
3120 GOSUB 64250
3130 IF H8=3 THEN PRINT TAB(21);
3140 GOSUB 64030
3150 PRINT
3160 H1(H8)=H1(H8)+1
3170 H(H8,H1(H8))=C
3180 GOSUB 64080
3190 IF H4<=21 THEN 3220
3200   PRINT "Too bad, Player goes over 21."
3210   H9(H8)=-1
3220 RETURN
3230     REM
3240     REM  PLAY THE DEALER'S HAND
3250     REM
3260 IF H1(3)=0 THEN D7=21 ELSE D7=42
3270 PRINT TAB(D7);
3280 C=H(1,1)
3290 GOSUB 64030
3300 PRINT
3310 PRINT TAB(D7);
3320 C=H(1,2)
3330 GOSUB 64030
3340 H8=1
3350 GOSUB 64080
3360 IF H4>17 THEN GOTO 3450
3370   GOSUB 64250
3380   PRINT
3390   PRINT TAB(D7);
3400   GOSUB 64030
3410   H1(1)=H1(1)+1
3420   H(1,H1(1))=C
3430   GOSUB 64080
3440   GOTO 3350
3450 PRINT
3460 IF H4>21 THEN GOTO 3490
3470   PRINT "The dealer stands at";H4
3480   GOTO 3500
3490 PRINT "The dealer goes over 21."
3500 RETURN
3510     REM
3520     REM  SETTLE THE BETS
3530     REM
3540 H8=1
3550 GOSUB 64080
```

```
3560 D2=H4
3570 IF H4<>21 OR H1(1)<>2 THEN GOTO 3600
3580    GOSUB 3680
3590    GOTO 3640
3600 IF H4<=21 THEN GOTO 3630
3610    GOSUB 3830
3620    GOTO 3640
3630 GOSUB 4070
3640 RETURN
3650       REM
3660       REM    DEALER HAS NATURAL
3670       REM
3680 PRINT
3681 PRINT "Dealer has a natural!"
3682 PRINT TAB(21);
3683 C=H(1,1)
3684 GOSUB 64030
3685 PRINT
3686 PRINT TAB(21);
3687 C=H(1,2)
3688 GOSUB 64030
3689 PRINT
3690 FOR H8=2 TO 3
3692    IF H1(H8)=0 THEN RETURN
3695    H2=H2+1
3700    IF H8=3 THEN PRINT "For the player's second hand:"
3710    GOSUB 64080
3720    IF H4<>21 THEN GOTO 3750
3730       PRINT "Standoff with naturals."
3740       GOTO 3780
3750    A1=A1-B
3760    C1=C1-B
3770    L1=L1+B
3780 NEXT H8
3790 RETURN
3800 -     REM
3810       REM    DEALER GOES OVER 21
3820       REM
3830 FOR H8=2 TO 3
3840    IF H1(H8)=0 THEN GOTO 4010
3845    H2=H2+1
3850    IF H8=3 THEN PRINT "For the player's second hand:"
3860    GOSUB 64080
3870    IF H4<>21 THEN GOTO 3930
3880    IF H1(H8)<>2 THEN GOTO 3930
3890       PRINT "Player wins with a natural, house pays extra."
3900       C1=C1+(1.5*B)
3910       L1=L1-(1.5*B)
3915       A1=A1+(1.5*B)
3916       H3=H3+1
3920       GOTO 4010
3930    IF H4<=21 THEN GOTO 3980
3940       PRINT "ERROR, YOU SHOULD NEVER GET HERE""
```

```
3970      GOTO 4010
3980      PRINT "Player wins!"
3990      C1=C1+B
4000      L1=L1-B
4005      A1=A1+B
4006      H3=H3+1
4010 NEXT H8
4020 IF L1<0 THEN GOSUB 4340
4030 RETURN
4040      REM
4050      REM   DEALER STANDS
4060      REM
4070 FOR H8=2 TO 3
4080    IF H1(H8)=0 THEN GOTO 4280
4085    H2=H2+1
4090    IF H8=3 THEN PRINT "For the player's second hand:"
4100    GOSUB 64080
4110    IF H4<>21 THEN GOTO 4170
4120    IF H1(H8)<>2 THEN GOTO 4170
4130      PRINT "Player wins with a natural, house pays extra."
4140      C1=C1+(1.5*B)
4150      L1=L1-(1.5*B)
4155      A1=A1+(1.5*B)
4156      H3=H3+1
4160      GOTO 4280
4170    IF H4>=D2 AND H4<=21 THEN GOTO 4220
4180      PRINT "Player loses."
4190      C1=C1-B
4200      L1=L1+B
4205      A1=A1-B
4210      GOTO 4280
4220    IF H4=D2 THEN GOTO 4270
4230      PRINT "Player wins!"
4240      C1=C1+B
4250      L1=L1-B
4255      A1=A1+B
4256      H3=H3+1
4260      GOTO 4280
4270    PRINT "Standoff with the dealer, nobody wins."
4280 NEXT H8
4290 IF L1<0 THEN GOSUB 4340
4300 RETURN
4310      REM
4320      REM   YOU BROKE THE BANK!
4330      REM
4340 PRINT
4350 PRINT "****** YOU HAVE BROKEN THE BANK ******"
4360 PRINT
4370 PRINT "The bank connot cover any more of its losses."
4380 PRINT "If you continue to play you will only lose"
4390 PRINT "   what you now have."
4400 PRINT
4410 L1=0
```

```
4420 C1=1200-L2
4430 RETURN
64000      REM
64010      REM   PRINTCARD
64020      REM
64030 PRINT V$(FNC(C));" OF ";S$(INT((C-1)/13)+1);
64040 RETURN
64050      REM
64060      REM   EVALUATE
64070      REM
64080 H4=0
64090 FOR C9=1 TO H1(H8)
64100   V=FNC(H(H8,C9))
64110   IF V>10 THEN V=10
64120   IF V=1 THEN V=11
64130   H4=H4+V
64140 NEXT C9
64145           REM   ADJUST FOR ACES
64150 C9=1
64160 IF H4<=21 THEN GOTO 64210
64170 IF C9>H1(H8) THEN 64210
64180   IF FNC(H(H8,C9))=1 THEN H4=H4-10
64190   C9=C9+1
64200 GOTO 64160
64210 RETURN
64220      REM
64230      REM   GET A CARD
64240      REM
64250 IF D1>104 THEN GOSUB 64320
64260 C=D(D1)
64270 D1=D1+1
64280 RETURN
64290      REM
64300      REM   SHUFFLE
64310      REM
64320 PRINT
64322 PRINT "Reshuffle the cards."
64325      REM   INITIALIZE DECK ARRAY
64330 FOR C9=1 TO 104
64340   D(C9)=0
64350 NEXT C9
64355      REM   LOAD NEW ARRAY
64360 FOR C9=1 TO 2
64370   FOR C=1 TO 52
64380     X=INT(RND(1)*104)+1
64390     IF D(X)=0 THEN GOTO 64430
64395           REM   FIND AN EMPTY POSTITION
64400       X=X+1
64410       IF X>104 THEN X=1
64420     GOTO 64390
64430     D(X)=C
64440   NEXT C
64450 NEXT C9
```

```
64460 D1=1
64470 RETURN
64480     REM
64490     REM  INPUT AND EDIT AN AMOUNT
64500     REM
64510 PRINT
64520 PRINT "Your amount: ";
64530 INPUT S1$
64540 A=VAL(S1$)
64550 IF STR$(A)=" "+S1$ THEN GOTO 64580
64560   PRINT "Please enter a number"
64570   GOTO 64520
64580 IF A>=M4 THEN GOTO 64610
64590   PRINT "Please enter an amount no less than ";M4
64600   GOTO 64520
64610 IF A<=M2 THEN GOTO 64640
64620   PRINT "Please enter an amount no greater than ";M2
64630   GOTO 64520
64640 IF A=INT(A) THEN GOTO 64670
64650   PRINT "Please enter an integer number"
64660   GOTO 64520
64670 RETURN
64680     REM
64690     REM  INPUT AND EDIT A CHOICE
64700     REM
64710 PRINT
64720 PRINT "Your choice: ";
64730 INPUT S1$
64740 IF X9<>1 THEN GOTO 64850
64750          REM  EDIT YES/NO
64760   IF LEN(S1$)>0 THEN GOTO 64790
64770     PRINT E1$
64780     GOTO 64720
64790   IF LEFT$(S1$,1)="Y" OR LEFT$(S1$,1)="N" THEN GOTO 64820
64800     PRINT E1$
64810     GOTO 64720
64820   IF LEFT$(S1$,1)="Y" THEN C2=1 ELSE C2=2
64830   RETURN
64840          REM  EDIT CHOICES
64850 C2=VAL(S1$)
64860 IF STR$(C2)=" "+S1$ THEN GOTO 64890
64870   PRINT E2$;X9
64880   GOTO 64720
64890 IF C2>=1 AND C2<=X9 THEN GOTO 64920
64900   PRINT E2$;X9
64910   GOTO 64720
64920 IF C2=INT(C2) THEN GOTO 64950
64930   PRINT "Please enter an integer number"
64940   GOTO 64720
64950 RETURN
```

VARIABLE NAMES FOR THE PASCAL PROGRAM

DATA NAMES

AMOUNT	AMOUNT
AMOUNTWON	AMTWON
BANKLIMIT	BANKLMIT
BET	BET
CARD	CARD
CHIPS	CHIPS
CHOICE	CHOICE
COUNT	COUNT
CURRENTHAND	THISHAND
DATAOK	DATAOK
DEALERCOLUMN	DLRCOLM
DEALERVALUE	DEALERV
DECK	DECK[204]
DECKCOUNT	DECKNEXT
DONE	DONE
HANDCOUNT	HANDCNT[3]
HANDONE	HANDONE[3]
HANDS	HANDS[3,15]
HANDSPLAYD	HANDPLAD
HANDSWON	HANDSWON
HANDVALUE	HANDVALU
MAXBET	MAXBET
MAXVAL	MAXVAL
MINBET	MINBET
MINVAL	MINVAL
OPTIONS	OPTIONS
PLAYLIMIT	PLAYLMIT
STRING	INSTRING
SUIT	SUIT[4]
V	V
VALUE	VALUE[13]
WONTHISHAND	WONHAND
X	X

PROGRAM ROUTINE NAMES

BANKER	BANKER
BETTING	BETTING
BROKENBANK	BROKEN
BUY	BUY
CARDVALUE	CARDVAL
CASHIN	CASHIN
DEAL	DEAL
DEALER	DEALER
DEALERNATURAL	DEALERN
DEALEROVER	DEALERO
DEALERSTANDS	DEALERS
EVALUATE	EVALUATE
GETCARD	GETCARD
INITIALIZE	INIT
INPUTAMOUNT	AMOUNTIN
INPUTCHOICES	CHOICEIN
MAINLINE	BLAKJACK
NATURALS	NATURALS
PLAYER	PLAYER
PLAYERHAND	PLYRHAND
PLAYHAND	PLAYHAND
PRINTCARD	SHOWCARD
RPTSTATUS	STATUS
SELECTACTIV	NEXTACTV
SETTLE	SETTLE
SHOWINSTRUCT	INSTRUCT
SHUFFLE	SHUFFLE
SPLITPAIRS	SPLIT
TERMINATE	TERM

BLACKJACK AS IMPLEMENTED IN PASCAL

```
(* BLACKJACK   VERSION 1.0
      THIS PROGRAM WILL PLAY THE PART OF THE
      DEALER IN A GAME OF BLACKJACK PLAYED
      ACCORDING TO HOYLE'S RULES

      WRITTEN BY JACK EMMERICHS,  1/1/82
      (COPYRIGHT MESSAGE GOES HERE IF YOU WANT ONE)   *)
```

```
PROGRAM BLAKJACK (INPUT, OUTPUT);

   VAR    AMOUNT,     CARD,
          CHOICE,     DECKNEXT,
          HANDVALU,   MAXVAL,
          MINVAL,     OPTIONS,
          THISHAND,   PLAYLMIT,
          BANKLMIT,   MINBET,
          MAXBET,     CHIPS,
          HANDPLAD,   HANDSWON,
          BET,        DLRCOLN,
          DEALERV,    AMTWON,
          SEED:          INTEGER;

          DECK:          ARRAY [1..104]       OF INTEGER;
          HANDCNT:       ARRAY [1..3]         OF INTEGER;
          HANDS:         ARRAY [1..3, 1..15]  OF INTEGER;
          SUIT:          ARRAY [1..4]         OF STRING [8];
          VALUE:         ARRAY [1..13]        OF STRING [5];
          HANDONE:       ARRAY [1..3]         OF BOOLEAN;

          INSTRING,
          ERROR1,
          ERROR2:        STRING;

          DONE:          BOOLEAN;


FUNCTION RAND (MAX: INTEGER): INTEGER;
   BEGIN
      SEED:=SEED*((SEED DIV 2)-1)+21845;
      RAND:=(SEED MOD MAX)+1;
   END;   (*  OF RANDOM NUMBER GENERATOR  *)


FUNCTION CARDVAL (CARD: INTEGER): INTEGER;
   BEGIN
      CARDVAL:=CARD-(((CARD-1) DIV 13) * 13);
   END;   (*  OF CARDVAL  *)


FUNCTION VAL (INSTRING: STRING): INTEGER;
   VAR COUNT, VALUE:  INTEGER;
       NUMBER:        BOOLEAN;
   BEGIN
      VALUE:=0;
      NUMBER:=TRUE;
      FOR COUNT:=1 TO LENGTH(INSTRING) DO
         IF INSTRING[COUNT] IN ['0'..'9'] THEN
            VALUE:=VALUE*10+ORD(INSTRING[COUNT])-ORD('0')
         ELSE
            NUMBER:=FALSE;
      IF NUMBER THEN
         VAL:=VALUE
      ELSE
         VAL:=-1;
   END;   (*  OF VAL  *)
```

```
PROCEDURE SHOWCARD;                    (*  PRINT A CARD  *)
    VAR   CHARS, COUNT: INTEGER;
    BEGIN
        WRITE (OUTPUT,VALUE[CARDVAL(CARD)],
                ' OF ',SUIT[((CARD-1) DIV 13) + 1]);
        CHARS:=LENGTH(VALUE[CARDVAL(CARD)])+
                LENGTH(SUIT[((CARD-1) DIV 13) + 1]);
        FOR COUNT:=1 TO (20-4-CHARS) DO
            WRITE (OUTPUT,' ');
    END;   (* OF SHOWCARD  *)



PROCEDURE EVALUATE;                    (*  EVALUATE A HAND  *)
    VAR V, COUNT: INTEGER;
    BEGIN
        HANDVALU:=0;
        FOR COUNT:=1 TO HANDCNT[THISHAND] DO
            BEGIN
                V:=CARDVAL(HANDS[THISHAND,COUNT]);
                IF V>10 THEN
                    V:=10;
                IF V=1 THEN
                    V:=11;
                HANDVALU:=HANDVALU+V;
            END;
        COUNT:=1;
        WHILE (HANDVALU>21) AND (COUNT<=HANDCNT[THISHAND]) DO
            BEGIN
                IF CARDVAL(HANDS[THISHAND,COUNT])=1 THEN
                    HANDVALU:=HANDVALU-10;
                COUNT:=COUNT+1;
            END;
END;   (* OF EVALUATE  *)

PROCEDURE SHUFFLE;                     (*  SHUFFLE THE DECK  *)
    VAR COUNT, X: INTEGER;
    BEGIN
        WRITELN (OUTPUT);
        WRITELN (OUTPUT,'Reshuffle the cards');
        FOR COUNT:=1 TO 104 DO
            DECK[COUNT]:=0;
        FOR COUNT:=1 TO 2 DO
            BEGIN
                FOR CARD:=1 TO 52 DO
                    BEGIN
                        X:=RAND(104);
                        WHILE DECK[X]<>0 DO
                            BEGIN
                                X:=X+1;
                                IF X>104 THEN
                                    X:=1;
                            END;
                        DECK[X]:=CARD;
                    END;
            END;
        DECKNEXT:=1;
    END;   (* OF SHUFFLE  *)
```

```
PROCEDURE GETCARD;                    (*  DEAL A CARD  *)
   BEGIN
      IF DECKNEXT>104 THEN
         SHUFFLE;
      CARD:=DECK[DECKNEXT];
      DECKNEXT:=DECKNEXT+1;
   END;  (*  OF GETCARD  *)


PROCEDURE AMOUNTIN;                   (*  GET AN AMOUNT  *)
   VAR DATAOK:   BOOLEAN;
   BEGIN
      DATAOK:=FALSE;
      WRITELN (OUTPUT);
      REPEAT
         WRITE  (OUTPUT,'Your amount: ');
         READLN (INPUT,INSTRING);
         AMOUNT:=VAL(INSTRING);
         IF AMOUNT=-1 THEN
            WRITELN (OUTPUT,'Please enter a number')
         ELSE
            IF AMOUNT<MINVAL THEN
               WRITELN (OUTPUT,
               'Please enter an amount no less than ',MINVAL)
            ELSE
               IF AMOUNT>MAXVAL THEN
                  WRITELN (OUTPUT,
                  'Please enter an amount no more than ',MAXVAL)
               ELSE
                  DATAOK:=TRUE;
      UNTIL DATAOK
   END;  (*  OF AMOUNTIN  *)



PROCEDURE CHOICEIN;                   (*  GET A CHOICE  *)
   VAR DATAOK:   BOOLEAN;
   BEGIN
      DATAOK:=FALSE;
      WRITELN (OUTPUT);
      REPEAT
         WRITE  (OUTPUT,'Your choice: ');
         READLN (INPUT,INSTRING);
         IF OPTIONS=1 THEN
            IF LENGTH(INSTRING)=0 THEN
               WRITELN (OUTPUT,ERROR1)
            ELSE
               IF NOT (INSTRING[1] IN ['Y','N']) THEN
                  WRITELN (OUTPUT,ERROR1)
               ELSE
                  BEGIN
                     DATAOK:=TRUE;
                     IF INSTRING[1]='Y' THEN
                        CHOICE:=1
                     ELSE
                        CHOICE:=2
                  END
```

```
            ELSE
               BEGIN
                   CHOICE:=VAL(INSTRING);
                   IF (CHOICE<1) OR (CHOICE>OPTIONS) THEN
                       WRITELN (OUTPUT,ERROR2,OPTIONS)
                   ELSE
                       DATAOK:=TRUE;
               END;
        UNTIL DATAOK
    END;   (* OF CHOICEIN *)


PROCEDURE SETTLE;                        (*  SETTLE BETS  *)

    PROCEDURE BROKEN;                        (*  YOU BROKE THE BANK  *)
       BEGIN
          WRITELN (OUTPUT);
          WRITELN (OUTPUT,'****** YOU HAVE BROKEN THE BANK *******');
          WRITELN (OUTPUT);
          WRITELN (OUTPUT,
                   'The bank cannot cover any more of its losses.');
          WRITELN (OUTPUT,
                   'If you continue to play you will only lose.');
          WRITELN (OUTPUT,'   what you now have.');
          WRITELN (OUTPUT);
          BANKLMIT:=0;
          CHIPS:=1200-PLAYLMIT;
       END;   (* OF BROKEN *)

    PROCEDURE DEALERS;                       (*  DEALER STANDS  *)
       BEGIN
          FOR THISHAND:=2 TO 3 DO
             IF HANDCNT[THISHAND]<>0 THEN
                BEGIN
                   HANDPLAD:=HANDPLAD+1;
                   IF THISHAND=3 THEN
                      WRITELN (OUTPUT,'For the player''s second hand');
                   EVALUATE;
                   IF (HANDVALU=21) AND
                      (HANDCNT[THISHAND]=2) THEN
                      BEGIN
                         WRITELN (OUTPUT,
                         'Player wins with a natural, house pays extra.');
                         CHIPS:=CHIPS+BET+(BET DIV 2);
                         BANKLMIT:=BANKLMIT-BET-(BET DIV 2);
                         AMTWON:=AMTWON+BET+(BET DIV 2);
                         HANDSWON:=HANDSWON+1;
                      END
                   ELSE
                      IF (HANDVALU<DEALERV) OR
                         (HANDVALU>21) THEN
                         BEGIN
                            WRITELN (OUTPUT,'Player loses');
                            CHIPS:=CHIPS-BET;
                            BANKLMIT:=BANKLMIT+BET;
                            AMTWON:=AMTWON-BET;
                         END
```

```
                    ELSE
                       IF HANDVALU>DEALERV THEN
                           BEGIN
                               WRITELN (OUTPUT,'Player wins!');
                               CHIPS:=CHIPS+BET;
                               BANKLMIT:=BANKLMIT-BET;
                               AMTWON:=AMTWON+BET;
                               HANDSWON:=HANDSWON+1;
                           END
                       ELSE
                           WRITELN (OUTPUT,'Standoff with dealer');
               END;
         IF BANKLMIT<0 THEN
             BROKEN;
      END;   (* DEALERS *)

PROCEDURE DEALERO;                      (* DEALER GOES OVER *)
   BEGIN
      FOR THISHAND:=2 TO 3 DO
         IF HANDCNT[THISHAND]<>0 THEN
             BEGIN
                HANDPLAD:=HANDPLAD+1;
                IF THISHAND=3 THEN
                    WRITELN (OUTPUT,'For the player''s second hand');
                EVALUATE;
                IF (HANDVALU=21) AND
                   (HANDCNT[THISHAND]=2) THEN
                    BEGIN
                       WRITELN (OUTPUT,
                       'Player wins with a natural, house pays extra.');
                       CHIPS:=CHIPS+BET+(BET DIV 2);
                       BANKLMIT:=BANKLMIT-BET-(BET DIV 2);
                       AMTWON:=AMTWON+BET+(BET DIV 2);
                       HANDSWON:=HANDSWON+1;
                    END
                ELSE
                    IF HANDVALU>21 THEN
                        WRITELN (OUTPUT,'ERROR HERE!!')
                    ELSE
                        BEGIN
                           WRITELN (OUTPUT,'Player wins!');
                           CHIPS:=CHIPS+BET;
                           BANKLMIT:=BANKLMIT-BET;
                           AMTWON:=AMTWON+BET;
                           HANDSWON:=HANDSWON+1;
                        END
             END;
         IF BANKLMIT<0 THEN
             BROKEN;
      END;   (* DEALERO *)

PROCEDURE DEALERN;                      (* DEALER NATURAL *)
   VAR   COUNT: INTEGER;
   BEGIN
      WRITELN (OUTPUT);
      WRITELN (OUTPUT,'Dealer has a natural!');
      CARD:=HANDS[1,1];
```

```
            FOR COUNT:=1 TO 20 DO
               WRITE (OUTPUT,' ');
            SHOWCARD;
            WRITELN (OUTPUT);
            CARD:=HANDS[1,2];
            FOR COUNT:=1 TO 20 DO
               WRITE (OUTPUT,' ');
            SHOWCARD;
            WRITELN (OUTPUT);
            FOR THISHAND:=2 TO 3 DO
               IF HANDCNT[THISHAND]<>0 THEN
                  BEGIN
                     HANDPLAD:=HANDPLAD+1;
                     IF THISHAND=3 THEN
                        WRITELN (OUTPUT,'For the player''s second hand');
                     EVALUATE;
                     IF HANDVALU=21 THEN
                        WRITELN (OUTPUT,'Standoff with naturals.')
                     ELSE
                        BEGIN
                           WRITELN (OUTPUT,
                                    'Dealer wins with a natural.');
                           CHIPS:=CHIPS-BET;
                           BANKLMIT:=BANKLMIT+BET;
                           AMTWON:=AMTWON-BET;
                        END;
                  END;
      END;   (* DEALERN *)


   BEGIN                          (* SETTLE BETS *)
      THISHAND:=1;
      EVALUATE;
      DEALERV:=HANDVALU;
      IF (HANDVALU=21) AND
         (HANDCNT[1]=2) THEN
         DEALERN                  (* DEALER NATURAL *)
      ELSE
         IF HANDVALU>21 THEN
            DEALERO               (* DEALER OVER *)
         ELSE
            DEALERS;              (* DEALER STANDS *)
   END;   (* OF SETTLE *)


PROCEDURE DEALER;                 (* PLAY DEALER HAND *)
   VAR   COUNT: INTEGER;
   BEGIN
      IF HANDCNT[3]=0 THEN
         DLRCOLM:=20
      ELSE
         DLRCOLM:=40;
      CARD:=HANDS[1,1];
      WRITELN (OUTPUT);
      FOR COUNT:=1 TO DLRCOLM DO
         WRITE (OUTPUT,' ');
      SHOWCARD;
```

```
        CARD:=HANDS[1,2];
        WRITELN (OUTPUT);
        FOR COUNT:=1 TO DLRCOLM DO
           WRITE (OUTPUT,' ');
        SHOWCARD;
        THISHAND:=1;
        EVALUATE;
        WHILE (HANDVALU<=17) DO
           BEGIN
              GETCARD;
              WRITELN (OUTPUT);
              FOR COUNT:=1 TO DLRCOLM DO
                 WRITE (OUTPUT,' ');
              SHOWCARD;
              HANDCNT[1]:=HANDCNT[1]+1;
              HANDS[1,HANDCNT[1]]:=CARD;
              EVALUATE;
           END;
        WRITELN (OUTPUT);
        IF HANDVALU<=21 THEN
           WRITELN (OUTPUT,'The dealer stands at ',HANDVALU)
        ELSE
           WRITELN (OUTPUT,'The dealer goes over 21');
     END;   (* OF DEALER *)

PROCEDURE PLAYER;                    (* PLAY PLAYER HAND *)

   PROCEDURE PLYRHAND;               (* DO A SINGLE PLAY *)
      VAR   COUNT: INTEGER;
      BEGIN
         IF HANDONE[THISHAND] THEN
            WRITELN (OUTPUT,'That hand is already over 21')
         ELSE
            BEGIN
               GETCARD;
               IF THISHAND=3 THEN
                  FOR COUNT:=1 TO 20 DO
                     WRITE (OUTPUT,' ');
               SHOWCARD;
               WRITELN (OUTPUT);
               HANDCNT[THISHAND]:=HANDCNT[THISHAND]+1;
               HANDS[THISHAND,HANDCNT[THISHAND]]:=CARD;
               EVALUATE;
               IF HANDVALU>21 THEN
                  BEGIN
                     WRITELN (OUTPUT,
                             'Too bad, player goes over 21');
                     HANDONE[THISHAND]:=TRUE;
                  END;
            END;
      END;   (* OF PLYRHAND *)


   BEGIN                             (* OF PLAYER *)
      HANDONE[2]:=FALSE;
      IF HANDCNT[3]=0 THEN
         HANDONE[3]:=TRUE
```

```
            ELSE
                HANDONE[3]:=FALSE;
            REPEAT
            WRITELN (OUTPUT,'What next?');
            IF HANDCNT[3]=0 THEN
                BEGIN
                    WRITELN (OUTPUT,'Stand on this hand?');
                    OPTIONS:=1;
                END
            ELSE
                BEGIN
                    WRITELN (OUTPUT,
                            '1: Done  2: Card for 1  3: Card for 2');
                    OPTIONS:=3;
                END;
            CHOICEIN;
            IF CHOICE<>1 THEN
                BEGIN
                    THISHAND:=CHOICE;
                    PLYRHAND;
                END;
        UNTIL (CHOICE=1) OR
              (HANDONE[2] AND HANDONE[3]);
        IF HANDONE[2] AND HANDONE[3] THEN
            DONE:=TRUE;
    END;   (* OF PLAYER *)


PROCEDURE SPLIT;                    (*  SPLIT PAIRS  *)
    BEGIN
        WRITELN (OUTPUT,'Do you wish to split your pair?');
        OPTIONS:=1;
        CHOICEIN;
        IF CHOICE=1 THEN
            IF CHIPS<(2*BET) THEN
                WRITELN (OUTPUT,'You cannot cover the bet.')
            ELSE
                BEGIN
                    HANDS[3,1]:=HANDS[2,2];
                    WRITELN (OUTPUT);
                    WRITELN (OUTPUT,
                        'PLAYER-1       PLAYER-2      DEALER');
                    WRITELN (OUTPUT);
                    CARD:=HANDS[2,1];
                    SHOWCARD;
                    CARD:=HANDS[3,1];
                    SHOWCARD;
                    WRITELN (OUTPUT,'XXXXX');
                    GETCARD;
                    HANDS[2,2]:=CARD;
                    SHOWCARD;
                    GETCARD;
                    HANDS[3,2]:=CARD;
                    SHOWCARD;
                    CARD:=HANDS[1,2];
                    SHOWCARD;
                    WRITELN (OUTPUT);
```

```
                 HANDCNT[3]:=2;
            END;
   END;   (* OF SPLIT *)


PROCEDURE NATURALS;                    (* HANDLE NATURALS *)
   BEGIN
      THISHAND:=1;
      EVALUATE;
      IF HANDVALU=21 THEN
         DONE:=TRUE;
   END;   (* OF NATURALS *)


PROCEDURE DEAL;                        (* DEAL THE HAND *)
   BEGIN
      WRITELN (OUTPUT);
      WRITELN (OUTPUT,'    PLAYER        DEALER');
      WRITELN (OUTPUT);
      GETCARD;
      HANDS[2,1]:=CARD;
      SHOWCARD;
      GETCARD;
      HANDS[1,1]:=CARD;
      WRITELN (OUTPUT,'XXXXX');
      GETCARD;
      HANDS[2,2]:=CARD;
      SHOWCARD;
      GETCARD;
      HANDS[1,2]:=CARD;
      SHOWCARD;
      WRITELN (OUTPUT);
      HANDCNT[1]:=2;
      HANDCNT[2]:=2;
      HANDCNT[3]:=0;
   END;   (* OF DEAL *)


PROCEDURE BETTING;                     (* PLACE YOUR BET *)
   BEGIN
      BET:=-1;
      MAXVAL:=10000;
      MINVAL:=0;
      REPEAT
         WRITELN (OUTPUT,'How much do you wish to bet?');
         AMOUNTIN;
         IF AMOUNT>MAXBET THEN
            BEGIN
               WRITELN (OUTPUT,'That is more than than the $',
                        MAXBET,' house limit.');
               MAXVAL:=MAXBET;
            END
         ELSE
            IF (AMOUNT<MINBET) AND
               (AMOUNT<>0) THEN
               WRITELN (OUTPUT,'That is below the $',
                        MINBET,' house minimum.')
```

```
            ELSE
                IF AMOUNT>CHIPS THEN
                    BEGIN
                        WRITELN (OUTPUT,'You only have $',
                                CHIPS,' in chips.');
                        MAXBET:=CHIPS;
                        END
                    ELSE
                        BET:=AMOUNT;
        UNTIL BET<>-1;
END;  (* OF BETTING *)


PROCEDURE PLAYHAND;                      (* PLAY A HAND OF CARDS *)
    BEGIN
        REPEAT
            DONE:=FALSE;
            BETTING;
            IF BET<MINBET THEN
                CHOICE:=2
            ELSE
                BEGIN
                    DEAL;
                    NATURALS;
                    IF NOT DONE THEN
                        BEGIN
                            IF CARDVAL(HANDS[2,1])=CARDVAL(HANDS[2,2]) THEN
                                SPLIT;
                            PLAYER;
                            IF NOT DONE THEN
                                DEALER;
                        END;
                    SETTLE;
                    WRITELN (OUTPUT,'Play again?');
                    OPTIONS:=1;
                    CHOICEIN;
                END;
        UNTIL CHOICE=2;
    END;  (* OF PLAYHAND *)


PROCEDURE STATUS;                        (* REPORT GAME STATUS *)
    BEGIN
        WRITELN (OUTPUT);
        WRITELN (OUTPUT,'Number of hands played: ',HANDPLAD);
        WRITELN (OUTPUT,'Number of hands won: ',HANDSWON);
        WRITE   (OUTPUT,'Percentage of hands won: ');
        IF HANDPLAD=0 THEN
            WRITELN (OUTPUT,0,' %')
        ELSE
            WRITELN (OUTPUT,((100*HANDSWON) DIV HANDPLAD),' %');
        WRITELN (OUTPUT);
        WRITELN (OUTPUT,'Current value of your cash: $',PLAYLMIT);
        WRITELN (OUTPUT,'Current value of your chips: $',CHIPS);
        WRITELN (OUTPUT,'Your current funds: $',PLAYLMIT+CHIPS);
        WRITELN (OUTPUT);
        WRITE   (OUTPUT,'Total amount ');
```

```
        IF AMTWON>=0 THEN
            WRITELN (OUTPUT,'won: $',AMTWON)
        ELSE
            WRITELN (OUTPUT,'lost: $',ABS(AMTWON));
        WRITE   (OUTPUT,'Average amount ');
        IF AMTWON>0 THEN
            WRITE   (OUTPUT,'won per hand: $')
        ELSE
            WRITE   (OUTPUT,'lost per hand: $');
        IF HANDPLAD=0 THEN
            WRITELN (OUTPUT,0)
        ELSE
            WRITELN (OUTPUT,ABS(AMTWON) DIV HANDPLAD);
        WRITELN (OUTPUT);
        WRITELN (OUTPUT,'        Press RETURN to continue');
        READLN   (INPUT,INSTRING);
    END;   (*  OF STATUS  *)


PROCEDURE BANKER;                      (*  DEAL WITH THE BANK  *)


    PROCEDURE BUY;                     (*  BUY CHIPS  *)
        BEGIN
            IF PLAYLMIT=0 THEN
                WRITELN (OUTPUT,'You have no more money.')
            ELSE
                BEGIN
                    MAXVAL:=10000;
                    MINVAL:=0;
                    REPEAT
                        WRITELN (OUTPUT,'How much do you wish to buy?');
                        AMOUNTIN;
                        IF AMOUNT>PLAYLMIT THEN
                            BEGIN
                                WRITELN (OUTPUT,'You only have $',
                                            PLAYLMIT);
                                MAXVAL:=PLAYLMIT;
                            END;
                    UNTIL AMOUNT<=PLAYLMIT;
                    PLAYLMIT:=PLAYLMIT-AMOUNT;
                    CHIPS   :=CHIPS   +AMOUNT;
                END;
        END;   (*  OF BUY  *)


    PROCEDURE CASHIN;                  (*  CASH IN CHIPS  *)
        BEGIN
            IF CHIPS=0 THEN
                WRITELN (OUTPUT,'You have no more chips.')
            ELSE
                BEGIN
                    MAXVAL:=10000;
                    MINVAL:=0;
                    REPEAT
                    WRITELN (OUTPUT,'How much do you wish to cash in?');
```

```
                    AMOUNTIN;
                    IF AMOUNT>CHIPS THEN
                        BEGIN
                            WRITELN (OUTPUT,'You only have ',
                                      CHIPS, 'chips.');
                            MAXVAL:=CHIPS;
                        END;
                UNTIL AMOUNT<=CHIPS;
                PLAYLMIT:=PLAYLMIT+AMOUNT;
                CHIPS   :=CHIPS   -AMOUNT;
            END;
    END;   (* OF CASH IN *)


    BEGIN                             (* OF BANKER *)
        WRITELN (OUTPUT);
        WRITELN (OUTPUT,'   You may do either of the following:');
        WRITELN (OUTPUT);
        WRITELN (OUTPUT,'       1. Buy more chips');
        WRITELN (OUTPUT,'       2. Cash in your chips');
        OPTIONS:=2;
        CHOICEIN;
        IF CHOICE=1 THEN
            BUY
        ELSE
            CASHIN;
    END;   (* OF BANKER *)



PROCEDURE INSTRUCT;                    (* PRINT GAME RULES *)
    BEGIN
        WRITELN (OUTPUT);
        WRITELN (OUTPUT);
        WRITELN (OUTPUT,'The rules in game are in the book:');
        WRITELN (OUTPUT);
        WRITELN (OUTPUT,'        HOYLE UP-TO-DATE');
        WRITELN (OUTPUT,'   OFFICIAL RULES OF CARD GAMES');
        WRITELN (OUTPUT);
        WRITELN (OUTPUT,'Please read the rules there.');
        WRITELN (OUTPUT);
        WRITELN (OUTPUT,'        Press RETURN to continue');
        READLN (INPUT,INSTRING);
    END;   (* OF INSTRUCT *)




PROCEDURE TERM;                        (* TERMINATION ROUTINE *)
    BEGIN
        STATUS;
        WRITELN (OUTPUT);
        WRITELN (OUTPUT,
            'Thank you for the game, please come again sometime.');
        WRITELN (OUTPUT,
            '  (Press RETURN to continue)');
        READLN (INPUT,INSTRING);
    END;   (* OF TERM *)
```

```
PROCEDURE NEXTACTV;                      (* NEXT ACTIV ROUTINE *)
   BEGIN
      REPEAT
         WRITELN (OUTPUT);
         WRITELN (OUTPUT,
            '    You may do any of the following things:');
         WRITELN (OUTPUT);
         WRITELN (OUTPUT,
            '         1.  Display the rules of the game.');
         WRITELN (OUTPUT,
            '         2.  Visit the bank.');
         WRITELN (OUTPUT,
            '         3.  Display the current status of the game.');
         WRITELN (OUTPUT,
            '         4.  Shuffle the deck.');
         WRITELN (OUTPUT,
            '         5.  Play a hand of cards.');
         WRITELN (OUTPUT,
            '         6.  Quit the game.');
         OPTIONS:=6;
         CHOICEIN;
         IF CHOICE<>6 THEN
            CASE CHOICE OF
               1:   INSTRUCT;
               2:   BANKER;
               3:   STATUS;
               4:   SHUFFLE;
               5:   PLAYHAND;
            END;    (*  OF CASE STATEMENT  *)
      UNTIL CHOICE=6;
   END;   (* NEXTACTV *)



PROCEDURE INIT;                          (* INIT ROUTINE *)
   BEGIN
      SUIT[1] := 'SPADES';        SUIT[2] := 'HEARTS';
      SUIT[3] := 'DIAMONDS';      SUIT[4] := 'CLUBS';
      VALUE[1] := 'ACE';    VALUE[2] := '2';     VALUE[3] := '3';
      VALUE[4] := '4';      VALUE[5] := '5';     VALUE[6] := '6';
      VALUE[7] := '7';      VALUE[8] := '8';     VALUE[9] := '9';
      VALUE[10] := '10';    VALUE[11] := 'JACK';
      VALUE[12] := 'QUEEN'; VALUE[13] := 'KING';
      SHUFFLE;
      PLAYLMIT:=2000;
      BANKLMIT:=10000;
      MINBET:=10;
      MAXBET:=500;
      CHIPS:=0;
      HANDPLAD:=0;
      HANDSWON:=0;
      AMTWON:=0;
      ERROR1:='Please enter YES or NO';
      ERROR2:='Please enter a number from 1 to ';
      WRITELN (OUTPUT);
      WRITELN (OUTPUT,
      'Welcome to the Blackjack table. We will be playing');
```

```
      WRITELN (OUTPUT,
      '   by the rules of Blackjack according to Hoyle.');
      WRITELN (OUTPUT,'   the house limits on bets are:');
      WRITELN (OUTPUT,'      minimum bet: $',MINBET);
      WRITELN (OUTPUT,'      maximum bet: $',MAXBET);
      WRITELN (OUTPUT,'   the house currently has $',
         BANKLMIT,' in the bank.');
      WRITELN (OUTPUT,'   You currently have $',
         PLAYLMIT,' in cash');
      WRITELN (OUTPUT);
      WRITELN (OUTPUT,
         '   Please sit down and play for a while.');
      WRITELN (OUTPUT, '        Press RETURN to continue');
      READLN  (INPUT,INSTRING);
   END;  (*  OF INIT  *)


BEGIN                              (* PROGRAM MAINLINE *)
   INIT;
   NEXTACTV;
   TERM;
END.  (*  OF PROGRAM  *)
```

Appendix F

The Final Programs

BLACKJACK (FINAL VERSION) AS IMPLEMENTED IN BASIC
(Program changes marked with underlining)

```
10        REM   BLACKJACK    VERSION 1.0
20        REM      THIS PROGRAM WILL PLAY THE PART OF THE
30        REM      DEALER IN A GAME OF BLACKJACK PLAYED
40        REM      ACCORDING TO HOYLE'S RULES
50        REM
60        REM  WRITTEN BY JACK EMMERICHS,   1/1/82
70        REM  (COPYRIGHT MESSAGE GOES HERE IF YOU WANT ONE)
72        REM
73        REM      CHANGED 2/1/80 TO FIX SCREENS, REMOVE
74        REM         PRINTING OF RULES, STANDARDIZE VARIABLES
75        REM         AND FIX DEALER'S CARDS.
76        REM
80        REM
90        REM  CARDVALUE FUNCTION AND ARRAYS
100       REM
110   DEF FNC(X)=X-(INT((X-1)/13)*13)
120       REM
121       REM  D8 = NUMBER OF DECKS BEING USED
122       REM  C8 = NUMBER OF CARDS BEING USED
123       REM  L8 = CREDIT LIMIT FOR THE PLAYER
124       REM  L9 = CREDIT LIMIT FOR THE BANK
125       REM  M1$ - M9$ = MESSAGES
126       REM
127   D8 = 2
128   C8 = D8 * 52
129   L8 = 2000
130   L9 = 10000
131   M1$ = "For the player's second hand:"
132   M2$ = "Player wins with natural, house pays extra."
133   M3$ = "Player loses."
134   M4$ = "Player wins."
```

```
135  M5$ = "Please enter an integer number."
136        REM
140        REM
149  DIM D(C8), H(3,15), H1(3), H9(3), S$(4), V$(13)
150        REM   PROGRAM MAINLINE
160        REM
170  GOSUB 240
180  GOSUB 610
190  GOSUB 900
195        REM
200  END
210        REM
220        REM   INITIALIZATION PROCEDURE
230        REM
240  RANDOMIZE
245        REM   INITIALIZE ARRAYS
250  DATA "SPADES","HEARTS","DIAMONDS","CLUBS"
260  DATA "ACE","2","3","4","5","6","7","8","9","10"
270  DATA "JACK","QUEEN","KING"
280  FOR X=1 TO 4
290    READ S$(X)
300  NEXT X
310  FOR X=1 TO 13
320    READ V$(X)
330  NEXT X
340  GOSUB 64320
345        REM   INITIALIZE VARIABLES
350  L1=L9
360  L2=L8
370  M1=500
380  M3=10
390  C1=0
400  H2=0
410  H3=0
420  E1$="Please enter YES or NO"
430  E2$="please enter a number from 1 to "
435        REM   PRINT WELCOME MESSAGE
436  GOSUB 64990
440  PRINT
450  PRINT "Welcome to the Blackjack table.  We will be playing"
460  PRINT "   by the rules of Blackjack according to Hoyle."
470  PRINT "   the house limits on bets are:"
480  PRINT "        minimum bet: $";M3
490  PRINT "        maximum bet: $";M1
500  PRINT "   The house currently has $";L1;" in the bank."
510  PRINT "   You currently have $";L2;" in cash."
520  PRINT "   You may exchange cash and chips at the bank."
530  GOSUB 65040
570  RETURN
580        REM
590        REM   SELECT THE NEXT ACTIVITY
600        REM
610  GOSUB 64990
612  PRINT
```

```
620   PRINT "   You may do any of the following things:"
630   PRINT
650   PRINT "        1.  Visit the bank."
660   PRINT "        2.  Display the current status of the game."
670   PRINT "        3.  Shuffle the deck."
680   PRINT "        4.  Play a hand of cards."
690   PRINT "        5.  Quit the game."
700   X9=5
710   GOSUB 64710
720   IF C2=5 THEN RETURN
730      REM 730-750 REMOVED
760   IF C2<>1 THEN GOTO 790
770      GOSUB 1130
780      GOTO 610
790   IF C2<>2 THEN GOTO 820
800      GOSUB 1600
810      GOTO 610
820   IF C2<>3 THEN GOTO 850
830      GOSUB 64320
840      GOTO 610
850   GOSUB 1880
860   GOTO 610
870         REM
880         REM    TERMINATION PROCEDURE
890         REM
900   GOSUB 1600
910   PRINT
920   PRINT "Thank you for the game, please come again sometime."
930         REM 930-940 REMOVED
950   RETURN
960         REM 960-1090 REMOVED
1100        REM
1110        REM    BANKER
1120        REM
1130  GOSUB 64990
1132  PRINT
1140  PRINT "   You may do either of the following:"
1150  PRINT
1160  PRINT "       1. Buy more chips"
1170  PRINT "       2. Cash in your chips"
1180  X9=2
1190  GOSUB 64710
1200  IF C2=1 THEN GOSUB 1260 ELSE GOSUB 1430
1220  RETURN
1230        REM
1240        REM   BUY CHIPS
1250        REM
1260  IF L2>0 THEN GOTO 1290
1270     PRINT "You have no more money."
1272     GOSUB 65040
1280     RETURN
1290  M2=L9
1300  M4=0
1310  PRINT "How much do you wish to buy?"
```

```
1320 GOSUB 64510
1330 IF A<=L2 THEN GOTO 1370
1340    PRINT "You only have $";L2
1350    M2=L2
1360    GOTO 1310
1370 L2=L2-A
1380 C1=C1+A
1390 RETURN
1400       REM
1410       REM  CASH IN CHIPS
1420       REM
1430 IF C1>0 THEN 1460
1440    PRINT "You have no more chips."
1442    GOSUB 65040
1450    RETURN
1460 M2=L9
1470 M4=0
1480 PRINT "How many chips do you wish to cash in?"
1490 GOSUB 64510
1500 IF A<=C1 THEN GOTO 1540
1510    PRINT "You only have";C1;" chips."
1520    M2=C1
1530    GOTO 1480
1540 L2=L2+A
1550 C1=C1-A
1560 RETURN
1570       REM
1580       REM  REPORT GAME STATUS
1590       REM
1600 GOSUB 64990
1602 PRINT
1610 PRINT "Number of hands played:";H2
1620 PRINT "Number of hands won:";ABS(H3)
1650 PRINT "Percentage of hands won:";
1670 IF H2=0 THEN PRINT 0;"%" ELSE PRINT (ABS(H3)/H2)*100;"%"
1690 PRINT
1700 PRINT "Current value of your cash: $";L2
1710 PRINT "Current value of your chips: $";C1
1720 PRINT "Your current funds: $";L2+C1
1730 PRINT
1740 PRINT "Total amount ";
1750 IF A1>=0 THEN PRINT "won: $"; ELSE PRINT "lost: $";
1760 PRINT ABS(A1)
1770 PRINT "Average amount ";
1780 IF A1>=0 THEN PRINT "won"; ELSE PRINT "lost";
1790 PRINT " per hand: $";
1800 IF H2=0 THEN PRINT 0 ELSE PRINT ABS(A1)/H2
1810 GOSUB 65040
1840 RETURN
1850       REM
1860       REM  PLAY A HAND OF CARDS
1870       REM
1880 D9=0
```

```
1882 GOSUB 64990
1890 GOSUB 2050
1900 IF B<M3 THEN RETURN
1910 GOSUB 2270
1920 GOSUB 2510
1930 IF D9<>0 THEN GOTO 1970
1940    IF FNC(H(2,1))=FNC(H(2,2)) THEN GOSUB 2580
1950    GOSUB 2910
1960    IF D9=0 THEN GOSUB 3260
1970 GOSUB 3540
1980 PRINT "Play again?"
1990 X9=1
2000 GOSUB 64710
2010 IF C2=1 THEN GOTO 1880 ELSE RETURN
2020       REM
2030       REM  BETTING
2040       REM
2050 M2=L9
2060 M4=0
2070 PRINT "How much do you wish to bet?"
2080 GOSUB 64510
2090 IF A<=M1 THEN GOTO 2130
2100    PRINT "That is more than the $";M1;" house limit."
2110    M2=M1
2120    GOTO 2070
2130 IF A=0 THEN GOTO 2180
2140 IF A>=M3 THEN GOTO 2180
2150    PRINT "That is below the $";M3;" house minimum."
2170    GOTO 2070
2180 IF A<=C1 THEN GOTO 2220
2190    PRINT "You only have $";C1;" in chips."
2200    M2=C1
2210    GOTO 2070
2220 B=A
2230 RETURN
2240       REM
2250       REM  DEAL THE CARDS
2260       REM
2270 GOSUB 64990
2272 PRINT
2280 PRINT "PLAYER";TAB(21);"DEALER"
2290 PRINT
2300 GOSUB 64250
2310 H(2,1)=C
2320 GOSUB 64030
2330 GOSUB 64250
2340 H(1,1)=C
2350 PRINT TAB(21);
2352 GOSUB 64030
2353 PRINT
2360 GOSUB 64250
2370 H(2,2)=C
2380 GOSUB 64030
```

```
2390 GOSUB 64250
2400 H(1,2)=C
2410 PRINT TAB(21);"XXXXX";
2420      REM THIS LINE REMOVED
2430 PRINT
2440 H1(1)=2
2450 H1(2)=2
2460 H1(3)=0
2470 RETURN
2480      REM
2490      REM  HANDLE DEALER NATURALS
2500      REM
2510 H8=1
2520 GOSUB 64080
2530 IF H4=21 THEN D9=-1
2540 RETURN
2550      REM
2560      REM  SPLIT A PAIR OF CARDS
2570      REM
2580 PRINT "Do you wish to split your pair?"
2590 X9=1
2600 GOSUB 64710
2610 IF C2=2 THEN RETURN
2620 IF C1>=2*B THEN GOTO 2650
2630    PRINT "You cannot cover the bet."
2640    RETURN
2650 H(3,1)=H(2,2)
2652 GOSUB 64990
2660 PRINT
2670 PRINT "PLAYER-1";TAB(21);"PLAYER-2";TAB(42);"DEALER"
2680 PRINT
2690 C=H(2,1)
2700 GOSUB 64030
2710 PRINT TAB(21);
2720 C=H(3,1)
2730 GOSUB 64030
2732 C=H(1,1)
2740 PRINT TAB(42);
2742 GOSUB 64030
2743 PRINT
2750 GOSUB 64250
2760 H(2,2)=C
2770 GOSUB 64030
2780 GOSUB 64250
2790 H(3,2)=C
2800 PRINT TAB(21);
2810 GOSUB 64030
2820      REM THIS LINE REMOVED
2830 PRINT TAB(42);"XXXXX";
2840      REM THIS LINE REMOVED
2850 PRINT
2860 H1(3)=2
2870 RETURN
```

```
2880       REM
2890       REM     PLAY THE PLAYER'S CARDS
2900       REM
2910 H9(2)=0
2920 IF H1(3)=0 THEN H9(3)=-1 ELSE H9(3)=0
2930 PRINT "What next?"
2940 IF H1(3)<>0 THEN GOTO 2980
2950___PRINT_"Do_you_want_another_card?"
2960    X9=1
2962___GOSUB_64710
2963___IF_C2=2_THEN_RETURN
2964___C2=2
2965___GOTO_3020
2980 PRINT "1: Done.  2: Card for 1.  3: Card for 2."
2990    X9=3
3000 GOSUB 64710
3010 IF C2=1 THEN RETURN
3020 H8=C2
3030 GOSUB 3090
3040 IF H9(2)=0 OR H9(3)=0 THEN GOTO 2930
3045 D9=-1
3050 RETURN
3060       REM
3070       REM     PLAY A PLAYER'S CARD
3080       REM
3090 IF H9(H8)=0 THEN GOTO 3120
3100    PRINT "That hand is already over 21."
3110    RETURN
3120 GOSUB 64250
3130 IF H8=3 THEN PRINT TAB(21);
3140 GOSUB 64030
3150 PRINT
3160 H1(H8)=H1(H8)+1
3170 H(H8,H1(H8))=C
3180 GOSUB 64080
3190 IF H4<=21 THEN 3220
3200    PRINT "Too bad, Player goes over 21."
3210    H9(H8)=-1
3220 RETURN
3230       REM
3240       REM     PLAY THE DEALER'S HAND
3250       REM
3260 IF H1(3)=0 THEN D7=21 ELSE D7=42
3270 PRINT TAB(D7);
3280 C=H(1,1)
3290 GOSUB 64030
3300 PRINT
3310 PRINT TAB(D7);
3320 C=H(1,2)
3330 GOSUB 64030
3340 H8=1
3350 GOSUB 64080
3360 IF H4>17 THEN GOTO 3450
```

```
3370    GOSUB 64250
3380    PRINT
3390    PRINT TAB(D7);
3400    GOSUB 64030
3410    H1(1)=H1(1)+1
3420    H(1,H1(1))=C
3430    GOSUB 64080
3440    GOTO 3350
3450 PRINT
3460 IF H4>21 THEN GOTO 3490
3470    PRINT "The dealer stands at";H4
3480    GOTO 3500
3490 PRINT "The dealer goes over 21."
3500 RETURN
3510       REM
3520       REM   SETTLE THE BETS
3530       REM
3540 H8=1
3550 GOSUB 64080
3560 D2=H4
3570 IF H4<>21 OR H1(1)<>2 THEN GOTO 3600
3580    GOSUB 3680
3590    GOTO 3640
3600 IF H4<=21 THEN GOTO 3630
3610    GOSUB 3830
3620    GOTO 3640
3630 GOSUB 4070
3640 RETURN
3650       REM
3660       REM   DEALER HAS NATURAL
3670       REM
3680 PRINT
3681 PRINT "Dealer has a natural!"
3682 PRINT TAB(21);
3683 C=H(1,1)
3684 GOSUB 64030
3685 PRINT
3686 PRINT TAB(21);
3687 C=H(1,2)
3688 GOSUB 64030
3689 PRINT
3690 FOR H8=2 TO 3
3692    IF H1(H8)=0 THEN RETURN
3695    H2=H2+1
3700    IF H8=3 THEN PRINT M1$
3710    GOSUB 64080
3720    IF H4<>21 THEN GOTO 3750
3730       PRINT "Standoff with naturals."
3740       GOTO 3780
3750    A1=A1-B
3760    C1=C1-B
3770    L1=L1+B
3780 NEXT H8
```

```
3790 RETURN
3800      REM
3810      REM   DEALER GOES OVER 21
3820      REM
3830 FOR H8=2 TO 3
3840    IF H1(H8)=0 THEN GOTO 4010
3845    H2=H2+1
3850    IF H8=3 THEN PRINT M1$
3860    GOSUB 64080
3870    IF H4<>21 THEN GOTO 3930
3880    IF H1(H8)<>2 THEN GOTO 3930
3890    PRINT M2$
3900       C1=C1+(1.5*B)
3910       L1=L1-(1.5*B)
3915       A1=A1+(1.5*B)
3916       H3=H3+1
3920       GOTO 4010
3930    IF H4<=21 THEN GOTO 3980
3940       PRINT "ERROR, YOU SHOULD NEVER GET HERE""
3970       GOTO 4010
3980    PRINT M4$
3990       C1=C1+B
4000       L1=L1-B
4005       A1=A1+B
4006       H3=H3+1
4010 NEXT H8
4020 IF L1<0 THEN GOSUB 4340
4030 RETURN
4040      REM
4050      REM   DEALER STANDS
4060      REM
4070 FOR H8=2 TO 3
4080    IF H1(H8)=0 THEN GOTO 4280
4085    H2=H2+1
4090    IF H8=3 THEN PRINT M1$
4100    GOSUB 64080
4110    IF H4<>21 THEN GOTO 4170
4120    IF H1(H8)<>2 THEN GOTO 4170
4130    PRINT M2$
4140       C1=C1+(1.5*B)
4150       L1=L1-(1.5*B)
4155       A1=A1+(1.5*B)
4156       H3=H3+1
4160       GOTO 4280
4170    IF H4>=D2 AND H4<=21 THEN GOTO 4220
4180    PRINT M3$
4190       C1=C1-B
4200       L1=L1+B
4205       A1=A1-B
4210       GOTO 4280
4220    IF H4=D2 THEN GOTO 4270
4230    PRINT M4$
4240       C1=C1+B
```

```
4250    L1=L1-B
4255    A1=A1+B
4256    H3=H3+1
4260    GOTO 4280
4270   PRINT "Standoff with the dealer, nobody wins."
4280 NEXT H8
4290 IF L1<0 THEN GOSUB 4340
4300 RETURN
4310    REM
4320    REM  YOU BROKE THE BANK!
4330    REM
4340 GOSUB 64990
4342 PRINT
4350 PRINT "****** YOU HAVE BROKEN THE BANK ******"
4360 PRINT
4370 PRINT "The bank connot cover any more of its losses."
4380 PRINT "If you continue to play you will only lose"
4390 PRINT "   what you now have."
4400 PRINT
4402 GOSUB 65040
4410 L1=0
4420 C1=(L8+L9)-L2
4430 RETURN
64000    REM
64010    REM  PRINTCARD
64020    REM
64030 PRINT V$(FNC(C));" OF ";S$(INT((C-1)/13)+1);
64040 RETURN
64050    REM
64060    REM  EVALUATE
64070    REM
64080 H4=0
64090 FOR C9=1 TO H1(H8)
64100   V=FNC(H(H8,C9))
64110   IF V>10 THEN V=10
64120   IF V=1 THEN V=11
64130   H4=H4+V
64140 NEXT C9
64145        REM  ADJUST FOR ACES
64150 C9=1
64160 IF H4<=21 THEN GOTO 64210
64170 IF C9>H1(H8) THEN 64210
64180   IF FNC(H(H8,C9))=1 THEN H4=H4-10
64190   C9=C9+1
64200 GOTO 64160
64210 RETURN
64220    REM
64230    REM  GET A CARD
64240    REM
64250 IF D1>C8 THEN GOSUB 64320
64260 C=D(D1)
64270 D1=D1+1
64280 RETURN
```

```
64290      REM
64300      REM   SHUFFLE
64310      REM
64320 PRINT
64322 PRINT "Reshuffle the cards."
64325      REM   INITIALIZE DECK ARRAY
64330 FOR C9=1 TO C8
64340    D(C9)=0
64350 NEXT C9
64355      REM   LOAD NEW ARRAY
64360 FOR C9=1 TO D8
64370    FOR C=1 TO 52
64380      X=INT(RND(1)*C8)+1
64390      IF D(X)=0 THEN GOTO 64430
64395         REM   FIND AN EMPTY POSTITION
64400         X=X+1
64410         IF X>C8 THEN X=1
64420         GOTO 64390
64430         D(X)=C
64440      NEXT C
64450 NEXT C9
64460 D1=1
64470 RETURN
64480      REM
64490      REM   INPUT AND EDIT AN AMOUNT
64500      REM
64510 PRINT
64520 PRINT "Your amount: ";
64530 INPUT S1$
64540 A=VAL(S1$)
64550 IF STR$(A)=" "+S1$ THEN GOTO 64580
64560    PRINT "Please enter a number"
64570    GOTO 64520
64580 IF A>=M4 THEN GOTO 64610
64590    PRINT "Please enter an amount no less than ";M4
64600    GOTO 64520
64610 IF A<=M2 THEN GOTO 64640
64620    PRINT "Please enter an amount no greater than ";M2
64630    GOTO 64520
64640 IF A=INT(A) THEN GOTO 64670
64650    PRINT M5$
64660    GOTO 64520
64670 RETURN
64680      REM
64690      REM   INPUT AND EDIT A CHOICE
64700      REM
64710 PRINT
64720 PRINT "Your choice: ";
64730 INPUT S1$
64740 IF X9<>1 THEN GOTO 64850
64750         REM   EDIT YES/NO
64760    IF LEN(S1$)>0 THEN GOTO 64790
64770       PRINT E1$
```

```
64780      GOTO 64720
64790      IF LEFT$(S1$,1)="Y" OR LEFT$(S1$,1)="N" THEN GOTO 64820
64800      PRINT E1$
64810      GOTO 64720
64820      IF LEFT$(S1$,1)="Y" THEN C2=1 ELSE C2=2
64830      RETURN
64840           REM  EDIT CHOICES
64850  C2=VAL(S1$)
64860  IF STR$(C2)=" "+S1$ THEN GOTO 64890
64870      PRINT E2$;X9
64880      GOTO 64720
64890  IF C2>=1 AND C2<=X9 THEN GOTO 64920
64900      PRINT E2$;X9
64910      GOTO 64720
64920  IF C2=INT(C2) THEN GOTO 64950
64930      PRINT M5$
64940      GOTO 64720
64950  RETURN
64960      REM
64970      REM  CLEAR THE SCREEN
64980      REM
64990  PRINT CHR$(11);
65000  RETURN
65010      REM
65020      REM  PAUSE FOR <RETURN>
65030      REM
65040  PRINT
65050  PRINT "         (Press RETURN to continue)"
65060  INPUT "",S1$
65070  RETURN
```

BLACKJACK (FINAL VERSION) AS
IMPLEMENTED IN PASCAL
(Program changes marked with underlining)

```
(*  BLACKJACK   VERSION 1.0
        THIS PROGRAM WILL PLAY THE PART OF THE
        DEALER IN A GAME OF BLACKJACK PLAYED
        ACCORDING TO HOYLE'S RULES

    WRITTEN BY JACK EMMERICHS,   1/1/82
    (COPYRIGHT MESSAGE GOES HERE IF YOU WANT ONE)   *)

(*  CHANGED 2/1/80 TO FIX SCREENS, REMOVE
        PRINTING OF RULES, STANDARDIZE VARIABLES
        AND FIX DEALER'S CARDS.   *)
```

```
PROGRAM BLAKJACK (INPUT, OUTPUT);

   CONST DECKS = 2;          (* NUMBER OF DECKS BEING USED  *)
         CARDS = 104;        (* NUMBER OF CARDS BEING USED  *)
         PLIMIT = 2000;      (* CREDIT LIMIT FOR THE PLAYER *)
         BLIMIT = 10000;     (* CREDIT LIMIT FOR THE BANK   *)

   VAR   AMOUNT,    CARD,
         CHOICE,    DECKNEXT,
         HANDVALU,  MAXVAL,
         MINVAL,    OPTIONS,
         THISHAND,  PLAYLMIT,
         BANKLMIT,  MINBET,
         MAXBET,    CHIPS,
         HANDPLAD,  HANDSWON,
         BET,       DLRCOLM,
         DEALERV,   AMTWON,
         SEED:      INTEGER;

         DECK:      ARRAY [1..CARDS]    OF INTEGER;
         HANDCNT:   ARRAY [1..3]        OF INTEGER;
         HANDS:     ARRAY [1..3, 1..15] OF INTEGER;
         SUIT:      ARRAY [1..4]        OF STRING [8];
         VALUE:     ARRAY [1..13]       OF STRING [5];
         HANDONE:   ARRAY [1..3]        OF BOOLEAN;
         INSTRING,
         ERROR1,
         ERROR2:    STRING;

         MSG1:      STRING [29];
         MSG2:      STRING [45];
         MSG3:      STRING [13];
         MSG4:      STRING [12];
         MSG5:      STRING [31];

         DONE:      BOOLEAN;

PROCEDURE PAUSE;
   BEGIN
      WRITELN (OUTPUT);
      WRITELN (OUTPUT,'         (Press RETURN to continue)');
      READLN (INPUT,INSTRING);
   END;    (*  OF PAUSE  *)

PROCEDURE CLEAR;
   BEGIN
      WRITE (OUTPUT,CHR(11));
   END;    (*  OF CLEAR SCREEN   *)

FUNCTION RAND (MAX: INTEGER): INTEGER;
   BEGIN
      SEED:=SEED*((SEED DIV 2)-1)+21845;
      RAND:=(SEED MOD MAX)+1;
   END;    (*  OF RANDOM NUMBER GENERATOR  *)
```

```
FUNCTION CARDVAL (CARD: INTEGER): INTEGER;
   BEGIN
      CARDVAL:=CARD-(((CARD-1) DIV 13) * 13);
   END;  (* OF CARDVAL *)


FUNCTION VAL (INSTRING: STRING): INTEGER;
   VAR COUNT, VALUE: INTEGER;
       NUMBER:          BOOLEAN;
   BEGIN
      VALUE:=0;
      NUMBER:=TRUE;
      FOR COUNT:=1 TO LENGTH(INSTRING) DO
         IF INSTRING[COUNT] IN ['0'..'9'] THEN
            VALUE:=VALUE*10+ORD(INSTRING[COUNT])-ORD('0')
         ELSE
            NUMBER:=FALSE;
      IF NUMBER THEN
         VAL:=VALUE
      ELSE
         VAL:=-1;
   END;  (* OF VAL *)


PROCEDURE SHOWCARD;                      (* PRINT A CARD *)
   VAR  CHARS, COUNT: INTEGER;
   BEGIN
      WRITE (OUTPUT,VALUE[CARDVAL(CARD)],
             ' OF ',SUIT[((CARD-1) DIV 13) + 1]);
      CHARS:=LENGTH(VALUE[CARDVAL(CARD)])+
             LENGTH(SUIT[((CARD-1) DIV 13) + 1]);
      FOR COUNT:=1 TO (20-4-CHARS) DO
         WRITE (OUTPUT,' ');
   END;  (* OF SHOWCARD *)


PROCEDURE EVALUATE;                     (* EVALUATE A HAND *)
   VAR V, COUNT: INTEGER;
   BEGIN
      HANDVALU:=0;
      FOR COUNT:=1 TO HANDCNT[THISHAND] DO
         BEGIN
            V:=CARDVAL(HANDS[THISHAND,COUNT]);
            IF V>10 THEN
               V:=10;
            IF V=1 THEN
               V:=11;
            HANDVALU:=HANDVALU+V;
         END;
      COUNT:=1;
      WHILE (HANDVALU>21) AND (COUNT<=HANDCNT[THISHAND]) DO
         BEGIN
            IF CARDVAL(HANDS[THISHAND,COUNT])=1 THEN
               HANDVALU:=HANDVALU-10;
            COUNT:=COUNT+1;
         END;
   END;  (* OF EVALUATE *)
```

```
PROCEDURE SHUFFLE;                      (*  SHUFFLE THE DECK  *)
   VAR  COUNT, X:  INTEGER;
   BEGIN
      WRITELN (OUTPUT);
      WRITELN (OUTPUT,'Reshuffle the cards');
      FOR COUNT:=1 TO CARDS DO
         DECK[COUNT]:=0;
      FOR COUNT:=1 TO DECKS DO
         BEGIN
            FOR CARD:=1 TO 52 DO
               BEGIN
                  X:=RAND(CARDS);
                  WHILE DECK[X]<>0 DO
                     BEGIN
                        X:=X+1;
                        IF X>CARDS THEN
                           X:=1;
                     END;
                  DECK[X]:=CARD;
               END;
         END;
      DECKNEXT:=1;
   END;  (*  OF SHUFFLE  *)

PROCEDURE GETCARD;                      (*  DEAL A CARD  *)
   BEGIN
      IF DECKNEXT>CARDS THEN
         SHUFFLE;
      CARD:=DECK[DECKNEXT];
      DECKNEXT:=DECKNEXT+1;
   END;  (*  OF GETCARD  *)

PROCEDURE AMOUNTIN;                     (*  GET AN AMOUNT  *)
   VAR DATAOK:   BOOLEAN;
   BEGIN
      DATAOK:=FALSE;
      WRITELN (OUTPUT);
      REPEAT
         WRITE  (OUTPUT,'Your amount: ');
         READLN (INPUT,INSTRING);
         AMOUNT:=VAL(INSTRING);
         IF AMOUNT=-1 THEN
            WRITELN (OUTPUT,MSG5)
         ELSE
            IF AMOUNT<MINVAL THEN
               WRITELN (OUTPUT,
               'Please enter an amount no less than ',MINVAL)
            ELSE
               IF AMOUNT>MAXVAL THEN
                  WRITELN (OUTPUT,
                  'Please enter an amount no more than ',MAXVAL)
               ELSE
                  DATAOK:=TRUE;
      UNTIL DATAOK
   END;  (*  OF AMOUNTIN  *)
```

```
PROCEDURE CHOICEIN;                     (*  GET A CHOICE  *)
   VAR DATAOK:    BOOLEAN;
   BEGIN
      DATAOK:=FALSE;
      WRITELN (OUTPUT);
      REPEAT
         WRITE  (OUTPUT,'Your choice: ');
         READLN (INPUT,INSTRING);
         IF OPTIONS=1 THEN
            IF LENGTH(INSTRING)=0 THEN
               WRITELN (OUTPUT,ERROR1)
            ELSE
               IF NOT (INSTRING[1] IN ['Y','N']) THEN
                  WRITELN (OUTPUT,ERROR1)
               ELSE
                  BEGIN
                     DATAOK:=TRUE;
                     IF INSTRING[1]='Y' THEN
                        CHOICE:=1
                     ELSE
                        CHOICE:=2
                  END
         ELSE
            BEGIN
               CHOICE:=VAL(INSTRING);
               IF (CHOICE<1) OR (CHOICE>OPTIONS) THEN
                  WRITELN (OUTPUT,ERROR2,OPTIONS)
               ELSE
                  DATAOK:=TRUE;
            END;
      UNTIL DATAOK
   END;  (*  OF CHOICEIN  *)
PROCEDURE SETTLE;                       (*  SETTLE BETS  *)

PROCEDURE BROKEN;                       (*  YOU BROKE THE BANK  *)
   BEGIN
      CLEAR;
      WRITELN (OUTPUT);
      WRITELN (OUTPUT,'****** YOU HAVE BROKEN THE BANK ******');
      WRITELN (OUTPUT);
      WRITELN (OUTPUT,
               'The bank cannot cover any more of its losses.');
      WRITELN (OUTPUT,
               'If you continue to play you will only lose.');
      WRITELN (OUTPUT,'   what you now have.');
      WRITELN (OUTPUT);
      PAUSE;
      BANKLMIT:=0;
      CHIPS:=(PLIMIT+BLIMIT)-PLAYLMIT;
   END;  (*  OF BROKEN  *)

PROCEDURE DEALERS;                      (*  DEALER STANDS  *)
   BEGIN
      FOR THISHAND:=2 TO 3 DO
         IF HANDCNT[THISHAND]<>0 THEN
            BEGIN
```

```
            HANDPLAD:=HANDPLAD+1;
            IF THISHAND=3 THEN
                WRITELN (OUTPUT,MSG1);
            EVALUATE;
            IF (HANDVALU=21) AND
               (HANDCNT[THISHAND]=2) THEN
                BEGIN
                    WRITELN (OUTPUT,MSG2);
                    CHIPS:=CHIPS+BET+(BET DIV 2);
                    BANKLMIT:=BANKLMIT-BET-(BET DIV 2);
                    AMTWON:=AMTWON+BET+(BET DIV 2);
                    HANDSWON:=HANDSWON+1;
                END
            ELSE
                IF (HANDVALU<DEALERV) OR
                   (HANDVALU>21) THEN
                    BEGIN
                        WRITELN (OUTPUT,MSG3);
                        CHIPS:=CHIPS-BET;
                        BANKLMIT:=BANKLMIT+BET;
                        AMTWON:=AMTWON-BET;
                    END
                ELSE
                    IF HANDVALU>DEALERV THEN
                        BEGIN
                            WRITELN (OUTPUT,MSG4);
                            CHIPS:=CHIPS+BET;
                            BANKLMIT:=BANKLMIT-BET;
                            AMTWON:=AMTWON+BET;
                            HANDSWON:=HANDSWON+1;
                        END
                    ELSE
                        WRITELN (OUTPUT,'Standoff with dealer');
        END;
    IF BANKLMIT<0 THEN
        BROKEN;
  END;    (*  DEALERS  *)


PROCEDURE DEALERO;                       (*  DEALER GOES OVER  *)
  BEGIN
    FOR THISHAND:=2 TO 3 DO
        IF HANDCNT[THISHAND]<>0 THEN
            BEGIN
                HANDPLAD:=HANDPLAD+1;
                IF THISHAND=3 THEN
                    WRITELN (OUTPUT,MSG1);
                EVALUATE;
                IF (HANDVALU=21) AND
                   (HANDCNT[THISHAND]=2) THEN
                    BEGIN
                        WRITELN (OUTPUT,MSG2);
                        CHIPS:=CHIPS+BET+(BET DIV 2);
                        BANKLMIT:=BANKLMIT-BET-(BET DIV 2);
                        AMTWON:=AMTWON+BET+(BET DIV 2);
                        HANDSWON:=HANDSWON+1;
                    END
```

```
            ELSE
                IF HANDVALU>21 THEN
                    WRITELN (OUTPUT,'ERROR HERE!!')
                ELSE
                    BEGIN
                        WRITELN (OUTPUT,MSG4);
                        CHIPS:=CHIPS+BET;
                        BANKLMIT:=BANKLMIT-BET;
                        AMTWON:=AMTWON+BET;
                        HANDSWON:=HANDSWON+1;
                    END
            END;
    IF BANKLMIT<0 THEN
        BROKEN;
    END;   (*  DEALERO  *)

PROCEDURE DEALERN;                      (*  DEALER NATURAL  *)
    VAR   COUNT: INTEGER;
    BEGIN
        WRITELN (OUTPUT);
        WRITELN (OUTPUT,'Dealer has a natural!');
        CARD:=HANDS[1,1];
        FOR COUNT:=1 TO 20 DO
            WRITE (OUTPUT,' ');
        SHOWCARD;
        WRITELN (OUTPUT);
        CARD:=HANDS[1,2];
        FOR COUNT:=1 TO 20 DO
            WRITE (OUTPUT,' ');
        SHOWCARD;
        WRITELN (OUTPUT);
        FOR THISHAND:=2 TO 3 DO
            IF HANDCNT[THISHAND]<>0 THEN
                BEGIN
                    HANDPLAD:=HANDPLAD+1;
                    IF THISHAND=3 THEN
                        WRITELN (OUTPUT,MSG1);
                    EVALUATE;
                    IF HANDVALU=21 THEN
                        WRITELN (OUTPUT,'Standoff with naturals.')
                    ELSE
                        BEGIN
                            WRITELN (OUTPUT,
                                'Dealer wins with a natural.');
                            CHIPS:=CHIPS-BET;
                            BANKLMIT:=BANKLMIT+BET;
                            AMTWON:=AMTWON-BET;
                        END;
                END;
    END;   (*  DEALERN  *)

    BEGIN                               (*  SETTLE BETS  *)
        THISHAND:=1;
        EVALUATE;
        DEALERV:=HANDVALU;
```

```
        IF (HANDVALU=21) AND
           (HANDCNT[1]=2) THEN
           DEALERN                (* DEALER NATURAL *)
        ELSE
           IF HANDVALU>21 THEN
              DEALERO             (* DEALER OVER *)
           ELSE
              DEALERS;            (* DEALER STANDS *)
     END;   (*  OF SETTLE  *)


PROCEDURE DEALER;                     (*  PLAY DEALER HAND  *)
   VAR   COUNT: INTEGER;
   BEGIN
      IF HANDCNT[3]=0 THEN
         DLRCOLM:=20
      ELSE
         DLRCOLM:=40;
      CARD:=HANDS[1,1];
      WRITELN (OUTPUT);
      FOR COUNT:=1 TO DLRCOLM DO
         WRITE (OUTPUT,' ');
      SHOWCARD;
      CARD:=HANDS[1,2];
      WRITELN (OUTPUT);
      FOR COUNT:=1 TO DLRCOLM DO
         WRITE (OUTPUT,' ');
      SHOWCARD;
      THISHAND:=1;
      EVALUATE;
      WHILE (HANDVALU<=17) DO
         BEGIN
            GETCARD;
            WRITELN (OUTPUT);
            FOR COUNT:=1 TO DLRCOLM DO
               WRITE (OUTPUT,' ');
            SHOWCARD;
            HANDCNT[1]:=HANDCNT[1]+1;
            HANDS[1,HANDCNT[1]]:=CARD;
            EVALUATE;
         END;
      WRITELN (OUTPUT);
      IF HANDVALU<=21 THEN
         WRITELN (OUTPUT,'The dealer stands at ',HANDVALU)
      ELSE
         WRITELN (OUTPUT,'The dealer goes over 21');
   END;   (*  OF DEALER  *)

PROCEDURE PLAYER;                   (*  PLAY PLAYER HAND  *)

   PROCEDURE PLYRHAND;                  (*  DO A SINGLE PLAY  *)
   VAR   COUNT:  INTEGER;
   BEGIN
      IF HANDONE[THISHAND] THEN
         WRITELN (OUTPUT,'That hand is already over 21')
```

```
      ELSE
          BEGIN
              GETCARD;
              IF THISHAND=3 THEN
                  FOR COUNT:=1 TO 20 DO
                      WRITE (OUTPUT,' ');
              SHOWCARD;
              WRITELN (OUTPUT);
              HANDCNT[THISHAND]:=HANDCNT[THISHAND]+1;
              HANDS[THISHAND,HANDCNT[THISHAND]]:=CARD;
              EVALUATE;
              IF HANDVALU>21 THEN
                  BEGIN
                      WRITELN (OUTPUT,
                                'Too bad, player goes over 21');
                      HANDONE[THISHAND]:=TRUE;
                  END;
          END;
  END;  (* OF PLYRHAND *)

BEGIN                            (* OF PLAYER *)
    HANDONE[2]:=FALSE;
    IF HANDCNT[3]=0 THEN
        HANDONE[3]:=TRUE
    ELSE
        HANDONE[3]:=FALSE;
    REPEAT
        WRITELN (OUTPUT,'What next?');
        IF HANDCNT[3]=0 THEN
            BEGIN
                WRITELN (OUTPUT,'Do you want another card?');
                OPTIONS:=1;
                CHOICEIN;
                IF CHOICE=1 THEN
                    CHOICE:=2
                ELSE
                    CHOICE:=1;
            END
        ELSE
            BEGIN
                WRITELN (OUTPUT,
                          '1: Done  2: Card for 1  3: Card for 2');
                OPTIONS:=3;
                CHOICEIN;
            END;
        IF CHOICE<>1 THEN
            BEGIN
                THISHAND:=CHOICE;
                PLYRHAND;
            END;
    UNTIL (CHOICE=1) OR
          (HANDONE[2] AND HANDONE[3]);
    IF HANDONE[2] AND HANDONE[3] THEN
        DONE:=TRUE;
END;  (* OF PLAYER *)
```

```
PROCEDURE SPLIT;                          (*  SPLIT PAIRS  *)
   BEGIN
      WRITELN (OUTPUT,'Do you wish to split your pair?');
      OPTIONS:=1;
      CHOICEIN;
      IF CHOICE=1 THEN
         IF CHIPS<(2*BET) THEN
            WRITELN (OUTPUT,'You cannot cover the bet.')
         ELSE
            BEGIN
               CLEAR;
               HANDS[3,1]:=HANDS[2,2];
               WRITELN (OUTPUT);
               WRITELN (OUTPUT,
                  'PLAYER-1          PLAYER-2          DEALER');
               WRITELN (OUTPUT);
               CARD:=HANDS[2,1];
               SHOWCARD;
               CARD:=HANDS[3,1];
               SHOWCARD;
               CARD:=HANDS[1,1];
               SHOWCARD;
               WRITELN (OUTPUT);
               GETCARD;
               HANDS[2,2]:=CARD;
               SHOWCARD;
               GETCARD;
               HANDS[3,2]:=CARD;
               SHOWCARD;
               WRITE (OUTPUT,'XXXXX');
               WRITELN (OUTPUT);
               HANDCNT[3]:=2;
            END;
   END;   (*  OF SPLIT  *)

PROCEDURE NATURALS;                       (*  HANDLE NATURALS  *)
   BEGIN
      THISHAND:=1;
      EVALUATE;
      IF HANDVALU=21 THEN
         DONE:=TRUE;
   END;   (*  OF NATURALS  *)

PROCEDURE DEAL;                           (*  DEAL THE HAND  *)
   BEGIN
      CLEAR;
      WRITELN (OUTPUT);
      WRITELN (OUTPUT,'   PLAYER          DEALER');
      WRITELN (OUTPUT);
      GETCARD;
      HANDS[2,1]:=CARD;
      SHOWCARD;
      GETCARD;
      HANDS[1,1]:=CARD;
      SHOWCARD;
```

```
           WRITELN (OUTPUT);
           GETCARD;
           HANDS[2,2]:=CARD;
           SHOWCARD;
           GETCARD;
           HANDS[1,2]:=CARD;
           WRITE (OUTPUT,'XXXXX');
           WRITELN (OUTPUT);
           HANDCNT[1]:=2;
           HANDCNT[2]:=2;
           HANDCNT[3]:=0;
      END;   (*  OF DEAL  *)

PROCEDURE BETTING;                        (*  PLACE YOUR BET *)
    BEGIN
        BET:=-1;
        MAXVAL:=BLIMIT;
        MINVAL:=0;
        REPEAT
           WRITELN (OUTPUT,'How much do you wish to bet?');
           AMOUNTIN;
           IF AMOUNT>MAXBET THEN
              BEGIN
                 WRITELN (OUTPUT,'That is more than than the $',
                          MAXBET,' house limit.');
                 MAXVAL:=MAXBET;
              END
           ELSE
              IF (AMOUNT<MINBET) AND
                 (AMOUNT<>0) THEN
                 WRITELN (OUTPUT,'That is below the $',
                          MINBET,' house minimum.')
              ELSE
                 IF AMOUNT>CHIPS THEN
                    BEGIN
                       WRITELN (OUTPUT,'You only have $',
                                CHIPS,' in chips.');
                       MAXBET:=CHIPS;
                    END
                 ELSE
                    BET:=AMOUNT;
        UNTIL BET<>-1;
      END;   (*  OF BETTING  *)



PROCEDURE PLAYHAND;                        (*  PLAY A HAND OF CARDS  *)
    BEGIN
        REPEAT
           CLEAR;
           DONE:=FALSE;
           BETTING;
           IF BET<MINBET THEN
              CHOICE:=2
```

```
        ELSE
            BEGIN
                DEAL;
                NATURALS;
                IF NOT DONE THEN
                    BEGIN
                        IF CARDVAL(HANDS[2,1])=CARDVAL(HANDS[2,2]) THEN
                            SPLIT;
                        PLAYER;
                        IF NOT DONE THEN
                            DEALER;
                    END;
                SETTLE;
                WRITELN (OUTPUT,'Play again?');
                OPTIONS:=1;
                CHOICEIN;
            END;
    UNTIL CHOICE=2;
  END;   (* OF PLAYHAND *)


PROCEDURE STATUS;                        (* REPORT GAME STATUS *)
  BEGIN
    CLEAR;
    WRITELN (OUTPUT);
    WRITELN (OUTPUT,'Number of hands played: ',HANDPLAD);
    WRITELN (OUTPUT,'Number of hands won: ',HANDSWON);
    WRITE   (OUTPUT,'Percentage of hands won: ');
    IF HANDPLAD=0 THEN
        WRITELN (OUTPUT,0,' %')
    ELSE
        WRITELN (OUTPUT,((100*HANDSWON) DIV HANDPLAD),' %');
    WRITELN (OUTPUT);
    WRITELN (OUTPUT,'Current value of your cash: $',PLAYLMIT);
    WRITELN (OUTPUT,'Current value of your chips: $',CHIPS);
    WRITELN (OUTPUT,'Your current funds: $',PLAYLMIT+CHIPS);
    WRITELN (OUTPUT);
    WRITE   (OUTPUT,'Total amount ');
    IF AMTWON>=0 THEN
        WRITELN (OUTPUT,'won: $',AMTWON)
    ELSE
        WRITELN (OUTPUT,'lost: $',ABS(AMTWON));
    WRITE   (OUTPUT,'Average amount ');
    IF AMTWON>0 THEN
        WRITE   (OUTPUT,'won per hand: $')
    ELSE
        WRITE   (OUTPUT,'lost per hand: $');
    IF HANDPLAD=0 THEN
        WRITELN (OUTPUT,0)
    ELSE
        WRITELN (OUTPUT,ABS(AMTWON) DIV HANDPLAD);
    PAUSE;
  END;   (* OF STATUS *)
```

```
PROCEDURE BANKER;                      (*  DEAL WITH THE BANK  *)

  PROCEDURE BUY;                       (*  BUY CHIPS  *)
     BEGIN
        IF PLAYLMIT=0 THEN
           BEGIN
              WRITELN (OUTPUT,'You have no more money.');
              PAUSE;
           END
        ELSE
           BEGIN
              MAXVAL:=BLIMIT;
              MINVAL:=0;
              REPEAT
                 WRITELN (OUTPUT,'How much do you wish to buy?');
                 AMOUNTIN;
                 IF AMOUNT>PLAYLMIT THEN
                    BEGIN
                       WRITELN (OUTPUT,'You only have $',
                                PLAYLMIT);
                       MAXVAL:=PLAYLMIT;
                    END;
              UNTIL AMOUNT<=PLAYLMIT;
              PLAYLMIT:=PLAYLMIT-AMOUNT;
              CHIPS   :=CHIPS   +AMOUNT;
           END;
     END;  (*  OF BUY  *)


  PROCEDURE CASHIN;                    (*  CASH IN CHIPS  *)
     BEGIN
        IF CHIPS=0 THEN
           BEGIN
              WRITELN (OUTPUT,'You have no more chips.');

              PAUSE;
           END
        ELSE
           BEGIN
              MAXVAL:=BLIMIT;
              MINVAL:=0;
              REPEAT
              WRITELN (OUTPUT,'How much do you wish to cash in?');
                 AMOUNTIN;
                 IF AMOUNT>CHIPS THEN
                    BEGIN
                       WRITELN (OUTPUT,'You only have ',
                                CHIPS, 'chips.');
                       MAXVAL:=CHIPS;
                    END;
              UNTIL AMOUNT<=CHIPS;
              PLAYLMIT:=PLAYLMIT+AMOUNT;
              CHIPS   :=CHIPS   -AMOUNT;
           END;
     END;  (*  OF CASH IN  *)
```

```
    BEGIN                           (*  OF BANKER  *)
       CLEAR;
       WRITELN (OUTPUT);
       WRITELN (OUTPUT,'   You may do either of the following:');
       WRITELN (OUTPUT);
       WRITELN (OUTPUT,'       1. Buy more chips');
       WRITELN (OUTPUT,'       2. Cash in your chips');
       OPTIONS:=2;
       CHOICEIN;
       IF CHOICE=1 THEN
          BUY
       ELSE
          CASHIN;
    END;  (*  OF BANKER  *)

       (* THE INSTRUCTION PROCEDURE HAS BEEN REMOVED *)

PROCEDURE TERM;                      (* TERMINATION ROUTINE *)
    BEGIN
       STATUS;
       WRITELN (OUTPUT);
       WRITELN (OUTPUT,
          'Thank you for the game, please come again sometime.');
       (* THE PAUSE HERE WAS REMOVED *)
    END;  (*  OF TERM  *)

PROCEDURE NEXTACTV;                   (* NEXT ACTIV ROUTINE *)
    BEGIN
       REPEAT
          CLEAR;
          WRITELN (OUTPUT);
          WRITELN (OUTPUT,
             '  You may do any of the following things:');
          WRITELN (OUTPUT);
          WRITELN (OUTPUT,
             '           1.  Visit the bank.');
          WRITELN (OUTPUT,
             '           2.  Display the current status of the game.');
          WRITELN (OUTPUT,
             '           3.  Shuffle the deck.');
          WRITELN (OUTPUT,
             '           4.  Play a hand of cards.');
          WRITELN (OUTPUT,
             '           5.  Quit the game.');
          OPTIONS:=5;
          CHOICEIN;
          IF CHOICE<>5 THEN
             CASE CHOICE OF
                1:  BANKER;
                2:  STATUS;
                3:  SHUFFLE;
                4:  PLAYHAND;
             END;  (*  OF CASE STATEMENT  *)
       UNTIL CHOICE=5;
    END;  (*  NEXTACTV  *)
```

```
PROCEDURE INIT;                         (* INIT ROUTINE *)
   BEGIN
      SUIT[1] := 'SPADES';        SUIT[2] := 'HEARTS';
      SUIT[3] := 'DIAMONDS';      SUIT[4] := 'CLUBS';
      VALUE[1] := 'ACE';   VALUE[2] := '2';   VALUE[3] := '3';
      VALUE[4] := '4';     VALUE[5] := '5';   VALUE[6] := '6';
      VALUE[7] := '7';     VALUE[8] := '8';   VALUE[9] := '9';
      VALUE[10] := '10';   VALUE[11] := 'JACK';
      VALUE[12] := 'QUEEN'; VALUE[13] := 'KING';
      SHUFFLE;
      PLAYLMIT:=PLIMIT;
      BANKLMIT:=BLIMIT;
      MINBET:=10;
      MAXBET:=500;
      CHIPS:=0;
      HANDPLAD:=0;
      HANDSWON:=0;
      AMTWON:=0;
      ERROR1:='Please enter YES or NO';
      ERROR2:='Please enter a number from 1 to ';
      MSG1:='For the player''s second hand:';
      MSG2:='Player wins with a natural, house pays extra.';
      MSG3:='Player loses.';
      MSG4:='Player wins.';
      MSG5:='Please enter an integer number.';
      CLEAR;
      WRITELN (OUTPUT);
      WRITELN (OUTPUT,
      'Welcome to the Blackjack table.  We will be playing');
      WRITELN (OUTPUT,
      '   by the rules of Blackjack according to Hoyle.');
      WRITELN (OUTPUT,'   the house limits on bets are:');
      WRITELN (OUTPUT,'      minimum bet: $',MINBET);
      WRITELN (OUTPUT,'      maximum bet: $',MAXBET);
      WRITELN (OUTPUT,'   the house currently has $',
         BANKLMIT,' in the bank.');
      WRITELN (OUTPUT,'   You currently have $',
         PLAYLMIT,' in cash');
      WRITELN (OUTPUT);
      WRITELN (OUTPUT,
      '   Please sit down and play for a while.');
      PAUSE;
   END;  (*  OF INIT  *)

BEGIN                                   (* PROGRAM MAINLINE *)
   INIT;
   NEXTACTV;
   TERM;
END.  (*  OF PROGRAM  *)
```

Glossary

This glossary contains words, names, and terms that may be new to beginning programmers and that are used in this book. Each definition reflects how an entry will be used here, and therefore may not include all possible definitions for the term. A more complete glossary of computer related terms can be found in *HOME COMPUTERS: A BEGINNER'S GLOSSARY AND GUIDE*, available from dilithium Press.

- **6800:** The Motorola M6800 is a single electronic component (a "chip") which is in itself a complete computer processor. It has been used as the basis for small computer systems (see 8080 and Z80 below).
- **8080:** The Intel 8080 is another single electronic component (another "chip") which is in itself a complete computer processor (see 6800 above and Z80 below). It has been used as the basis for several small computer systems. The instruction set for the Intel 8080 has also been included in several newer processors so that programs that run on the 8080 can usually be made to run on these newer processors.
- **ABS(X):** The mathematical function that returns the absolute value (the positive) of the variable X (eg. five is the absolute value of plus five and minus five). See FUNCTION below.
- **Acceptance testing:** Testing a completed computer program or system of programs to see if it performs in an acceptable manner.

- **Address:** The location of a specific unit in a computer's memory (see BYTE below). The first position of memory is usually address zero. The highest possible address in most small computer systems is 65535.
- **ALGOL:** A computer language developed in Europe during the 1960's. It was one of the first structured languages. The name is derived from the term ALGO-rythmic Language.
- **Alpha numeric:** Information that can be either alphabetic or numeric. This includes just about any combination of printable characters shown on your terminal's keyboard.
- **APL:** A computer language that is very powerful when working with large arrays or matrices. It uses a set of special characters which makes it difficult for a beginning programmer to learn. The name is derived from the term A Programming Language.
- **Array:** A data structure made up of repetitions of a single type of data. A list of numbers may be represented as an array with each number being one element of the array. A table of numbers arranged in rows and columns may be represented by a two-dimensional array: one dimension indicates an element's row, and the other indicates the column. In most computer languages there is no limit to the number of dimensions that an array may have (except for the amount of memory available).
- **Assembler:** A program that translates an assembly language program into a machine language program. It replaces the programmer's labels and data names with appropriate memory addresses, and it translates each instruction's mnemonic name into the proper machine instruction.
- **Assembly language:** A computer language that requires one program instruction for each machine instruction. The program is translated into machine language by an assembler (see above). There is an assembly language for each type of computer processor.
- **BASIC:** A computer language developed as a teaching aid that has received broad acceptance as a high-

level general purpose language. It is the language most commonly used on small computer systems. The name is an acronym for Beginner's All-purpose Symbolic Instruction Code.

- **Bit:** The primary unit of information storage in computer memory. A bit is a "switch" that may store either of two values: "on" or "off." Eight bits are usually gathered together into a *byte* (see below) which may store any of 256 (2 to the 8th power) values.

- **Black box:** A process that uses a single type of input or has a single entry point; and performs a single function or yields a specific result. It is called a black box because the way in which the process works internally need not be known outside of the function itself.

- **Block:** A common expression for a small, easily identified portion of a computer program. The instructions for attaching wheels to shafts in the Frammis instructions make up a *block* of program instructions.

- **Boolean:** A term derived from the name of the mathematician George Boole; usually meaning "relating to logic". Boolean algebra is the algebra of formal logic, and the logical TRUE/FALSE data elements in the Pascal computer language are called BOOLEAN data.

- **Bug:** An error that prevents a program from working correctly. Insidious little things that are virtually impossible to get rid of or prevent. The bane of the programmer's existence.

- **Byte:** A collection of eight bits in a computer's memory. For most small computers, memory is measured in bytes. Each byte may contain any of 256 (2 to the 8th power) values (see BIT above).

- **CALL:** The type of programming statement used to invoke a subroutine. The RETURN at the end of the subroutine will return processing to the next statement after the CALL.

- **Calculator:** A simple device used to perform arithmetic calculations. Unlike the computer the calculator cannot change its operation by changing a program because its "program" is built into its wiring. Programmable calculators are really small computers because they do not have this limitation.

- **CASE statement:** The type of programming statement used to choose one condition from a list of conditions.

- **Chaining:** The practice of invoking a new program with the terminating statement of another program. A computer system built up from several small programs can operate like one large program if each part of the system automatically chains to the next part of the system.

- **Character:** A single printable letter, numeral, or punctuation mark (including the blank). In most small computers one character can be stored in byte of memory.

- **Clause:** A portion of a programming instruction. The IF-THEN-ELSE statement has a condition clause, a THEN clause, and an ELSE clause.

- **COBOL:** A computer language developed in the early 1960's. It has traditionally been the most commonly used language for large business systems. The name is an acronym for COmmon Business Oriented Language.

- **Code:** A common term for programming instructions. A program written in a high level language is often called the *source code* because it is the source of the translation program's information.

- **Comment:** Explanatory information added to a computer program to make the program listing easier to understand. Comments are ignored when the program is executed. In BASIC a comment is called a REMARK.

- **Compiler:** A program that translates high-level language statements into a machine-level program. The compiler will figure out where data must be stored and what machine instructions must be used to make the program work (contrast this with ASSEMBLER above, and INTERPRETER below).

- **Computer:** A machine that will process textual and numeric information according to instructions stored in its memory. A computer is usually distinguished from a calculator (see above) by the fact that it is directed from an internal stored program which can easily be changed, and it can communicate with external devices such as printers, terminals, and disk or tape drives.

- **Condition:** A situation that is tested for being true or false. When several possible situations are logically combined into a more complicated test it is called a *conditional expression.* Conditions are tested in CASE, IF-THEN, DO-UNTIL, and DO-WHILE statements.

- **Constant:** A value in a program that never changes. Constants may be numeric or character data, and are written directly into the program's instructions.

- **Counter:** A variable used to count something within a program. Most DO LOOPS are controlled by a counter that will allow the loop to be executed a specific number of times.

- **Coupling:** The interaction between modules within a system. In a well-structured system, there is little need for one module to know how the other modules work. They can therefore be loosely coupled by simply sharing some common information (see BLACK BOX above). Modules that depend on the internal processing of other modules are tightly coupled and represent a poorly structured system.

- **Data:** The information used within a computer system. The processing of this information has led to the term DATA PROCESSING. The singular form of the word is datum, but it is common to use data as both singular and plural.

- **Data allocation:** The process of assigning a memory location to each constant and variable that a program will use. In low-level languages this must be done by the programmer. In high-level languages it is often done by the translation program with little or no direction from the programmer.

- **Data definition:** Specification of what data type each constant and variable in a program will be. Allowable ranges of values may also be defined for each data item.

- **Data dictionary:** A compilation of all the data items in a system showing the item, its name, its type, and its allowable range of values.
- **Data element:** The lowest level of data item available to a program. Files, records, arrays, and other data structures are all made up of data elements.
- **Data structure:** Several related items of information that have been gathered together into a single group and can be treated as a single complex data type. An array is a data structure made up of a list of items rather than a single item. Records and files are even more complex data structures.
- **Data type:** The identification of how information stored in a computer's memory is to be used. The same pattern of bytes in memory may be part of a number or may be characters in a text message. In this book we have dealt primarily with numeric data and character data.
- **Debugging:** The process of trying to remove the bugs (see above) from a program. Bugs are usually found by testing or by demonstrating a program to a friend.
- **Design:** To plan the steps of a project so that you know what you are doing during the development of a computer system. A system should be thoroughly designed before the first programs are written.
- **Detailed design:** The third step of a computer programming project. The detailed design refines the general design and produces the data dictionary and the functional dictionary. The entire system exists in the form of sketch code at the end of this step.
- **Device:** A piece of equipment connected to, and usually controlled by, a computer. Printers and terminals are communication devices. Tape drives and disk drives are storage devices which can hold information from the computer's memory when the computer is turned off. Because they are outside of the computer itself these items are often called *external devices*.
- **Dialect:** A specific version of a computer language. Most high-level languages are changed by each manufacturer just enough so that one dialect of a

language will usually not work on a computer that uses a different dialect of the same language.

- **Digital:** Using discrete values such as 0 or 1 instead of smoothly changing values such as the movement of a phonograph needle. A stereo system is an ANALOG device which can produce any tone or sound. A digital computer can only operate with the 256 possible values of a byte of memory (which is itself made up of the two possible values for each bit of memory)*.
- **Dimensions:** The number of indices required to identify an element of an array. A one-dimensional array is a list of numbers that requires one index to identify an item in the list. A two-dimensional array can be visualized as a table of rows and columns that requires two indices to indicate an item (where a row and column intersect in the table). There may be no limit to the number of dimensions that an array may have.
- **Directive statement:** The type of programming statement used to change a value, read a variable, print a result, or to perform in some other way the actual processing that is to be done. The other types of statements may control the execution of the program, but it is the directive statements that actually get the work done.
- **Disk drive:** A mechanical device that allows a computer to store information on a magnetic disk in much the same way that music can be stored on a stereo system's magnetic tapes. The disk is very fast, and it can access any piece of information on command without having to read through all the other information ahead of it. (a bit like being able to play any selection on a phonograph record).
- **DO-LOOP:** The type of programming statement that allows a block of instructions to be executed a preset number of times by using a counter that increases (or decreases) with each execution until it eventually

---

*Note: digital audio recordings are now being made. These cannot reproduce extremely high frequencies, but they can reproduce the sounds we can hear much more accurately than analog recordings can.

reaches the preset number. In BASIC, the DO-LOOP is called a FOR-NEXT loop.

- **DO-UNTIL:** The type of programming statement that allows a block of instructions to be executed until a specific condition has been satisfied. The condition is checked at the end of the loop, so the block of code will always be executed at least once.

- **DO-WHILE:** The type of programming statement that allows a block of instructions to be executed as long as a specific condition is satisfied. The condition is checked at the beginning of the loop, so the block of code will never be executed if the condition is never met.

- **Driver program:** A small program written to test a subroutine before the subroutine is added to the final program.

- **Dummy subroutine:** A small subroutine that is written to test a program before the final subroutine is completed. The dummy routine usually prints messages and sets conditions that will help test the developing program.

- **Dynamic variable:** A variable that will constantly change its value throughout the operation of a program (eg. the number of chips that a player currently has).

- **Editing input:** The process of checking information when it is first entered into a computer system to see that it is correct. If all information in a system is completely edited when it is first obtained, there will be no need for checking it again later on.

- **ELSE:** The clause of an IF-THEN-ELSE statement that controls processing when the IF condition is false.

- **END statement:** The type of programming statement used to end a program and possibly chain to another program. Note, however, that in Pascal, END is used throughout the program to terminate blocks of instructions. Pascal ends the program by reaching the end of the last instruction. For this reason, we have called this type of statement STOP in this book.

- **Error checking:** Checking to be sure that some abnormal condition does not exist before beginning an operation. All abnormal conditions and how each is to be handled must be defined in a program. Only when it is known that no errors exist should normal processing proceed.
- **Evaluate:** To find the value of. When a condition or expression is evaluated, it is reduced to a simple true or false. Mathematical expressions and functions are evaluated to produce a single value (eg. (5+3)/2 becomes 4 when it is evaluated).
- **Execute:** To process. The term may be used to indicate that a program instruction, subroutine, or entire program is being used.
- **Expression:** a (usually complex) programming statement. If an IF-THEN statement tests several conditions together, they are called a condition of expression. (5+3)/2 is a mathematical expression which is equal to four.
- **Feasibility study:** The first step in a programming project. The feasibility study should determine what is to be done, and if it is a reasonable project.
- **File:** A data structure that is usually made up of records (which are usually data structures themselves) and kept on an external storage device like a tape or disk drive. A payroll file, for example, may contain a record for each employee, and may be processed once each week.
- **Flag:** A simple data type that indicates a logical TRUE/FALSE condition. In Pascal a flag is a BOOLEAN variable.
- **Flow chart:** A programming aid that allows a programmer to visualize how a process will work before a program is written. It was developed before the era of "structured programming" and has several shortcomings. On occasion, however, it can be useful.
- **FOR-NEXT:** The type of programming statement that controls repeated execution of a block of instructions. See DO-LOOP above.
- **FORTH:** A programming language that provides a simple basic language and allows the programmer to

develop additional procedures that can actually become a new part of the language. The name is derived from the fact that the fourth version of the language was kept on a computer that only allowed file names up to five characters long.

- **FORTRAN:** A programming language that was developed in the late 1950's. This was one of the first high-level languages. It is efficient with calculations and is often found in engineering and statistical applications. The name is derived from the term FORmula TRANslation.

- **Frammis:** A child's toy that comes in a box marked "Some assembly required." The articulated type is the most popular for obvious reasons.

- **Function:** A specific operation. In designing a program, the operations that must be performed are defined as functions. At the level of a specific instruction, a function is an operation that receives a specific value and returns a unique answer. The absolute value function, ABS(X), receives any number X and returns the positive value of the number (see above). Functions can deal with numbers or characters, are provided with most high-level languages, and (in some cases) may be defined by the programmer.

- **Functional dictionary:** This is one of the products of the detailed design. It is a compilation of sketch code for every function within a program. Creating the functional dictionary is the heart of a program's design.

- **General purpose language:** A high-level computer language that is not restricted by its design to a specific type of application. Most of the languages that a beginning programmer would be likely to use are general purpose languages.

- **General design:** The second step of a programming project. The general design develops the processing functions and the items of information that will be needed to complete the project.

- **GOTO:** A type of statement that transfers processing to another part of a program. A program full of GOTO statements is almost impossible to understand so it has not been included in the list of structured programming statements. In simple versions of BASIC, however, the GOTO may be required to build up some of the more complex types of structured statements.

- **Graphics:** Pictorial information in computer form. Many small computers include a limited capability to draw pictures on a terminal screen or printer. Detailed graphics processing usually requires specialized equipment, large amounts of storage capacity, and very complex programs.

- **Hierarchy:** An organization in which the overall system (represented by the highest level of detail) is broken down into lower levels of detail. Each level is made up of several individual modules. Each module is a part of the next higher (or *parent*) module, and is made up of all the elements at the next lower (or *offspring*) module.

- **High-level language:** A computer language in which the programmer does not need to know the internal structure of the computer. A compiler program (see above) or an interpreter (see below) will translate the high level language program into whatever machine-level instructions are required to run the program.

- **Housekeeping functions:** Utility operations that are found in almost all programs. Initialization operations like initializing variables and loading arrays with specific values are done at the beginning of the program. Termination operations like final reports and messages are done at the end of the program.

- **IF-THEN Statement:** The type of programming statement used to test current conditions and then select the proper processing to be done depending on the result of that test. A more complex form of the statement also includes an ELSE clause (see above).

- **Implementation:** The last step of a programming project. This is where the actual programs are written, tested, and used. This is also the first step in many projects, followed by discovery, design, and then re-implementation.

- **Index:** An pointer to a specific valve in an array. Each dimension of an array is represented by an index value when the array is used. The second element of a one-dimensional array is written ARRAY(2), and the value two is the index.

- **Initialization procedure:** The first procedure of a program; used to perform the start-up housekeeping (see above) functions.
- **Input:** Information that is entered into a program while it is running. Input may come from the person using the computer, a tape or disk drive, or any other source outside the program. All input is stored in variables within the program.
- **Instruction:** A direction for the computer to perform a specific operation. A machine language program uses one instruction for each operation available in the computer. A single high-level instruction (eg. set the value of a variable to the sum of two numbers) may require many machine language instructions to be executed.
- **Instruction set:** The instructions that have been built into a computer. Each computer has its own instruction set. In some cases, a new computer (like the Z80) will include all of the instructions of an older computer (the 8080 in this case) so that programs that ran on the older computer will also run on the new one.
- **INT(X):** The integer function. For any number X, INT(X) will return the whole number value of the number without any fractional amounts. The integer portion of 1.23, for example, is 1.
- **Integer:** A whole counting number like 1, 2, 3, etc. Integers may be positive or negative and of any size. In many computer languages, the integers from –32768 to +32767 can be stored in two bytes of memory. Such a language may restrict "integer" variables to these values.
- **Integration testing:** Testing a completed program or system of programs (see Acceptance testing above).
- **Intelligence:** A measure of thinking ability. Unfortunately, it is almost impossible to define or measure. Computer systems developed to explore thinking processes are often referred to as *artificial intelligence* systems since the apparent intelligence was supplied by a person's program.

- **Interpreter:** A program (usually written in machine language with an assembler) that reads a high-level language program and carries out each instruction as it is read. This means that the interpreter must be in memory along with the high-level language program and that the instructions of the program are constantly being re-interpreted as they run. Most common versions of BASIC are interpreters.
- **Language:** A format for exchanging information. Languages spoken by people are called *natural languages*. Computer languages are the vocabulary and syntax that an assembler, interpreter, or compiler program requires for its input.
- **LISP:** A computer programming language developed to work with lists of information. LISP is uaually an interpreter that is very powerful with textual data but somewhat clumsy with calculations. It is not an easy language for a beginning programmer to learn. The name is derived from the expression LISt Processing.
- **Listing:** A printed representation of a program. The program itself is really the pattern of bits in the computer's memory when the program is running. A programmer will work with a listing of the assembly or high-level language version of the program.
- **Literal:** Another name for a constant (see above).
- **Logic:** A common term for a program's structure as in: "the program's logic looks okay to me." Logical operations also refer to the use of AND, OR, and NOT as described in chapter one to evaluate a conditional expression.
- **Loop:** A programming structure that allows a block of instructions to be executed repetitively. A program with a few hundred instructions that contains lots of loops may make a computer execute billions of instructions.
- **Machine instruction:** An operation that has been built into the circuitry of a computer.
- **Machine language:** The numeric codes for a computer's instructions. In most small computers each instruction is stored in one byte of memory so the machine's language consists of 256 codes or fewer.

More powerful computers may use more than one byte per instruction and may therefore have a much larger set of codes in their language.

- **Mainline:** The main controlling logic of a program. The mainline module may call an initialization routine, control the operation of the program, and then call a termination routine when the program has finished.

- **Memory:** The circuits of a computer that store information. Most memory is made up of bits that can hold an "on" or "off" condition. The pattern of the bits indicates the information stored in memory.

- **Module:** An easily identified portion of a system, hierarchy, network, or other structure. In a well-structured system, each module represents a single function and is loosely coupled to a few other modules.

- **Murphy's demon:** A nasty little creature who is constantly trying to find ways to make your programs misbehave. The only way to outwit the demon is to try to think of all possible abnormal conditions during a system's design and then include ways to handle each condition in each program. This is almost never completely successful.

- **Natural language:** Languages such as English, French, and Swahili that people use to communicate with each other as opposed to computer languages which are used to communicate with a computer.

- **Nested statements:** Programming statements that are controlled by other programming statements. This may include any combination of IF-THEN-ELSE statements within other IF-THEN-ELSE statements, loops within-loops, or any other such combination of statements.

- **Network:** An organization in which the overall system (represented by the highest level of detail) is broken down into lower levels of detail. Each level is made up of several individual modules. Unlike a hierarchy (see above), any one module may be part of several other higher level modules in the network. Most programs are networks with a set of utility subroutines that may be called from any module in the program.

- **Number:** A value representing an amount. A number may be positive or negative, it may be an integer (see above) or a fractional value such as 1.234, and it may be exact (like the integer 1) or approximate (like 0.33333 for 1/3).
- **Numeric:** A type of data that deals with numbers.
- **Offspring:** Sub-modules within a hierarchy or network. Each module is part of its *parent* or higher level and is made up of its *offspring* or lower levels.
- **Output:** Information that is produced by a program. This may be numeric, alphanumeric, constant, or variable data, and it may be sent to a terminal screen, printer, or other external device. Creating the output is the reason for writing the program.
- **Parent:** The module within a hierarchy or network for which a specific module is a sub-element. Each module is part of its *parent* or higher level and is made up of its *offspring* or lower levels.
- **Pascal:** A structured programming language that was derived from ALGOL. Pascal is a general purpose high-level language that is rapidly becoming widely used with small computers. It is named after the French mathematician-philosopher, Blaise Pascal.
- **PL/I:** A structured programming language that was designed to provide all the advantages of COBOL and FORTRAN, and was organized somewhat like ALGOL. It is a large and complex language which has a subset that is just now starting to become available on small computer systems.
- **Precision:** A measure of the accuracy of a number. To represent 1/3 as a decimal number, 0.333 has less precision than 0.33333333. Most computer languages have a limit to the number of digits a number may have, and thus a limit to their precision.
- **Printer:** An external device that prints information from a computer on paper rather than showing it on a terminal screen or writing it to a file on magnetic tape or disk.
- **Processing:** What a computer does. To process information is to act upon it as directed by a program.
- **Processor:** The central controlling mechanism of a computer. The circuits of the processor define the

instructions that may be used in the computer. The processor may read or write in memory, and may communicate with external devices in the "real" world.

- **Program:** An ordered set of instructions. The program tells the processor what to do next. If a computer program is changed, the computer's actions are changed. Any set of instructions from a recipe for oatmeal muffins to a payroll system is a program.
- **Project life cycle:** The complete plan for building a program. The steps of the cycle make up the steps of program development.
- **Project:** An organized programming activity with a specific goal, and an organized method (top-down structured programming) of operation.
- **Project definition:** The first step of a project. If we have not defined what we are to do, we will have no specific goal, and will not be able to proceed in a reasonably organized way.
- **Project plan:** Another term for PROJECT LIFE CYCLE (see above).
- **Prompt:** A message to an operator explaining what will be needed for the next input item.
- **Pseudo-random number:** A computer generated number that appears to be a random value. In fact, the number is calculated from the previous pseudo-random number using a complex calculation. The first random number used is calculated from a seed. From any specific seed, the same group of pseudo-random numbers will always be generated.
- **Pseudo-code:** Programming logic written as general instructions and calculation notes. See SKETCH CODE below.
- **Random number:** A number picked at random that does not relate to anything else. This is almost impossible to achieve, so most small computer systems use pseudo-random numbers (see above) to control "random" events.
- **Real number:** Any positive or negative value including integers and the fractional amounts between the integers. 3.14159 is a real number. A real number may be exact like 0.25 for 1/4, or approximate like

0.33333 for 1/3. (See PRECISION and INTEGER above).

- **Record:** A data structure that contains other data structures and elements that relate to a specific entity. All of the information about an employee, for example, may be kept on one employee RECORD. A collection of records is usually kept in a file on an external storage device.

- **Regression testing:** Retesting procedures that have already been tested after part of a program has been changed. Major changes to a program may interfere with functions that are already working. A regression test re-tests everything tested so far to ensure that this has not happened.

- **RETURN:** The type of programming statement used at the end of a subroutine. The RETURN transfers control of the program back to the instruction following the CALL statement that invoked the subroutine in the first place.

- **Routine:** A reasonably small, homogeneous block of code that performs a specific function. Also see MODULE.

- **Run-time package:** A program in a semi-compiler system that runs in memory with the "compiled" program and performs common complex functions like mathematics calculations, input, output, and file handling. By having these functions in the run-time package, the "compiled" program can be much smaller.

- **Seed:** The initial value used to generate a series of pseudo-random numbers (see above).

- **Semi-compiler:** A program that translates most of the simple statements of a high-level language program into a machine language program (or something much like it). For complex operations like input, output, and arithmetic, calls are made to routines in a *run-time package* (see above). The "compiled" program and the run-time package are then run together as the final "program" under the control of the run-time package.

- **Siblings:** Modules in a hierarchy or network that are offsprings of the same parent.

- **Significant digits:** The number of digits of precision (see above) available for a programming language's real numbers (see above). Many languages support single-and double-precision numbers; the latter numbers offer more significant digits but require more room in memory.
- **Sketch code:** A representation of program logic at a very high level of abstraction using general structured statements and processing notes. This is a design "program" which can later be translated into the proper detailed computer language instructions.
- **Space character:** The printable character represented by the space bar at the bottom of a terminal's keyboard. This is not an "empty space" in the text, but a specific character that prints a space.
- **Statement:** A program instruction (see above).
- **Static variable:** A variable that is given a specific value at the beginning of a program, but is never changed. Using such a variable for a value such as the bank's credit limit allows you to change the limit throughout the program by changing the one line of the program where the variable is set.
- **STOP statement:** The type of programming statement that stops the program and, optionally, chains to another program (see END above).
- **Strength:** A measure of the internal consistency of a programming module. If all of the instructions within a module contribute to the module's specific function, the strength is high. If there are instructions that set conditions or modify values for other modules, the strength is low. A well structured system will usually be made up of loosely coupled (see above) strong modules.
- **String:** A data type consisting of zero or more textual characters. Most data in a program is either a number or a character string.
- **Structure:** The organization of all of the parts within a whole system. Structured programming is an organized method of building up a system. The *hierarchy* and the *network* (see above) are two types of structures.

- **Structured programming:** The technique of writing a program using the design and development steps explained in this book. Each programming instruction has a specific structure so that the project as a whole is well organized, easy to complete, and easy to maintain.

- **Style:** A programmer's own inimitable way of writing a program. While structured design offers specific procedures for developing a program, it by no means eliminates a programmer's freedom of style.

- **Sub-element:** A further breakdown of a function, program, or other element of a structure (see OFF-SPRING and STRUCTURE above).

- **Subroutine:** A block of programming instructions that may be invoked from within a program by using the CALL statement. The RETURN statement at the end of the subroutine returns control of the program to the next instruction after the CALL.

- **Switch:** See FLAG.

- **Symbol:** The most common building block of information used within a computer. Most small computers use the 256 possible symbols that can be formed by the eight-bit BYTE of the computer's memory.

- **Syntax:** The rules for proper usage of the words in a language. Natural languages like English and French have fairly complex syntax rules. Computer languages have very simple and specific syntax rules because the languages are so limited. The syntax for a high-level language defines how the interpreter/compiler expects proper statements to be formed. Any other types of statements are errors.

- **System:** A complete collection of programs, files, equipment, and people required to perform a specific function or group of functions. Most computer systems are usually divided into the equipment (hardware system) and the programs (software system). This, unfortunately, leaves out the people and is therefore incomplete. This book on programming deals primarily with the software system and how it is to be developed and used by people.

- **Table:** A small data structure or file that contains common information that can be looked up when the information is needed. The array of suit names in our Blackjack example is a "table" of names.
- **Tape drive:** An external device for storing information on magnetic tape in much the same way that music signals are stored by a stereo system's tape recorder. Information from a computer, however, is saved in digital (see above) form. Information saved on a magnetic tape can be read in again as input at a later time.
- **Termination procedure:** The procedure used at the end of a program to print final totals, messages, or any other utility functions required as the program ends.
- **Terminal:** The most common communication device between an operator and a small computer. Input from the operator is typed on the terminal's keyboard and output to the operator is displayed on the terminal's screen.
- **Testing:** Exercising a program to make sure that all functions are performed correctly. If errors are found, the program must be "debugged." All programs must be tested, however, even if only to prove that there were no bugs to find (fat chance!)
- **Top-down:** The design approach that starts with an overall description of what is to be done, and then works down to ever increasing levels of detail until every last detail has been completed. Throughout the design you will always know how the function you are currently working on relates to its controlling function and to the system as a whole.
- **Transient variable:** A variable that is only used to hold temporary values during a calculation. When the calculation has been completed, the variable is ignored or available for use elsewhere.
- **Translation:** The act of changing the form of a language from something that is meaningful to one party (the programmer) into a form that is meaningful to another party (the computer). This translation

may take place once, or it make take place line by line as the program is run.

- **User-defined function:** A programming function (see above) that is defined by the programmer rather than being provided as a part of a computer language.
- **Utility subroutine:** A subroutine that provides a common function and may be called from anywhere within a program.
- **Value:** The current state of a variable or constant. A constant's value is always the same, but a variable may not have had a value assigned yet, so that its value is undefined, or it will have the last value assigned to it.
- **Variable:** Data used within a computer program that may change its value (see above).
- **Variable name:** The name assigned to a variable by a programmer in an assembly language or high-level language program. The high-level program always refers to the data by this name. Once the program is translated for the computer, however, the processor always refers to the data by its address in memory.
- **Volume test:** Extensive use of a program or system of programs that has passed specific tests of each function. The hardest bugs to find are those that are only caused by a unique sequence of operations. All possible sequences of operations are not likely to be tried until a large volume of information has been processed by the program or system.
- **Z80:** The Zilog Z80 is a single electronic component (a "chip") which is in itself a complete computer processor. The Z80 is an expansion of the Intel 8080 and includes all of the 8080 instructions within its instruction set. This means that programs that run on the 8080 will also run on the Z80. It has been used as the basis for small computer systems (see 6800 and 8080 above).

Bibliography

This bibliography contains references to other books in the dilithium Press library that may be of use to beginning programmers.

Instant (Freeze-Dried Computer Programming in) BASIC by Jerald R. Brown. This is a somewhat whimsical but sound introduction to the BASIC language for the beginner; a good place to start.

Introduction to BASIC by Jeffrey B. Morton. This is a more advanced introduction to the BASIC language. It starts with an introduction to the language itself and, then presents a series of projects to be developed in BASIC.

Pascal by Paul M. Chirlian. An detailed introduction to Pascal with the emphasis on structured programming.

Home Computers: A Beginner's Glossary and Guide by Merl K. Miller and Charles J. Sippl. An introduction in glossary form to the terminology and ideas used by those who work with computers.

Understanding Computers by Paul M. Chirlian. A good introduction to the design and operation of computers. This will be of special interest to those who enjoyed the information about computer equipment contained in Chapter Two.

Computers for Everybody by Jerry Willis and Merl K. Miller. A broad introduction to personal computers: how to choose one; how to use one; and how to get the most enjoyment out of one.

Index